Teaching the Holocaust

Practical approaches for ages 11–18

Michael Gray

Routledge
Taylor & Francis Group

LONDON AND NEW YORK

First published 2015
by Routledge
2 Park Square, Milton Park, Abingdon, Oxon OX14 4RN

and by Routledge
711 Third Avenue, New York, NY 10017

Routledge is an imprint of the Taylor & Francis Group, an informa business

© 2015 Michael Gray

British Library Cataloguing in Publication Data
A catalogue record for this book is available from the British Library

Library of Congress Cataloging-in-Publication Data
Gray, Michael, 1984– author.
Teaching the Holocaust : practical approaches for ages 11–18 / Michael Gray.
pages cm
1. Holocaust, Jewish (1939–1945)--Study and teaching (Secondary) I. Title.
D804.33.G735 2015
940.53'1807--dc23
2014041456

ISBN: 978-1-138-79099-5 (hbk)
ISBN: 978-1-138-79100-8 (pbk)
ISBN: 978-1-315-76328-6 (ebk)

Typeset in Bembo
by Saxon Graphics Ltd, Derby

Teaching the Holocaust

Teaching the Holocaust is an important but often challenging task for those involved in modern Holocaust education. What content should be included and what should be left out? How can film and literature be integrated into the curriculum? What is the best way to respond to students who resist the idea of learning about it?

This book, drawing upon the latest research in the field, offers practical help and advice on delivering inclusive and engaging lessons, along with guidance on how to navigate through the many controversies and considerations when planning, preparing, and delivering Holocaust education. Whether teaching the subject in history, religious education, English, or even in a school assembly, there is a wealth of wisdom which will make the task easier for you and make the learning experience more beneficial for the student.

Topics include:

- The aims of Holocaust education
- Ethical issues to consider when teaching the Holocaust
- Using film and documentaries in the classroom
- Teaching the Holocaust through literature
- The role of online learning and social media
- The benefits and practicalities of visiting memorial sites.

With lesson plans, resources, and schemes of work which can be used across a range of different subjects, this book is essential reading for those who want to deepen their understanding and deliver effective, thought-provoking Holocaust education.

Michael Gray teaches at Harrow School, UK. He has a Ph.D. in Holocaust education and has published widely on the subject. He is a member of both the International Network of Genocide Scholars and the British Association of Holocaust Studies.

Contents

Chapter 1

What was the Holocaust?

If we are going to be teaching about the Holocaust it seems imperative that we understand exactly what we mean by the word 'Holocaust'. From where does its use originate and does it have the same definition and connotations for everyone? If we are to teach about the Holocaust then it seems important that we as practitioners know exactly what we are referring to; after all, if we are confused about what we mean by the word, there seems little hope of our students grasping it. As with so many areas of the Holocaust – and perhaps especially Holocaust education – there is little consensus, and practitioners ought to know where the key areas of contention lie in formulating an accurate and appropriate definition.

Before doing this, it is worth acknowledging that there is by no means any agreement on whether or not the word 'Holocaust' is the most suitable term to use. Etymologically, 'Holocaust' derives from the Greek *Holókauston*, meaning whole burnt sacrifice, and carries with it religious implications whereby animals were offered as sacrifices by fire. This suggests that the murder of the Jews was some form of martyrdom or voluntarily offering, which is highly problematic to say the least. Consequently, the Hebrew word *Shoah* (meaning 'catastrophe' or 'calamity') is generally preferred, especially among Jewish and Israeli audiences, not least because it does not carry with it any religious implications. In addition to *Shoah*, other terms have been employed to challenge and replace the word 'Holocaust', such as *Churban Europa*, meaning 'European destruction' and in ultra-orthodox communities the term *Gezerot tash–tashah* (the Decrees of 1939–45) are sometimes employed. Despite this, the popularity and common usage of the term 'Holocaust' means that it seems unlikely to be replaced globally outside of specialised or scholarly use.

Specific words and phrases connected to the Holocaust are naturally very significant and should only be employed when one wants to convey their precise meaning. Alas, it seems that some practitioners use terminology reminiscent of the euphemistic code which the Nazis utilised to disguise the extent of their operations against the Jews. The phrase 'Final Solution' is characteristic of that and should not simply be considered as an appropriate synonym for the Holocaust. The 'Final Solution' was a specific shift in policy by the Nazi regime at some point between the summer of 1941 and the spring of 1942, which was the culmination of other attempts to answer what they referred to as the *Judenfrage* or Jewish question. Similarly, terms such as 'extermination' were employed to de-humanise the victims and teachers should take care that they do not inadvertently do so in their classrooms. It seems much more appropriate to talk about the murder of the Jews than their extermination.

Teaching about defintions

When teaching the Holocaust I often start by asking my students to define the Holocaust in fewer than fifty words. While this works very effectively for older students, many children within younger classes are not familiar with the term and may not be able to define it. Very often, however, they are aware that the Nazis persecuted and killed the Jews and other groups during the Second World War. Consequently, those who have not come across the word Holocaust are asked to describe how the Nazis treated people they did not like. If pupils have no background knowledge whatsoever, then it is necessary to teach some of the key content first and encourage pupils to establish a definition at a later point in the course.

The answers in Box 1.1 are taken from year 9 (ages 13 and 14) students in comprehensive schools in London and Oxford, UK.

Box 1.1 What was the Holocaust? Some student definitions

The Germans felt strongly that all Jews were bad and that they should be destroyed. This movement was known as the Holocaust.

(John, aged 13)

Nazis thought the gypsies, Jews, blacks and disabled people were a waste of space and should be executed.

(Leonie, aged 13)

Hitler, the leader of the Nazis, hated blacks, Jews and gypsies.

(Kabir, aged 14)

Encouraging students to produce their own definitions helps to highlight the preconceptions that they hold. It also enables them to understand that legitimate differences of opinion can exist, although students also need to be aware that not any definition is correct or appropriate.

As demonstrated in the examples above, it is often common for adolescents to write about black people being victims of the Holocaust. It was undoubtedly the case that black people within Nazi-occupied territory (including black prisoners of war) were sometimes subject to isolation, persecution, sterilisation and even murder. Interestingly, far fewer students refer to Poles or Soviet prisoners of war – two groups which suffered several millions of deaths at the hands of the Nazi regime during the Second World War.

When students do define the Holocaust, the range of answers that are read back highlight to the class the wide range of definitions that have been produced. Very often they fall into three broad categories:

- The Holocaust was the murder of various groups such as Jews, communists, homosexuals and prisoners of war.
- The Holocaust was the persecution and murder of the Jews by the Nazis.
- The Holocaust was the murder of the Jews by the Nazis.

These three types of responses highlight two controversial questions which those who attempt to define the Holocaust must answer. The first of these is, Who should be included in the definition? The second is, When did the Holocaust take place? Needless to say, both of these questions are connected and how one answers the first of them will certainly influence how one deals with the second. For example, if one were to include the murder of disabled persons in a definition of the Holocaust, then the Holocaust might start in 1939 when the Nazi regime introduced their child 'euthanasia' programme. However, if the compulsory sterilisation of those with hereditary diseases was considered a part of the Holocaust then the date would have to shift back to as early as 1933. Similarly, the year of Hitler's appointment as chancellor of Germany would also be considered the start date of the Holocaust if the definition only applied to Jewish victims but included persecution and state-sponsored discrimination in addition to murder.

How the Holocaust is defined can have a number of important implications both inside and outside of the classroom. The issue has increasingly taken on a political significance and the historical, semantic and even pedagogic arguments on both sides can often be driven by particular agendas. As a practitioner, there is some flexibility on how the Holocaust is defined, although it seems helpful that students recognise that there is no universal consensus. It also seems important that you know both why you have chosen to define it in such a way and what the potential implications may be of opting for such a definition. The teaching guidelines of the International Holocaust Remembrance Alliance (IHRA) – an intergovernmental body of thirty-one countries – are particularly helpful in this regard when they state: 'a clear definition of the term Holocaust is essential. Many teachers apply this term in a very broad sense to encompass all victims of Nazi persecution. Yet most historians of the period use a more precise definition' (IHRA 2014a).

This statement is supported by a national survey of trends, perspectives and practice in Holocaust education in English schools, conducted by the Holocaust Education Development Programme (HEDP) (now called the Centre for Holocaust Education) in 2009. The study, which was conducted on over 2,000 practitioners teaching various subjects, found that when given seven definitions to choose from, over 50 per cent of respondents believed that the Holocaust was 'the persecution and murder of a range of victims perpetrated by the Nazi regime and its collaborators'. Conversely, fewer than 10 per cent of the sample defined it as 'the systematic, bureaucratic, state-sponsored persecution and murder of approximately six million Jews by the Nazi regime and its collaborators' (Pettigrew et al. 2009: 62–63), which as discussed below, is the definition used by the United States Holocaust Memorial Museum (USHMM) in Washington DC. Interestingly, the HEDP study analysed the relationship between teachers' definitions and three other factors: the subject they taught, their experience of teaching the Holocaust and their knowledge of the Holocaust. The research concluded that 'a teacher's knowledge has more of an impact on how they understand the term "the Holocaust" than either their subject background or their prior experience of teaching in this area'. Moreover, the greater the knowledge, the more likely they were to reject a broad definition in favour of recognising 'the specificity of the targeting of European Jews' (ibid., 68).

It can be beneficial – and certainly thought-provoking – to encourage one's students to think about the difficulties and implications of defining the Holocaust and for them to be aware of the lack of consensus among teachers. The 'Defining the Holocaust' worksheet aims to facilitate this by providing a number of events which might or might not be included in a definition. This can be adapted or developed on the basis of the students' definitions.

If, for example, they believe that the Holocaust only began after systematic mass murder commenced in 1941, then did the thousands of Jews who had starved to death in the ghettos of Poland before this date not die in the Holocaust? Moreover, if students include those who died on the death marches, does that include British prisoners of war who perished on the torturous journeys west? If so, should Britons who died in the Blitz also be included, as they too died as a consequence of Nazi aggression? The objective of such questioning is not to make their definitions watertight and certainly not to compare the extent of suffering, but rather to encourage them to see how problematic and difficult it is to define the Holocaust and to understand why there is such a divergence of opinion.

Established definitions of the Holocaust

Rather than create your own definition, it is often helpful to use one that has already been established by one of the major institutions involved in Holocaust remembrance and education. As the IHRA guidelines intimated, most historians use a precise definition and this is typically reflected in the examples of many of the leading Holocaust museums and organisations. The USHMM states on its website that:

> The Holocaust was the systematic, bureaucratic, state-sponsored persecution and murder of approximately six million Jews by the Nazi regime and its collaborators … During the era of the Holocaust, German authorities also targeted other groups because of their perceived 'racial inferiority': Roma (Gypsies), the disabled, and some of the Slavic peoples (Poles, Russians, and others). Other groups were persecuted on political, ideological, and behavioral grounds, among them Communists, Socialists, Jehovah's Witnesses, and homosexuals.
>
> (USHMM 2014)

No doubt a great deal of care and attention took place in articulating this definition. The museum has defined the Holocaust itself as the 'persecution and murder' of Jews, thus including all aspects of antisemitism which pre-dated the invasion of the Soviet Union in June 1941 and the commencement of systematic mass murder. While stating that it was Jewish deaths which constituted the Holocaust, other groups are not excluded nor marginalised as they are included in the paragraph. Nevertheless, the targeting of 'other groups' occurred 'during the era of the Holocaust', not as a part of the Holocaust itself. Consequently, the USHMM have been able to maintain the Jewish specificity of the Holocaust but ensure the inclusion of other groups, which helps them to fulfil their broader goals of confronting hatred, preventing genocide and promoting human dignity rather than simply remembering Jewish deaths and tackling antisemitism. A more generalised set of aims seems more appropriate for an organisation which receives tens of millions of dollars each year in federal funds in a contemporary and multicultural America. Yet at the same time, the narrower definition of the Holocaust maintains the Jewishness of the phenomenon, which is likely to be welcomed by the Jewish community.

There are both similarities and differences between the definition used by the USHMM and that employed by Yad Vashem – the official memorial and national museum to Holocaust victims in Israel:

> The Holocaust was the murder of approximately six million Jews by the Nazis and their collaborators. Between the German invasion of the Soviet Union in the summer

of 1941 and the end of the war in Europe in May 1945, Nazi Germany and its accomplices strove to murder every Jew under their domination. Because Nazi persecution of the Jews began with Hitler's accession to power in January 1933, many historians consider this the start of the Holocaust era. The Jews were not the only victims of Hitler's regime, but they were the one single group that the Nazis sought to destroy entirely.

Like that of the USHMM, Yad Vashem's definition also draws a distinction between 'the Holocaust' and the 'Holocaust era'. However, it does this to distinguish between the periods of mass murder and of persecution, rather than between Jewish and non-Jewish victims. Both definitions also draw attention to the role of collaborators. Experience suggests that many students are not aware that the Holocaust was also perpetrated by those who chose to collaborate with the Nazi regime, and it is helpful if practitioners include this often-forgotten group in their definition. It is noteworthy that while Yad Vashem acknowledges that 'the Jews were not the only victims of Hitler's regime', they seek to explain why they adopt a narrow rather than a broad definition, stating that the Jews were 'the one single group that the Nazis sought to destroy entirely'. The focus of Yad Vashem is exclusively on the fate of the Jews, while the USHMM includes educational resources and exhibitions on non-Jewish victims as well as post-Holocaust genocides. The geo-political context is likely to be influential in this regard, seeing that the USHMM is operating within a secular rather than a Jewish state.

While it may be helpful for teachers to adopt an institution's definitions or at least be influenced by them, it is also important that they understand some of the practical and political reasons for their definitions.

The Holocaust Memorial Day Trust – the government-funded charity which promotes Holocaust Memorial Day – adopts the following definition:

> Between 1941 and 1945, the Nazis attempted to annihilate all of Europe's Jews. This systematic and planned attempt to murder European Jewry is known as the Holocaust.
>
> (HMDT 2014)

Again, it is only Jewish victims included in this definition, which commences in 1941 and therefore excludes Jewish deaths during *Kristallnacht* as well as those who perished in the ghettos before this date.

Why do defintions matter?

There are a number of reasons why the definition of the Holocaust that is chosen really matters, and it is probable that it will have significant implications on many aspects of one's teaching. Ultimately, how we define the Holocaust determines what we mean when we say we are teaching the Holocaust or that we are engaged in Holocaust education. For some practitioners, therefore, they may believe that when they are teaching the treatment of communists and political opponents or the persecution of the disabled they are teaching the Holocaust. Others would argue that they are not.

Definitions impact on content choices

Teaching the Holocaust involves making important decisions about what content we include and what we omit. It seems probable that the definition that we adopt will influence this decision-making process. If we say that the Holocaust refers to all victims of Nazi persecution then it seems possible that a teacher may choose to spend an equal amount of time on non-Jewish groups. A teacher who adopts a restricted definition of the Holocaust may also select course content on the basis of his or her approach. This does not automatically mean that they will exclude other victims from their teaching, yet if they believe that the term 'Holocaust' only applies to the treatment of Jews, then they may hold to the view that there was something unique and intrinsically different about Nazi policy in this area. Such a position may lead to the belief that the persecution and murder of the Jews is thus more worthy of study than other groups. Conversely, practitioners may simply prefer a narrow definition because it is more precise and may feel that using the word as an umbrella term muddies rather than clears the water as each victim group's unique experiences are unceremoniously lumped together. In such instances, the definition employed may have less of an impact on content choice.

Definitions impact on aims

The aims of Holocaust education are discussed in the next chapter, yet there is undoubtedly a link between how teachers define the Holocaust and what they attempt to achieve through their teaching of the subject. Clearly some definitions are more compatible with certain aims than others. For example, if one believes the purpose of children learning about the Holocaust is to ensure that they are tolerant and accepting of all people irrespective of race, religion, sexual orientation or physical ability, then it is more helpful to include the persecution of Poles, Jehovah's Witnesses, homosexuals and the disabled in a definition. If the Holocaust is only defined in terms of Jewish deaths, then this aim is significantly less easy to fulfil. One may, however, suggest that the aims of Holocaust education ought not to determine its definition but rather the other way round. It seems logical to argue that only when we know what the Holocaust was, can we be in a position to decide how and why we want to teach it. The ambitions of many teachers to promote certain values and attitudes through Holocaust education may explain why the IHRA remarked that many teachers encompass all victims groups while most historians use a precise definition.

Definitions can help tackle Holocaust denial

Those who distort or deny the Holocaust often deny their own denial; they frequently state that they do not deny the Holocaust. Clearly in such instances, they are using a different definition of the Holocaust. In other words they are not denying their own definition of the Holocaust. By establishing clear, precise and accurate definitions of the Holocaust, then it means that so-called 'revisionist historians' can no longer deny their own denial.

As we have already seen, there is no absolute consensus on one particular definition and this is in many senses both understandable and natural. However, the accommodating of different definitions should not be so open-ended as to allow the very essence of the Holocaust to be challenged or undermined by those who would seek to deny its key features. Definitions thus matter if Holocaust denial is to be successfully exposed and challenged.

Definitions can affect students' attitudes

However a teacher chooses to define the Holocaust is unlikely to please everyone or be wholly unproblematic. Nevertheless, it is important to be aware that some students may be unhappy with the definition and in some cases feel that the suffering of a particular group with which they identify has been overlooked, marginalised or ignored. For example, if a teacher states that the Holocaust only referred to Jewish deaths then an adolescent from Poland or from a Roma community may feel that their history is not being included and consequently develop negative attitudes towards either the teacher or the subject of the Holocaust. While it seems highly questionable for a definition of the Holocaust to be determined by the demographic composition of a class, it is important to recognise the possible implications of the definition that is chosen. Perhaps the best way round this problem is to adopt a restricted definition if one so wishes, but to emphasise, explain and teach about the other victims as well, highlighting that the Nazis conducted various genocides, politicides and mass murders.

It is also possible that Jewish students may feel equally aggrieved if a definition of the Holocaust adopts a broad approach. They may believe that the experiences of the Jews at the hands of the Nazi regime and its collaborators was unique and that grouping it with the persecution of Jehovah's Witnesses, for example, who had the opportunity to recant, or homosexuals, who were not systematically mass-murdered, is trivialising the Jewish experience or even piggybacking on it in order to fulfil a political or social agenda. Teachers need to be aware of the potential attitudes with which they might be confronted and the requisite sensitivity to handle these feelings with care and understanding.

Definitions can affect students' engagement

Connected to students' attitudes are their levels of engagement. If an adolescent believes that the experiences of the group with which they identify are being marginalised or trivialised then they may fail to engage appropriately, and this will severely limit the effectiveness of their Holocaust education. Moreover, it may breed resentment towards the victim group that is being focused on, and rather than promote tolerance and harmony their pedagogic experiences may lead to divisions, jealousy and bitterness.

Research by the HEDP found that some teachers purposefully adopted a broad definition because many of their students had much more familiarity and regular encounters with adolescents who associated with other victim groups. Some practitioners did so to try and make the Holocaust more 'relevant':

TEACHER A: One of the ways that you can make it relevant to the pupils, because we're in a multi-racial school, is the fact that anybody who is of a different race, who is not of the 'Aryan' race, would not be living here if the Nazis had actually won the war.

TEACHER B: I think that's really relevant in a school like this, isn't it? Where we've got such a high number of Asian kids.

TEACHER C: Yes, so we try and look at it in a much broader way than just the Jews.

(Pettigrew et al. 2009: 70)

While it is no doubt commendable that teachers want to engage their students, there seems something slightly perverse about adjusting how the Holocaust is defined and how students learn to define it simply because a school has a lot of non-Jewish minorities. After all, if the Holocaust is being taught for its own sake and because it was a significant historical event, then whether or not it is 'relevant' is not particularly important in the same way that the Norman Conquest or French Revolution may not seem relevant to contemporary adolescents but are not re-defined to make them so. If, however, the Holocaust is being taught to promote values such as respect for human life, tolerance and the like, it seems strange that teachers feel the need to include groups which are most like their students. After all, it is impossible to 'tolerate' a group with which one associates, and with concerning levels of antisemitism in the UK, it seems plausible that Holocaust education may be an effective and relevant way of confronting it.

Summary of defintions

Table 1.1 Summary of definitions

Definition	Some benefits and problems
The persecution and murder of the Jews by the Nazi regime and its collaborators between 1933 and 1945.	This definition has the advantage of including Jews who were murdered during *Kristallnacht* or who starved to death in the Polish ghettos before the summer of 1941. If the Holocaust includes all Nazi persecution, it means that a Jewish shopkeeper whose business was boycotted in April 1933 and then emigrated to Britain is technically a victim of the Holocaust.
The systematic mass murder of the Jews by the Nazi regime and its collaborators between 1941 and 1945.	The advantage of this definition is that it recognises that Nazi policy dramatically and fatally shifted in 1941 to adopt a policy of systematic mass murder. By excluding persecution before this date, it justifies applying the term Holocaust to Jewish deaths alone, for while other groups suffered persecution and deaths (as the Jews did before 1941) no other group experienced systematic mass murder. Nevertheless, it seems problematic and inconsistent to say that Jews who were shot in cold blood in the ghettos before the summer of 1941 did not die in the Holocaust, while those who were shot in similar circumstances after this date did.
The persecution and murder of various groups by the Nazi regime and its collaborators between 1933 and 1945.	This definition recognises the fate of various victim groups who were persecuted and murdered by the Nazis. It acknowledges that Jews were not the only group to be killed but fails to appreciate that Jews were the only group to be systematically mass murdered simply for existing, and with the intent of utterly destroying them.

Recommended reading

Bauer, Y. (2001) 'What Was the Holocaust?' (Chapter 1) in *Re-Thinking the Holocaust* (New Haven CT: Yale University Press).

Russell, L. (2006) 'What Was "The Holocaust"?' (Chapter 2) in *Teaching the Holocaust in School History: Teachers or Preachers?* (London: Continuum).

Why teach about the Holocaust?

When students ask, 'Why are we learning about the Holocaust?' it seem reasonable to provide them with a more compelling answer than simply because it is on the syllabus. It is important for both teachers and learners alike to understand why they are studying the Holocaust, even though these reasons may differ from classroom to classroom or from school to school. In a similar way to how we define the Holocaust, the aims that we adopt when teaching it are likely to have implications for our entire approach to the subject. It is important that teachers understand the different aims which exist in Holocaust education, as well as the arguments for and against them, and are thus able to formulate their own pedagogic goals and objectives. Box 2.1 shows some of the commonly held aims of teachers and educators.

Box 2.1 Some commonly held aims of Holocaust teaching

- To increase knowledge and understanding of the Nazi regime and the Second World War.
- To encourage thinking about the moral and ethical dilemmas which the Holocaust generates.
- To ensure that the memory of the victims is not forgotten.
- To promote tolerance and acceptance within society.
- To demonstrate where prejudice, antisemitism and racism can lead to within a society.
- To uphold the values of democracy and liberalism.
- To highlight what can happen when people remain silent or apathetic towards injustice.
- To encourage thinking about the Holocaust for its own sake.
- To generate theological discussions.
- To prevent future genocides and human rights abuses from occurring again.

Developing a rationale

The Holocaust is taught through a large number of subject areas from history to drama, including English, RS and citizenship, to name just a few of the most common disciplines. Undoubtedly, each of these subjects has their own precise aims, many of which may be quite different from each other. After all, encouraging students to express themselves through acting involves dissimilar methods to contemplating the nature of evil and suffering, even though someone who can effectively do the latter may be better positioned to do the former. Teaching about the Holocaust usually involves integrating the topic into the overarching themes of the subject discipline, for example, a play that is set in a ghetto typically includes the same pedagogic rationales as any other piece of theatre, even if it adds a new dimension to them or a new way of achieving them. This chapter seeks to lay aside subject-specific objectives and discuss the precise aims of Holocaust education which are relevant to every discipline. It highlights the different views which exist, and areas of compatibility and incompatibility between the various positions.

Generally speaking, there are two main schools of thought regarding the aims of Holocaust education. On the one hand are those who believe that the only purpose of teaching this subject is to educate adolescents about the factual, historical past and that all learning objectives should have this goal as their end. On the other hand are those who see the principal and primary aim of Holocaust education as a moralising one, whereby students learn the lessons of the past to prevent any repetition of such horrors in the future. There are some who hold to an extreme position on this issue and who believe that these two aims are irreconcilable. Others suggest a mutualism between them with disagreements focusing simply on where the emphasis ought to lie.

The Holocaust as history

Whether one is teaching about the mass murder of Europe's Jews during the Second World War, the emancipation of serfs in Russia or the religious reforms of Alfred the Great, the aims of such education are to ensure that students know and understand about the past; why things happened, how things happened and the consequences of these happenings. Such is the position of those who reject the notion that contemporary lessons can be acquired from the past. They argue that history is extremely complex, multi-faceted and so sophisticated that it transcends generalisability. Moreover, it is so context-specific that it is does not produce maxims or instruction which is transferable to the present. A Latvian collaborator in 1942 for example, with a unique set of characteristics, education, experiences and socio-political prejudices, acting in the specific context of Nazi-occupied Europe, does not bear relevance for a 13-year-old girl in twenty-first-century London who is faced with moral choices. Advocates of this position argue that to attempt to teach lessons from the Holocaust means de-contextualising and simplifying the past to fit it into a neat framework of modern ethical beliefs. Herbert writes:

> The didactic challenge of the history of the Holocaust lies precisely in the fact that it does not lend itself to explanations involving pithy formulations and simple, readily-digested concepts or theories … The Holocaust possesses no theory or redemptive formula.
>
> (Herbert 2000: 44)

Those who argue that there are no real lessons to be learnt from the Holocaust sometimes hold to this position because it is the inevitable conclusion of the belief that the Holocaust was unique. The debate about uniqueness is discussed in Chapter 9, but it suffices to say here, that if the Holocaust is without parallel then it has no moral relevance to contemporary students. Nevertheless, there are many who argue that the aims of Holocaust education ought to be purely historical while rejecting the idea that it was unique. Novick, for example, who considers the notion of uniqueness to be 'vacuous'

(Novick 1999: 32), believes that lessons cannot be learnt because the circumstances of the Holocaust are too extreme to have resonance or bearing on everyday life. Kinloch, who also rejects the idea that the Holocaust was unique, writes:

> Apart from the most general lessons, however, the Shoah probably has no more to teach British students than any other genocide of modern – or for that matter medieval – times. There may be good reason to teach children that killing other human beings is generally undesirable. Whether the history class is really the place for such lessons, however remains debatable. There is less of a consensus here than most of those called upon to teach it might realise.
>
> (Kinloch 2001: 13)

Learning moral lessons

In distinction to the view that the Holocaust ought simply to be taught as history is the belief that there are in fact many contemporary lessons which can be learnt through the Holocaust. Advocates of this view may not necessarily stipulate that these lessons need to be exclusively taught in history, although many of them agree that this is one of the purposes of the discipline. The moral value of the Holocaust in producing civilised, tolerant and responsible citizens is therefore to be demonstrated whenever the subject is taught, whether in English, RS, or citizenship.

One of the strongest voices for the moralising qualities of Holocaust education is Geoffrey Short, who has been critical of the bleak and pessimistic outlook that historians of the Holocaust have often demonstrated. He also responds to the accusation that post-Holocaust genocides are not evidence of the failure of Holocaust education, and cites examples of how modern political leaders have justified military intervention through references to the mass murder of the Jews during the Second World War. Box 2.2 shows three specific lessons which Short believes can be drawn out from the Holocaust.

Box 2.2 Short's three specific lessons

'The Holocaust leaves students in no doubt where racism can lead.'

'Students familiar with the Holocaust can hardly fail to realise the perils of turning a blind eye to evil.'

'The final lesson that the Holocaust teaches individual students is that their attitudes are, to some extent at least, culturally determined.'

(Short 2003: 285–86)

Remembering the past

In addition to teaching the Holocaust for its own sake or for the sake of society, another reason which is sometimes put forward for teaching the subject is so that the event is remembered. The focus on memory and commemoration is often closely connected to the arguments put forward by those who advocate moral lessons from history – arguing the maxim of Santayana that those who forget the past are doomed to repeat it. Some, like Eckmann, have been critical of making this the cardinal learning objective for Holocaust education. She writes:

> It is important to counter a common misinterpretation: that Holocaust education is above all a duty of memory. In fact, it is first and foremost a duty of history: the duty to transmit and to teach and learn the history.
>
> (Eckmann 2010: 10)

Even if memory and commemoration is not the focal point or the purpose of Holocaust education, students who learn about the horrors of Nazi genocide will inevitably be assisting in the cause of remembering the past.

Division or consensus?

As discussed above, it seems that there is often a lack of consensus among teachers, historians and educators regarding the aims and purposes of Holocaust education. In a study conducted by the HEDP in 2009 on over 2,000 teachers, there was almost universal consent on certain propositions, with 94 per cent agreeing or strongly agreeing that 'it will always be important to teach about the Holocaust'. Moreover, 85.1 per cent agreed that 'it is right that teaching about the Holocaust is compulsory in the history school curriculum' (Pettigrew et al. 2009: 71). Clearly therefore, most teachers believe that teaching the Holocaust is important and its place on the National Curriculum – not to mention the vast sums of taxpayers' money which are designated to Holocaust education – suggests that governments, irrespective of their party colours, agree.

The consensus soon falls apart, however, when enquiry is made into why teachers believe that the Holocaust is important. The HEDP study found that some practitioners struggled to articulate why studying the Holocaust was important and simply took its educational significance for granted. Many talked in vague terms about the moral and social lessons which could be learned. When given thirteen suggestions and asked to state which three most closely matched their aims when teaching the Holocaust, the most common statement marked was: 'to develop an understanding of the roots and ramifications of prejudice, racism, and stereotyping in a society'. This was listed by over 60 per cent of all respondents, while fewer than 30 per cent of history teachers considered deepening their students' knowledge of World War II and twentieth-century history to be one of their aims (Pettigrew et al. 2009: 73).

Asking teachers what their aims are when teaching the Holocaust may not necessarily reflect the multifarious objectives which are likely to exist. After all, it seems unlikely that every lesson is going to have identical aims. A lesson which focuses on the controversial issues of collaboration, acquiescence, apathy and resistance is likely to try and offer some sort of insight into issues of morality and human nature, which may not be so central when teaching about the contribution of the pre-war Jewish communities to European culture. Moreover, the purpose of a lesson may shift mid-course in response to a specific question or remark. Even a teacher who thinks that the Holocaust should only be taught as a historical phenomenon will no doubt seek to tackle and correct an antisemitic comment or answer an enquiry which suggests a student has been influenced by Holocaust denial websites. Consequently, in such lessons on the Holocaust, social and moral aims have emerged, which were not pre-planned, but rather reactionary in nature. It is perfectly fair to hold to the position that the Holocaust should not be used to teach moral lessons, but even those who adopt such a stance have to be flexible enough in their approach to recognise that the Holocaust will always generate social and ethical issues and questions which have contemporary relevance, and which no practitioner can or should avoid. This does not mean that the Holocaust cannot be taught for its own sake, but surely this should not be done in such a way that removes the moral responsibility of a teacher.

While those who advocate 'lessons' from the Holocaust would emphasise the unavoidability of moral issues and a practitioner's sense of responsibility, those who reject this agenda would rightly highlight the duty of historical detail and accuracy which rests upon all Holocaust educators. In the same way that a teacher cannot escape from the ethical dimensions of the subject, neither can there be any avoidance of the fact that the Holocaust is rooted and grounded in the historical past and to detach it from context is to commit a grave injustice. Decisions, actions and policies were all driven by specific circumstances and particular stimuli which cannot be ignored and should be carefully understood if one is to attempt to understand why people adopted a course of action and how that might have some contemporary relevance. By suggesting that someone in the Holocaust and someone in twenty-first-century Europe both think and act in a vacuum will be thoroughly unconvincing to any student and offer no social or moral benefit to learners. Box 2.3, produced by the United States Holocaust Memorial Museum (USHMM) in Washington DC, suggests that the Holocaust can be used to teach young people about the dangers of racism and the importance of tolerance. Yet rather than doing so at the expense of the history, the Museum argues that 'relevant connections for all learners often surface as the history is analyzed' (USHMM 2014b), suggesting a compatibility between the two positions.

Box 2.3 USHMM's view on some benefits of Holocaust study

Studying the Holocaust also helps students to:

- Understand the roots and ramifications of prejudice, racism, and stereotyping in any society.
- Develop an awareness of the value of pluralism and an acceptance of diversity.
- Explore the dangers of remaining silent, apathetic, and indifferent to the oppression of others.
- Think about the use and abuse of power as well as the roles and responsibilities of individuals, organizations, and nations when confronted with civil rights violations and/or policies of genocide.
- Understand how a modern nation can utilize its technological expertise and bureaucratic infrastructure to implement destructive policies ranging from social engineering to genocide.

(USHMM 2014b)

A false dichotomy?

In light of this, it may be reasonable to suggest that the long-standing division over the aims and purposes of Holocaust education is something of a false dichotomy. While this is not to deny that there are clearly differences of perspective and emphasis – and of course argument – the existing schism is perhaps more reconcilable than it first appears, and perhaps teachers should adopt the strengths of both sides. There are clearly merits to both perspectives, but perhaps neither position must be held to exclusively. Even if one holds to the view that the Holocaust is unique and has no lessons of contemporary relevance, such practitioners must recognise that even teaching the history of the Holocaust will almost always generate questions about contemporary antisemitism, Holocaust denial and the like, not to mention the fact that *how* the Holocaust is taught will affect children's perceptions and understandings of Jews and Judaism. Therefore, even though the Holocaust might not offer neatly packaged lessons for today – it almost certainly doesn't – Holocaust education provides a natural link with themes and issues which are of contemporary relevance. Thus, even if one explicitly rejects the notion that the Holocaust should be taught for the purpose of moralising students, it does not mean that discussions of a moral nature which are of contemporary relevance cannot be welcomed and developed. Surely, to quash such questions and enquiries would be to ignore one's duty as a teacher, which should, after all, be to inspire and enthuse learners, making them well-rounded individuals. Believing that the past should not be plundered or exploited for a contemporary moral agenda is a virtuous position, but to be so inflexible and rigid in that position that children receive such a narrow education whereby they are not permitted to consider present-day issues which have some connection with the past, is not virtuous but rather inconsiderate and problematic.

Moreover, pedagogic flexibility can allow for different aims at different times. It seems perfectly reasonable to have historically grounded aims in one subject, in one lesson or even in one part of a lesson, and yet to discuss and focus on the moral implications of the Holocaust in the next lesson, in a different subject or when the appropriate question or comment demands a shift in rationale.

It seems that a balance is needed when teaching the Holocaust. There is minimal value in producing educated and knowledgeable individuals, who may be able to explain complex multi-causal phenomena and reel off countless dates and statistics, if they leave their schooling without any moral compass or understanding of contemporary ethical issues. If students are aware of the intricate facts of Nazi antisemitism but have no conception that discrimination and persecution of Jews continues in some instances, then such adolescents have failed to receive a well-rounded and balanced education. Similarly, however, there seems little use in encouraging students to hold pro-democratic and anti-racist attitudes if they are grounded upon tenuous and spurious links with the past. Adolescents will not be able to benefit from a moralising education if they do not know, understand and appreciate why dictatorship, racial theory and both popular and state-sponsored antisemitism are so concerning and where they have sometimes led. Therefore, comparing the life-risking actions of Raoul Wallenberg or the self-sacrificing altruism of Maximilian Kolbe to someone who stands up to a playground bully is simply facile as it de-contextualises the historical past and ignores the complexities and specific circumstances which people faced during the Holocaust. If teaching the Holocaust is to have any moralising effects on its learners, these will only occur when the subject is grounded in factual accuracy and precise detail; when the teacher avoids simplification and generalisations which undermine the complexities of the past and the intelligence of the student. Box 2.4 is an excerpt from the International Holocaust Remembrance Alliance's (IHRA) guidelines on *How to Teach about the Holocaust in Schools*. While it correctly draws a distinction between the history of the Holocaust and its moral messages, it suggests that with care, there is a compatibility and mutualism between the two which can be achieved.

> **Box 2.4** The IHRA on history and morality
>
> Be careful to distinguish between the history of the Holocaust and the moral lessons one can draw from a study of that history. There is a danger of distorting the historical narrative if it is oversimplified or shaped to better serve the particular moral lesson that teachers wish their students to learn.
>
> Learning about these events can sensitise young people to modern-day examples of prejudice and injustice; the Holocaust can confront students with stereotypes, myths, and misconceptions and enable them to test received prejudices against historical evidence. But moral lessons will not be well founded unless they are based upon an accurate and objective reading of the historical record.
>
> (IHRA 2014a)

In contrast to the ideas discussed above, Short (2005: 378) has argued that the so-called lessons of the past need to be explicitly drawn out by teachers, because students are often incapable of doing so by themselves. Others, such as Hondius, have argued that an overt moralising of the Holocaust in the classroom simply makes learners reluctant and disengaged. Hondius remarks:

> Some Holocaust education projects, for instance, have a pronounced moral tone, which can provoke irritation and resistance among students, who tend to dislike being preached to. The end result can be the opposite of what one attempts to accomplish.
>
> (Hondius 2010: S64)

Ultimately, it seems that teachers should discuss the moral issues as and when they arrive. If this is student-driven and student-centred then it seems unlikely that they will feel the irritation to which Hondius alludes. Answering questions, responding to student comments and generating discussion can help to develop and shape students' ethical framework. This avoids the explicitly moral-driven style of Holocaust education but firmly places the contemporary ethical issues in the context and history of the Holocaust. Allowing for the students to generate the moral issues does not mean that they dictate the direction of the lesson. It does, however, mean that they feel the freedom to ask questions and that the lesson has sufficient flexibility to answer them without deviating too far off course. Such an approach appears to be very beneficial for the students and appreciates the broader picture of a learner's education.

This method fuses the two principal schools of thought regarding the aims of Holocaust education. Nevertheless, it also supports the additional purpose of Holocaust remembrance. By teaching about this chapter of human history, be it in RS, history or any other subject, the past is remembered. The ubiquity of the Holocaust within Western education, society and the media suggests that there is minimal chance that it will be forgotten or marginalised any time soon. The establishment of Holocaust Memorial Day by the United Nations in 2004 also suggests this. Salmons argues that commemoration and remembrance are undoubtedly taking place, but that 'the danger is that unless commemoration is accompanied by detailed study and depth of understanding then the old myths and misconceptions will continue, and the memory of the Holocaust will remain shallow and insecure'. Consequently, what is at stake is not 'whether we choose to remember but what form that memory takes' (Salmons 2013).

The consequences of our aims

Along with how we define the Holocaust, deciding on our aims will have the biggest impact on how we approach Holocaust education. Why we are teaching the Holocaust will affect what content we want to include and what we want to omit; the pedagogic methods that we employ; whether or not we use sensitive or traumatic images; and what we want the students to still remember in one, five or even ten years' time. It is thus vital that teachers understand what they are trying to achieve and why they hold to this view before designing and delivering their Holocaust curriculum. By recognising what the Holocaust is and why it should be studied, solid foundations can be laid. If such questions are not satisfactorily answered, it is likely that there will be inherent contradictions in the teaching which may soon become apparent to both the practitioner and the students.

In addition to the broader implications of a teacher's views on the aims of Holocaust education, there are also consequences on the interaction between practitioner and student as well as how Holocaust content is delivered. Table 2.1 shows some of the things that should be encouraged and avoided if balance and moderation are to be employed.

Table 2.1 Strategies for achieving balance and moderation

	Encourage …	*Avoid …*
The Holocaust as history	• Students to think carefully about the decisions that people made in the past and to develop historical empathy. • Students to recognise that the Holocaust was a complex phenomenon and that general terms such as 'perpetrator', 'victim' and 'bystander' are not as simple as one may first think.	• Marginalising or ignoring questions or comments which seek to make comparisons with contemporary issues such as racism or antisemitism. • Suggesting that the Holocaust was so context-specific that nothing similar could happen again. • Insensitivity to those who make comparisons between the Holocaust and other human rights abuses.
Learning moral lessons	• Students to make their own connections between the past and the present. • Moral lessons to be grounded in the history and context of the Holocaust. • Students to consider what influences existed on peoples' thinking and course of actions.	• Trivialising the Holocaust by attempting to draw inappropriate comparisons. • Making generalised points which fail to understand the complexities and variation which existed in the Holocaust. • Distorting the past to make it fit in with a particular moral goal. • Simplifying the past or ignoring the context in which decisions were made.

Recommended reading

Eckmann, M. (2010) 'Exploring the Relevance of Holocaust Education for Human Rights Education', *Prospects*, 40: 7–16.

Leyman, T. and Harris, R. (2013) 'Connecting the Dots: Helping Year 9 to Debate the Purposes of Holocaust and Genocide Education', *Teaching History*, 153: 4–10.

Salmons, P. (2010) 'Universal Meaning or Historical Understanding? The Holocaust in History and History in the Curriculum', *Teaching History*, 141: 57–63.

Short, G. (2003) 'Lessons of the Holocaust: A Response to the Critics', *Educational Review*, 55, no. 3: 277–87.

Chapter 3

How should the Holocaust be taught?

Within many schools today, students are likely to learn about the Holocaust in a number of different subjects. No longer is the topic only taught within history lessons but research by the HEDP found that in England, it can on some occasions even be taught in maths, science, business studies and psychology. Nevertheless, in a study of 1,084 practitioners who taught the Holocaust, 55 per cent principally did so in history, 25 per cent in religious education, 7 per cent in English and three per cent in each of citizenship and PSHE (Pettigrew et al. 2009: 29). This important piece of research conducted by the HEDP also found that in many schools, students' first encounter with the Holocaust in the classroom came in a subject other than history, where the topic typically did not appear on the syllabus until year 9 when they were aged 13–14. Consequently, a number of learners may first study the Holocaust through the prism of morality and ethics or through a fictional text or play. Teachers of other subjects must remember this when they are considering what they include within their Holocaust courses and ensure that their students leave with a sound contextual understanding, accurate knowledge of the past and as few misconceptions as possible. This is not to say that those who teach students about the Holocaust before they have learnt it in history should try and cover everything that their colleagues will go on to look at, but it is to suggest that adolescents should be given the intellectual foundations to understand any encounter with the Holocaust (or its representations) within their appropriate historical contexts. When planning and preparing Holocaust curricula, teachers should therefore make enquiries into what their students will have already learnt about the Holocaust in other subjects. This prevents needless repetition, as well as ensuring that they have sufficient understanding to appropriately interpret a particular book, play or conceptualisation of the Holocaust.

Although it is important to emphasise the historical basis of students' ideas about the Holocaust, it is also apposite to recognise that the discipline of history does not and should not have a monopoly on it. The Holocaust is a phenomenon which in many ways can only be understood through various forms of expression and representation and if learners are to appreciate its nuances, complexities and aspects, then multiple approaches and angles will be required.

Although a student's understanding of the Holocaust must come from multiple sources, ultimately however, when answering the question 'What should a Holocaust curriculum include?' the answer must be subject-driven. After all, education is organised by subject and therefore the content of a Holocaust programme within a particular discipline should dovetail together the general aims of the subject with the principles and practices of sound Holocaust pedagogy.

Teaching the Holocaust in history

One of the biggest problems when teaching the Holocaust in history is the designing of the curriculum, due to the sheer volume of content which one would like to cover. With limited teaching time, it will probably be impossible to include everything and thus the key is to understand your learning objectives and produce your curriculum accordingly.

Providing context

Students are unlikely to gain as much as they can from learning about the Holocaust if it is not placed within a suitable historical context. Yet how far back should the teacher go? Do students need to know the long history of antisemitism either in Germany itself or within Europe more generally? What about the history of the Jewish people? Even within the history classroom, it will be necessary to discuss who the Jews are and something of their past. In an ideal world, this will already have been done in some depth by the religious studies department and thus it may only be necessary to recap. Nevertheless, it is important to explain the complexities of Jewish identity and also how the Nazis viewed the Jews in strictly racial terms. It will be necessary for learners to appreciate that the attitudes of National Socialism towards the Jews were not unique and that antisemitism had existed for many centuries. Yet as discussed in Chapter 12, students should also be made aware of the positive contributions of Jews to European social and cultural life and not view Jews simply as outsiders or victims within the meta-narratives of history.

In addition to the Jewish context, students should also understand something of the political climate and the emergence of Nazism as well as its subsequent establishment within Germany. Learners should appreciate why there was significant popular support for the NSDAP and examine the popularity (or lack thereof) of anti-Jewish measures such as the boycott of Jewish shops in April 1933, the Nuremberg Laws and *Kristallnacht*. In many schools the Holocaust is part of a more general course on German history, typically covering the period 1918–45. In such instances, teaching about Nazi as well as popular attitudes towards the Jews can be integrated into the course, and care should be taken to show how the Holocaust can only be understood within its context. Other schools teach the Holocaust as a stand-alone unit, which provides greater scope to go into depth on the subject. In such instances, students may never have studied Weimar or Nazi Germany and so providing a suitable political framework for understanding the Holocaust is important. It is not uncommon for the Holocaust to still be taught as part of a study of the Second World War. If this is to be done effectively, then the direction of anti-Jewish policy before 1939 should not be ignored.

When teaching the Holocaust – especially when doing so as a stand-alone unit – it is easy to forget that the Nazis' decision-making processes were governed by their involvement in the Second World War. This does not mean that every decision that they took regarding the Jews was in the interest of winning of the war – on many occasions they were counter-productive in that regard. Yet the direction of the Second World War did simultaneously determine the direction and levels of acceleration within the Holocaust. After all, the invasion of the Soviet Union led to a cataclysmic, irreversible and fatal shift in the very nature of Nazi Jewish policy, while the bombing of Hamburg by the British in September 1941 led its *Gauleiter*, Karl Kaufmann, to write to Hitler requesting the deportation of Jews from the city to make way for Germans who had had their homes destroyed. Hitler agreed to the request and the Jews of Hamburg were sent to Łódź.

Failing to place the Holocaust within the context of the Second World War will provide a one-dimensional aspect which prevents students from understanding the subject as fully as they ought to.

Moving beyond Auschwitz and moving beyond the camps

The camps which were established by the Nazi regime were a central part of the apparatus and infrastructure which was necessary to conduct the Holocaust. Consequently Auschwitz, where around 1 million Jews were murdered, has become a synonym of the word 'Holocaust'. Auschwitz frequently appears in literature, films and documentaries on the Holocaust and many students arrive in the classroom with at least some conception of what went on there. The importance of Auschwitz should certainly not be marginalised but at the same time, it should not be emphasised to such an extent that it overshadows other extermination camps. Students should recognise that before Auschwitz became the central feature of the Nazi programme of murder, camps such as Treblinka, Sobibor, Chelmno, Madjanek and Belzek were killing Jews in their hundreds of thousands.

Moreover, the complex arrangement of Nazi camps throughout Europe varied dramatically, serving various functions and purposes. A place such as Westerbork in northeast Netherlands was a transit camp where Jews would be held before their deportation to concentration and extermination camps in other parts of Europe. Drancy, located in a Parisian suburb, was also an internment and detention camp where Jews were situated before their journeys east. These were different from Dachau, which in turn had many distinctions from Theresienstadt concentration camp in Czechoslovakia or Mauthausen in Austria. Many adolescents arrive in the classroom with the misconception that all camps were practically identical, where the weak were sent to the gas chambers and the strong forced to work. Learners should finish their Holocaust curriculum in history with the appreciation that the thousands of camps across Europe served different goals but were all a brutal part of the Nazi programme of murderous antisemitism.

While it would seem peculiar in the extreme to omit the camps from a history syllabus on the Holocaust, so one might argue that it is equally strange to not teach about the other ways in which Jews were murdered. Yet some curricula seem to marginalise a study of the ghettos, where many Jews were shot or starved to death. Moreover, the systematic murder of Jews in the East by the *Einsatzgruppen* is perhaps the most commonly ignored and forgotten aspect of the Holocaust. While studying Auschwitz and the camps is important, teachers must ensure that they go beyond this; that their lessons give sufficient detail and attention to the other places of murder.

The decision of the Nazi regime to establish ghettos in Poland from 1939 onwards was an important step towards systematic murder, even though the 'Final Solution' had not been conceived at this stage of the war. Students need to know that many Jews who ended up in the camps did not come directly from their homes. Instead they were placed in cramped and horrific conditions where disease was rife and where many starved to death. Students need to appreciate that Polish Jews (as well as Jews from many other countries) were placed within ghettos which were then liquidated by sending the inhabitants to the camps (principally the extermination camps). Such an understanding is necessary for a number of reasons:

• It helps students to realise how the Nazis were able to implement their murderous programme so quickly and effectively.

- It enables students to see the evolution of Nazi policy and the journey that many Jews took from their homes to their eventual deaths.
- It highlights how a number of Jews did not think that things were going to get worse and how some (especially in the early years of extermination) believed that being deported from the ghettos would be better for them.
- It provides an opportunity for teachers to study Jewish resistance within the ghettos, which is an often overlooked topic.
- It helps students to appreciate why those arriving at the camps were incredibly weak and largely incapable of putting up any resistance.

Moving beyond an exclusive focus on the camp system entails more than including the ghettos. Another frequently overlooked area is the mass shooting of Jews in the East. In June 1941 when the Nazis invaded the Soviet Union, mobile killing squads called *Einsatzgruppen*, which had previously operated in Poland, implemented a murderous programme against communist officials and Jews. The mass shooting of Jews in the Baltic States, Ukraine, Russia and other parts of the East was a central part of the Holocaust and very influential in the evolution of what was to become known as the 'Final Solution'. Students need to learn about this important part of the Holocaust if they are to have a proper and meaningful understanding of what took place. By failing to include the mass shootings within a history curriculum, it excludes the experiences of Jews living in that part of the world and focuses too heavily on the fate of Jews in Central and Western Europe. In addition to that, students who add up the death tolls from the largest of the camps will find that the figure is some way off from the approximately 6 million who perished during the Holocaust. One of the key claims of those who distort the Holocaust is that this figure is too high and if students are not aware that over 1 million were shot in the East, then they will struggle to defend their case.

Highlight the complexity of the past

When studying the Holocaust, students are only going to have a genuine understanding of the past if practitioners appreciate that generalisations and simplifications may do more harm than good. Learners must recognise that many aspects of the Holocaust defy generalisations and that there are very often individual stories which present a unique insight into the Holocaust's complexity.

Trends in Holocaust education over recent years have rightly emphasised the consideration of individuals' experiences, which helps to personalise and realise the horrors of the Holocaust when faced with overwhelming statistics such as 6 million deaths. Yet it is important that students who look at one person's account recognise that this was likely to be very different from another's. In many senses there was no typical story of either a survivor or one who was never able to record their experiences. It therefore seems beneficial if learners appreciate that the Holocaust in France was different to the Holocaust in Poland, which in turn was different to the Holocaust in Germany, Latvia or Hungary. Even within these individual countries there were varying experiences, and a sound history education should enable students to understand this, even if there is no possibility of studying the details of Nazi policy towards the Jews in each of these countries.

Students must also recognise similar levels of complexity when studying the topic of resistance. Learners often perceive the only form of meaningful opposition to the Nazis as that which was violent, and can thus overlook the nuances of what it meant to challenge the regime. Cultural, spiritual and religious resistance should thus be included in a history curriculum. In addition to this, teachers should provide examples which show this range, perhaps including partisan resistance, the celebrating of *Shabbat* in a ghetto or the performing of plays in Theresienstadt.

Liberation and beyond

With serious curriculum constraints existing for almost every teacher of the Holocaust, it is understandable that tough decisions have to be made regarding what is included and what is not. Unfortunately, it seems that for many practitioners they run out of lessons and consequently fail to give proper attention to the way that the Holocaust ended. If students have been taught the subject within the context of the Second World War, then they will be better placed to understand the way that the camps were liberated by the Allied forces. When learning about this final chapter of the Holocaust, they should also be aware of how the Nazis sought to cover up the evidence and how they forced inmates to go on the death marches. Students also benefit from considering what happened to survivors after the war, and misconceptions that they simply went home should be challenged. In addition to this, some mention of the Nuremberg trials, as well as other famous court cases such as the Eichmann trial, will also help provide closure on the topic and provide a fascinating angle for learners. If students appreciate the significance and legacy of the Holocaust then they will be better positioned to understand its relevance and place on the curriculum.

Naturally, a number of factors (most of all teaching time) will affect what can be included in the curriculum. Yet with careful planning, a very meaningful and beneficial programme can be constructed. Box 3.1 shows the key themes and sub-topics that a broad and detailed curriculum might include.

Box 3.1 Key themes and sub-topics of a broad curriculum

Jewish identity, religion and history
Nazi persecution of Jews in Germany (1933–39)
    Boycott of Jewish shops; Nuremberg Laws; *Kristallnacht*; emigration
The experiences of Jews in Europe (1939–40)
    Antisemitic legislation; life in the ghettos
The evolution of the 'Final Solution' (1941–42)
    Invasion of the Soviet Union; *Einsatzgruppen*; Wannsee Conference
The destruction of Europe's Jews (1942–45)
    The camp system; life in the camps; Operation Reinhard
    Resistance; decisions and actions
The ending of the Holocaust (1945 onwards)
    Liberation; the death marches; the experiences of survivors; post-war trials;
    the legacy of the Holocaust.

To see how this fits into a specific scheme of work, see the example in Chapter 14.

Teaching the Holocaust in religious studies

The Holocaust raises all sorts of moral and ethical issues. It challenges some very fundamental values and beliefs and thus its inclusion within a religious studies curriculum seems paramount. Within the subject, the Holocaust is often used as an example or case study when dealing with broader ethical or moral themes. The scheme of work in Chapter 14 shows how a specific Holocaust scheme of work can be constructed which pulls together its inclusion from a range of different areas.

Providing context

For some students, their first encounter with the concepts of Judaism or Jewish people will be through a study of the Holocaust. They are thus likely to have little, if any understanding of the long and vibrant history of Jews and Jewish identity; of the millions of Jews who had lived throughout the world for thousands of years long before Hitler, Nazism or Auschwitz had ever existed. It is thus imperative that teachers ensure that a student's knowledge of Jews is not defined by the Holocaust. A study of Judaism as one of the three ancient monotheisms helps to ensure that this problem is avoided. Learners should recognise the rich cultural heritage as well as the important religious practices and teachings, which occurred before, often during and certainly after the Holocaust. While the Holocaust has cast a long shadow on post-war Jewish life, it ought not and must not narrowly define how students view Judaism or Jewish identity.

Context is not only important when developing students' conceptions of Jews and Judaism, but also when including the Holocaust in any teaching on ethics and moral decision making. It is easy to sit in a classroom and pass moral judgement on those who lived in the past without a sense of the context and climate in which such individuals were operating. Assessing the decisions made by individuals, families and groups within the Holocaust can only be a meaningful exercise if students have the best possible understanding of the factors that were shaping their decision making. It is unacceptable for them to simply apply their contemporary rationale to someone living in 1930s Germany, a Polish ghetto or a concentration camp. Moral lessons cannot be served to students void of context. Clearly, the Holocaust has the potential to challenge myths, stereotypes and prejudices, but this will only be effective by comparing and contrasting popularly held ideas with the record of the past. As the IHRA teaching guidelines state, 'moral lessons will not be well founded unless they are based upon an accurate and objective reading of the historical past' (IHRA 2014a).

Detaching the Holocaust from its context can also take place when teaching about prejudice, hatred or racism. Too often the horrors of the Holocaust are evoked by teachers in attempts to discourage unpleasant behaviour or playground nastiness. In other words, the Holocaust is used as a political tool to try and modify behaviour or combat bullying. Whether or not such aims are appropriate has been discussed in Chapter 2, but it is certainly the case that the power of the Holocaust should not be inappropriately harnessed to achieve politically motivated goals. Moreover, there is a strong chance that the Holocaust will be trivialised by using it in such a fashion. While name calling and playground bullying are not justifiable, permissible or tolerable, they remain qualitatively worlds away from the mass shootings and gas chambers of Auschwitz. Assuming that the former inevitably leads to the latter is an abuse of history and removes the Holocaust from its specific historical context.

This is not to say that the Holocaust should not be used as an example of prejudice, hatred or racism. Clearly it serves as a very chilling and powerful example. Yet clear distinctions need to be drawn between the history of the Holocaust and any potential lessons which practitioners may attempt to draw from it. When there is a lack of explicit distinction and clarity, the Holocaust is in danger of being exploited. Any moral lesson therefore which uses the Holocaust as its basis, must ensure that there is transparency, context, objective and critical analysis of the past and an avoidance of oversimplification in order to accommodate the most palatable moral conclusion.

Issues of forgiveness, reconciliation and justice

People's views on forgiveness are likely to be very varied and derive from a variety of religious traditions and ethical frameworks. Within the context of the Holocaust – or genocide more generally – the issues surrounding forgiveness, reconciliation and justice are particularly sensitive. Yet, they remain very pertinent and relevant debates as efforts continue to be made to bring the last few surviving perpetrators to trial.

It seems likely that within a class, students will have different views on many of these issues. Respecting such positions is important, as is encouraging learners to articulate the reasons why they hold to such views. When reflecting on these issues, it is often unhelpful to think in too generalised a way. Not all those involved in the Holocaust thought or acted in the same way or for the same reasons. It is far more beneficial if students have the opportunity to look at individual cases and then reflect on the appropriate response. It is unhelpful to simply talk of categories such as perpetrators and victims when there is a very grey area somewhere in the middle. How do the ideas of forgiveness and justice relate to someone like Rudolf Kastner, who was found guilty by an Israeli court of collaborating with the Nazis and yet saved over a thousand Jews who were otherwise destined for Auschwitz? Undoubtedly, students would look more favourably on him than on someone like Adolf Eichmann. With the case of the latter, teachers can also explore the ethics of his capture and whether the severity of his crimes justified the operation in 1960 which violated Argentina's sovereign rights.

Yet when dealing with these issues, it is also important to stand back and engage with some of the broader questions. Perhaps at the forefront of these is regarding the definition and meaning of justice. If justice is the application and administration of equity and due reward, then can true justice ever exist? For someone like Eichmann who was a central part of the implementation of the Holocaust, is justice even possible? Can there really be due reward when hanging was his only fate? Similar questions could be applied to those individuals in their eighties or nineties who are arrested and put on trial for Holocaust crimes. They have lived in relative freedom for the vast majority of their lives. The idea that a custodial sentence in their final years is justice for their crimes is certainly worthy of being called into question. Consequently, how we use and define terms is very important and specificity of language and terminology is particularly important.

Yet the broader questions go beyond the definition of justice. When reflecting on the theme of forgiveness, it is worth considering whether or not forgiveness is possible when there is an absence of contrition or repentance in the individual concerned. Yet even when words of regret are expressed and forgiveness requested, who is able to offer that forgiveness? Was it right for a Roman Catholic priest to receive the confession of Rudolf Hoess, the former commandant of Auschwitz? Despite his words of penitence, was it acceptable that he was given Holy Communion in his prison cell? Recognising the complexity of the issues is central to any effective teaching of these themes within the context of the Holocaust.

Where was God in the Holocaust?

One of the key religious and ethical dilemmas that the Holocaust produces is regarding the role of God. Does the Holocaust suggest that there is no God? Does it mean that he was not interested in what was going on? Was he not powerful enough to stop it and if he was powerful enough, why did he not intervene? Did God suffer with his people during the Holocaust? Questions such as these do not have easy answers and resist simplistic or straightforward responses.

Clearly these are important questions, both to the Jewish community and to those of other faiths. When reflecting upon them it is imperative that there is great sensitivity, as these lines of enquiry may challenge the very basis of established worldviews. While it seems perfectly reasonable to pose these questions, they should not be driven by an agenda to undermine any pre-existing religious beliefs. Teachers should ensure that in addition to posing these questions, they provide many of the answers that have been constructed by various Jewish thinkers. Learners need to know what these answers are so that they are in a position to either accept them or reject them. To challenge a student's belief in or conception of the divine without providing a balanced case can be damaging and harmful.

Teaching the Holocaust through English

Although the Holocaust is more commonly taught in subjects such as history and religious studies, it is also sometimes covered in English language and literature classes. Both provide a very helpful dimension to the subject which would not be included elsewhere.

When teaching the Holocaust through English it is important to consider whether or not students have studied the topic in other subjects. Learning about the Holocaust in history provides the foundation for studying it in other disciplines, and students are likely to be much better equipped to look at language or texts if they have a knowledge and understanding of what actually happened during the Holocaust. If learners have not previously studied the Holocaust in history lessons, then teachers of English will need to reflect carefully on how the use of literary texts may be interpreted and whether or not they may establish misconceptions. Providing a detailed historical background is also likely to be very necessary.

One particularly interesting way of exploring the Holocaust in English lessons is through a study of the Nazis' use and control of language. As McGuinn notes: 'The Nazis mounted a fundamental assault upon the integrity of words … just as they sought to deny Jewish people access to the channels of communication, so they manipulated the spoken and written word to their own ends' (McGuinn 2000: 119–20). A valuable study of the Nazis' use of language could include their use of euphemism to disguise their crimes through phrases such as 'resettlement' or 'Final Solution'. Their use of lies and deceit to convince Jews to be deported and enter the camps and then gas chambers with minimal suspicion could also be considered. Other areas of study might include how the Nazis used specific words and terms to dehumanise their victims.

Many English teachers choose to use non-fictional Holocaust texts such as diary accounts or post-war testimonies. Among the most commonly used are: *Anne Frank:*

Diary of a Young Girl; *Night* by Elie Wiesel; and *If This Is a Man* by Primo Levi. Not only are these three books seminal in the canon of Holocaust literature, but provide an important insight and dimension to the subject. Yet just because these texts are not fictional does not mean that they cannot pose problems for adolescents' understanding of the Holocaust or should not be subject to rigorous scrutiny. In research by Gray on students' knowledge and understanding of the Holocaust, there was evidence to suggest that students held an exaggerated belief in the number of Jews who hid during the Holocaust as well as their levels of success in doing so. The importance of Anne Frank's experiences and her diary was considered the most probable reason for this (Gray 2014: 176). It seems sensible therefore, that teachers place emphasis on the range of very different experiences that Jews had during the Holocaust. What happened to Anne Frank differed greatly from Primo Levi, who endured different circumstances to countless others. Practitioners should assess with their students the typicality of one set of experiences, not to mention the fallibility of memory and the various issues which are associated with post-war testimonies.

By contrast, some teachers choose to study fictional texts about the Holocaust with their classes, such as *Friedrich* by Hans Peter Richter, *The Devil's Arithmetic* by Jane Yolen or Lois Lowry's novel *Number the Stars*. There are undoubtedly pros and cons to studying any book, but perhaps of equal if not more significance is how the book is studied. Even within a book with very limited and questionable historical accuracy such as *The Boy in the Striped Pyjamas* by John Boyne, there is an interesting discussion of life in the Krakow ghetto between Shmuel and Bruno which could be meaningfully explored. The book also generates discussion of whether or not Bruno's naivety would have been maintained and how many people really knew what was happening to Europe's Jews.

Fictional texts which use the Holocaust as their central theme can play a very valuable role in Holocaust education. Nevertheless, it is imperative that teachers of English literature provide a constant and critical analysis of the historical accuracy of the book. Failure to do this can lead to a wide range of misconceptions being established and end up doing far more harm than good to children's understanding of the subject. Practitioners should choose their texts carefully and think about what the implications of studying a particular text are likely to be (see Chapter 5). By ensuring that the historical accuracy is critically assessed and that the book is studied in its context, then literary works can be very effective in Holocaust education.

Conclusion

Teaching the Holocaust in any subject offers a wide range of challenges and opportunities. Delivering an effective programme relies upon constantly reflecting on the issues; on what is good practice; and on how what is taught in the classroom will affect the students concerned.

Recommended reading

Foster, S. and Mercier, C. (2000) 'Teaching the Holocaust through Religious Education', in Davies, I. (ed.), *Teaching the Holocaust: Educational Dimensions, Principles and Practice* (London: Continuum), pp. 151–62.

Haydn, T. (2000) 'Teaching the Holocaust through History', in Davies, I. (ed.), *Teaching the Holocaust: Educational Dimensions, Principles and Practice* (London: Continuum), pp. 135–50.

Shawn, K. (2001) 'Choosing Holocaust Literature for Early Adolescents', in Totten, S. and Feinberg, S. (eds), *Teaching and Studying the Holocaust* (Boston: Allyn and Bacon), pp. 139–55.

Chapter 4

What do students already know?

When children arrive in the classroom they come with a whole range of ideas about life and how the world works. Rather than being empty vessels waiting to be filled with knowledge, their experiences, observations and encounters with people, places and the things around them have shaped the way that they approach their learning. When it comes to a subject like the Holocaust, students will have a wide range of preconceptions – and misconceptions – about the Jews, the Nazis, Hitler, concentration camps and the gas chambers. Only by discovering what students understand by terms such as these, can a teacher ensure that their students are learning what they intend them to learn. After all, if two adolescents have very different conceptions of Jews and Nazis, a simple statement such as 'The Nazis tried to murder all the Jews of Europe' will have two distinct meanings. Consequently it is vital that teachers take the time to explore what ideas and understandings their students have brought with them before they begin to teach the Holocaust.

Why are preconceptions important?

The ideas that students bring with them into the classroom can be either a benefit or a hindrance to their learning. The key to effective teaching is to build on their existing knowledge and understandings, while challenging and replacing their misconceptions with that which is accurate and evidence-based. There are various reasons why recognising preconceptions is so important.

It tackles ignorance and error

Enabling students to learn, lies at the very heart of education. This includes disseminating knowledge, developing their understanding, highlighting where their existing thinking needs to change and filling in the areas where there is an absence of awareness. Teaching is most effective when it tackles erroneous ideas and dispels the myths, misconceptions and ignorance which previously existed. Yet teachers are only able to do this as effectively as possible when they take the time and effort to find out what a class knows, doesn't know or thinks it knows, about a particular subject.

It helps determine curriculum content

If a history teacher discovers that a class already possesses considerable knowledge of Jews, Jewish identity, life and culture as a consequence of religious studies lessons, then it will not be necessary to teach the same thing again. Similarly, if as a result of studying a book in English literature classes, students know a great deal about camp life, then this may influence how much teaching time is dedicated to this area of the Holocaust. Conversely, if students are lacking in meaningful knowledge of the ghettos or pre-war Jewish life, then this may encourage the teacher to spend more time on this topic than previously planned. Moreover, if it is clear that students have acquired misconceptions of what it means to be Jewish or are under the impression that one person's experiences were typical of everyone in the Holocaust, then these concerns may need to be addressed more specifically.

It ensures that students accept new knowledge

Within a student's mind their ideas need to cohere. Their brain tells them that two contradictory statements cannot both be true. If adolescents arrive in the classroom with existing misconceptions, which are not deconstructed, then they may reject new knowledge which is incoherent with their original ideas. For example, if a student erroneously believes that there were millions of Jews in Germany during the 1930s and their teacher then states that Jews were not taking up lots of jobs in the country, then they are likely to reject this new statement because it is incoherent with their original misconception. If, however, the teacher is able to tackle their erroneous view and enable the student to understand that Jews made up less than 1 per cent of the 1933 German population, then they will not reject the idea that Jews were not taking up all the jobs.

It prevents students reverting to misconceptions

Unless the misconceptions that students hold are discovered and actively tackled, then students may learn the new information that they acquire in the classroom, repeat it in a test, but then revert to their original misunderstandings. Learners must recognise why their existing views may be incorrect and be shown the evidence to prove it. This is only possible when the teacher explores the existing ideas.

It enables students to understand other aspects of the Holocaust

As a consequence of the need for internal coherence in one's thinking, students often develop new misconceptions as a result of existing ones. For example, students who have no awareness of the mass shootings in the East are likely to think that the Jews of the Soviet Union, Latvia, Estonia and Lithuania were typically gassed in extermination camps rather than shot by the *Einsatzgruppen*.

How can preconceptions be discovered?

Discovering the ideas that pupils hold about the Holocaust is a continuous part of good practice when teaching the subject. Even in the last lesson, new preconceptions may come to light. Despite this, it is useful to invest time and energy into directly investigating what knowledge and ideas the class has about the topic before the teaching commences. This investigation does not need to take place in the first lesson of the course programme; often it is better to do it a few weeks prior to the first lesson so that the results can be analysed and resources and curriculum adjusted accordingly so that existing knowledge is built upon and developed, while misconceptions are specifically addressed. There are various ways in which this can be done.

Writing down their questions

It can be very beneficial to ask one's students what they would like to know about the Holocaust when they study it. This has multiple benefits. First, it gives students a sense that they are contributing to their own learning and that they can have an input into the content of their curriculum. Second, it highlights the existing level of knowledge and can highlight some key misconceptions. Third, students may be inclined to engage with a subject when they recognise how many things they do not know about it. Interesting pre-course questions which some students have generated have included: 'Why was Hitler so keen to kill the Jews?', 'How did the Nazis know who was Jewish?', and 'Did anyone fight back?'.

Spider diagrams or clusters

One simple way of exploring preconceptions is give students a sheet of paper with the word 'Holocaust' in the middle of it and then ask them to write anything they know about the subject in a spider diagram format. It is important to remember that many young people are not familiar with the term 'Holocaust' but do know about the treatment of the Jews during the Second World War. Consequently, explaining the word first is likely to make the exercise more productive. If a class is able to do this successfully, it can be developed into a cluster whereby each word or fact becomes the centre of mini spider diagrams and the exercise is taken onto the next level. Some students may find it easier to write down what they associate with the treatment of the Jews during the Second World War rather than what they know about it. These answers will also help to demonstrate the nature and extent of their existing knowledge and understanding.

Questionnaire

Another way of discovering students' prior understandings is to produce a short and simple questionnaire. While no method will bring to light every idea that even one child holds, let alone a whole class, it does enable students' thinking on the main questions to be seen. These are questions such as 'Who carried out the Holocaust?', 'Why was it carried out?' and 'How was it carried out?'. Open-ended questions are much more effective than closed questions or multiple choice answers, as they show a student's thinking more clearly. With open-ended questions, a wrong answer may be more informative and insightful about how a learner is thinking than a correct response.

What are the sources of students' preconceptions of the Holocaust?

A key part of getting to grips with students' preconceptions of the Holocaust is to understand the sources of their existing ideas. Being able to pinpoint the exact origins of students' thinking is impossible but research has shown that films and books can have a large impact on the way that many young people think about the subject (Gray 2014).

Perhaps the largest influence on thinking has come from John Boyne's novel *The Boy in the Striped Pyjamas*, which was turned into a film in 2008. In Gray's research in 2013 on a sample of 298 13- and 14-year-olds in England, 75.8 per cent had either read the book or watched the film compared with 48.9 per cent for *Anne Frank: The Diary of a Young Girl*. With so many students having been exposed to these specific sources of

Holocaust knowledge, it seems that teachers need to be familiar with them too if they want to understand what their students think and why they hold to those particular views. After all, if the majority of a class have seen the film of *The Boy in the Striped Pyjamas* one can understand why students would be surprised when they are told that children arriving in Auschwitz were gassed on arrival. Moreover, it is easy to see why those who have read the diary of Anne Frank may think that it was very typical of Jews in Europe to go into hiding in secret annexes.

In addition to being aware of some of the more popular and mainstream Holocaust representations, it is also important to recognise that a particular class may have all studied a book in literature lessons or all watched a certain film in religious studies. If such is the case, then engaging with the text or film may be of great benefit when it comes to appreciating why students hold particular misconceptions. Only when one knows why they think in a certain way is one best equipped to respond, and thus some consideration of from where students have acquired their knowledge and understanding of the Holocaust is most beneficial indeed.

What are the common preconceptions about the Holocaust?

Within even a single class, there is likely to be a wide range of prior conceptions which will exist. Nevertheless, research demonstrates that some knowledge and understanding of the Holocaust is more common, while there are also certain misconceptions which are popularly held. It is also worth remembering that preconceptions are likely to change as students go through their education. As students encounter the subject in various disciplines their preconceptions will be modified. Nevertheless, the areas discussed below highlight some of the most common preconceptions which currently exist according to the latest studies.

Jews and Jewish identity

Central to any understanding of the Holocaust is knowledge of Jews and their identity. Teachers of the Holocaust therefore, cannot assume that their students have an accurate conception of who Jews are; their culture, history and identity. Short et al. correctly state:

> It is … essential that teachers spend some time, *prior* to starting work on the Holocaust, exploring and challenging any misconceptions their pupils may have either about Jews or Judaism. These religious and secular misconceptions are woven into the fabric of western culture and, because the vast majority of schools in Europe are in places where there are few or no Jews, the misconceptions, if not challenged by teachers, will inevitably influence pupils' reactions to the Holocaust.
>
> (Short et al. 1998: 20)

Box 4.1 shows some answers that 13- and 14-year-olds gave in response to the question: 'who are Jews?'

While some of the students saw Jews simply as a religious group, others understood the term to refer to a particular ethnic group. This appears to be common among adolescents. Many see Jews simply as a religious group, others simply as a race. Few seem to appreciate the complexity of defining Jewishness, concepts of consanguinity and cultural identity, for example. Integrating this multi-layered and more sophisticated understanding into

---

Box 4.1 Who are Jews? Answers from 13- and 14-year-olds

'It's just like being a Catholic or like a Christian.'
'They're normal people who just have a religion that is different to Christianity.'
'As well as a religious group they are an ethnic group as well. If your parents were Jewish then you count as Jewish even if you don't believe.'
'Is it like when, like I'm Greek, you're English, you're English, is it like, you're Jewish?'

---

students' framework of thinking is very helpful for laying sound foundations for teaching the Holocaust. Often learners' thinking can be challenged by posing examples which do not fit into their existing definitions, such as the notion of secular Jews, as characterised by Albert Einstein or Sigmund Freud.

Religious studies curricula often address questions such as 'Who are Jews?' and 'What is Judaism?' Teachers of the Holocaust in other subjects may therefore find it very helpful to ask their colleagues whether or not their students have already come across these issues and what the nature of their thinking has tended to be. If adolescents commence a study of the Holocaust without first considering who Jews are – their history, culture and contribution to pre-war European life – then they may have fundamental misconceptions which affect their entire understanding of the course and severely reduce the positive impact of their learning.

The causes

One of the most commonly asked questions that a teacher receives when delivering Holocaust education is 'Why did Hitler hate Jews?' Adolescents are always keen to know what caused the Holocaust and if their enquiries are not satisfactorily answered then students may leave thinking that there was something fundamentally wrong with Jews themselves.

When explaining why the Holocaust took place, it is important to recognise some popular misconceptions that often exist in the minds of adolescents. The first of these is the belief that Jews were ubiquitous within Germany. A recent study found that many students in England believed that Jews made up between 21 and 40 per cent of the 1933 German population (Gray 2014: 194); a misconception which was also shared (although to a lesser extent) by teachers of all subject disciplines (Pettigrew et al. 2009: 54). Consequently, many adolescents believed that Jews were taking 'all the jobs' in Germany, failing to recognise that according to the census of 16 June 1933, Jews made up less than 1 per cent of the population and that 80 per cent of them had German citizenship and were thus German.

Another popular misconception that is often held is the belief that Jews were not integrated into German society. This directly contradicts Gilbert's statement that: 'the Jews of Germany had been among Europe's most assimilated, most cultured, most active contributors to the national life of the state in which they lived. Hundreds of thousands of them had become an integral part of German society' (Gilbert 1986: 35).

By dispelling these erroneous beliefs, the idea that popular antisemitism within Germany drove Nazi policy towards the Jews becomes a far less tenable cause of the Holocaust. It then allows for a discussion of how racial theory – the belief that race determines one's nature and character as well as one's physical appearance and that there is a strict racial hierarchy – lay at the heart of Nazi ideology and was the driving force in their approach to the Jews.

Only by appreciating the biological antisemitism that the Nazis possessed, their obsession with the *Judenfrage* (the 'Jewish question', i.e. what to do with Jews) and the relationship between the evolution of the 'Final Solution' and the Second World War can students really begin to grasp the complexity of the Holocaust's causes and avoid the simplistic mono-causal explanations which fail to provide a truly satisfactory answer. Adolescents already have a tendency to simplify the origins of the Holocaust and, as characterised by the question 'Why did Hitler hate the Jews?', often see its causes in purely Hitler-centric terms. It is important that Holocaust education goes beyond Hitler's antisemitism, tackles misconceptions and provides a more sophisticated and historically grounded explanation for the murder of Europe's Jews during the Second World War.

The perpetrators

Hitler-centrism has a large impact on students' thinking when considering who perpetrated the Holocaust. Very often, adolescents do not go beyond Hitler in explaining who implemented the murder of Europe's Jews, and those who do typically just refer to the Nazis. An effective way of helping shift students away from their Hitler-centric perspective is to ask them who actually murdered the 6 million Jews of the Holocaust. It is beneficial for learners to recognise that to conduct such a vast European-wide programme of annihilation, a large number of personnel was needed, which went far beyond an inner clique of brainwashed Hitler-worshippers and included countless men and women who were willing and determined to implement genocidal antisemitism.

An important part of providing students with a sophisticated understanding of the Holocaust is to first remove simplistic preconceptions. Only then can a teacher begin to introduce the various perpetrators into the course programme such as the *Einsatzgruppen*, the camp guards and the desk-bound killers who administered the transportations.

Chronology

Unsurprisingly, most students do not have anything close to a detailed or accurate chronological knowledge of the Holocaust. Nevertheless, perhaps as a consequence of films and literature – or even the influence of the media – students do have various ideas which they tend to patch together in a loose chronology. Figure 4.1 demonstrates how many students tend to see both the order of events and the actual chronology of the Holocaust (albeit in simplified form).

As indicated by Figure 4.1, the majority of students have minimal awareness of the ghettos and the mass shootings in the East. Instead they seem to think that Jews were simply taken directly from their homes to the camps. While this obviously happened in some instances, for most of Europe's Jews – especially those living in Poland – they arrived at the camps from ghettos like the one at Warsaw, Lublin or Krakow. When teaching about the camps or the Holocaust in general, it is important not to assume any knowledge of the ghettos and to highlight their role in the Nazis' policies towards the Jews.

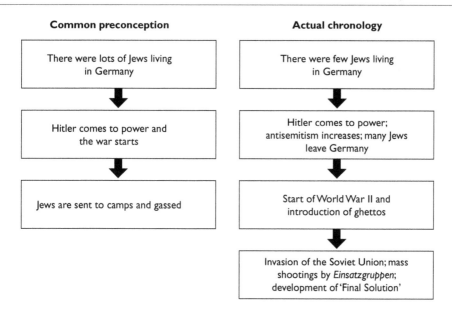

Common preconception

There were lots of Jews living in Germany

↓

Hitler comes to power and the war starts

↓

Jews are sent to camps and gassed

Actual chronology

There were few Jews living in Germany

↓

Hitler comes to power; antisemitism increases; many Jews leave Germany

↓

Start of World War II and introduction of ghettos

↓

Invasion of the Soviet Union; mass shootings by *Einsatzgruppen*; development of 'Final Solution'

Figure 4.1 Holocaust chronologies: preconceived versus actual

The same can also be said about the work of the *Einsatzgruppen*. These mobile killing squads which accompanied the German Army into the Soviet Union and systematically murdered Jews in their hundreds, thousands and tens of thousands, are little known among most adolescents. It is important that students are aware that these murderous units were responsible for over 1 million Jewish deaths and played a crucial role in the evolution and implementation of the Holocaust.

The camps

The word 'Auschwitz' is now used even as a synonym for the Holocaust and students generally have greater knowledge of the camps than they do of other aspects. Research suggests that many adolescents are aware that there were lots of camps, although few are able to distinguish between the different types or know the names of them other than Auschwitz. Nevertheless, something of the barbaric conditions, the striped uniform, the shaving of heads, the starvation and the frequent beatings is generally known and understood (Gray 2014: 261).

Students also have a tendency to universalise the experiences of inmates at Auschwitz and make the assumption that what happened there occurred in every camp. For example, the tattooing of numbers on an inmate was a unique characteristic of Auschwitz, while the selection processes for work or the gas chambers did not take place in every camp. In many instances the decisions affecting life and death had already been made in the ghettos with those arriving at places like Belzec or Treblinka II already sentenced to death before the train pulled into the station.

Many students therefore have a one-dimensional approach to the camps, failing to recognise that there were many different types and that the experiences of one inmate in a particular camp were not necessarily the same as somebody else's. Providing a multi-layered and multi-dimensional understanding of the camp system is very important and helps to dispel the myth that all camps were like Auschwitz.

Resistance

Students have a tendency to think of resistance in very black and white terms, as seen in the examples in Box. 4.2.

Box 4.2 Students' simplified ideas about Jewish resistance

'Fighting is the only form of resistance that matters.'
'Jews just accepted what was happening to them – I don't know why they didn't fight back.'

They understand that engaging in violence against the Nazi regime was resistance, but struggle to see how the term can be applied to religious or cultural acts of defiance. This simplified misconception can often be tackled by drawing analogies to occasions when non-violent acts have had large effects, such as the Black Power salute in the Mexico City Olympics or the Freedom Rides of the 1960s. By explaining how those who resisted – in any form – were breaking the law, defying the wishes of the regime and putting their own lives in danger, helps students to recognise that resistance was far more than acts of aggression.

Nevertheless, focusing on specific uprisings conducted by Jews against their Nazi oppressors is also important, as research suggests that few students are aware of the Warsaw Ghetto Uprising or the revolt of the *Sonderkommando* in Birkenau in 1944 (Gray 2014: 265). Consequently, it seems that most adolescents believe that all Jews went passively to their deaths. Highlighting why some Jews did not resist (i.e. disbelief; optimism; Nazi deception and violence; physical exhaustion) and why and how others chose to do so is an important part of providing a more developed understanding of the issues, and helps to avoid the simplifications and generalisations which often exist.

Scale and geography

In a society where knowledge and discussion of the Holocaust is ubiquitous, it is easy to almost take it for granted that students already know that around 6 million European Jews were murdered by the Nazis. However, such assumptions are problematic and fail to take into account that many students perceive that the Holocaust was the murder of German Jews in Germany and that they are not familiar with the figure of 6 million. Seeing that most learners have no knowledge of the *Einstazgruppen*, it is perhaps unsurprising that they lack awareness of the full scale of the killings or that they stretched from the Channel Islands to the Soviet Union. Unless students know which territories were occupied by the Nazi regime and its allies, then they will not be able to appreciate the far-reaching extent of the Holocaust.

If students learn that Jews in Germany constituted less than 1 per cent of the population of Germany in 1933, they may well wonder how it was possible for the Nazis to murder six million. In other words, where did the Jews that were murdered come from? Moreover, if only around 1 million Jews were murdered in Auschwitz-Birkenau, where were the others killed? These are important questions, which must be answered confidently and effectively. The rise of Holocaust denial and so-called 'revisionism' means that it is very helpful if teachers can give a clear breakdown of the figures.

The ending

Many of the popular films and books with which adolescents engage, do not address in any detail how the Holocaust ended. Teachers should not be surprised therefore when their students demonstrate various misconceptions about it. One of the most common of these is the belief that Hitler's death caused the end of the Holocaust. In other words, many adolescents are aware that Hitler committed suicide but believe that this event caused the end of the Holocaust. This is undoubtedly connected to students' Hitler-centric explanation of Nazi policy towards the Jews. In other words, Hitler's fanatical antisemitism and total control over Germany forced the country into a genocidal policy which terminated only when Hitler killed himself, as though his death broke some sort of spell over the German people. This is a problematic and worrying misconception for a number of reasons. First, this idea is not supported by the available evidence. While Hitler was no doubt very important in the development of the Holocaust he was not driving the minutiae, which were propelled by a range of figures within the regime, not least of all Himmler, Eichmann and, up to his assassination in June 1942, Heydrich. Second, such a misconception provides a simplistic and grossly generalised view of the past and will support other misconceptions. Moreover, by marginalising the involvement of so many thousands of individuals in the process of mass murder, one is also ignoring their guilt, complicity and criminality.

To truly understand any aspect of the Holocaust, it cannot be detached from the context of the Second World War. This is especially true of its ending. Learners must recognise that the camps were liberated by Allied soldiers who were doing so to end the War. Some adolescents hold the idea that the Allies invaded Europe to end the Holocaust and that this is what the whole conflict was all about. Challenging this idea is very needful.

Other misconceptions that students sometimes demonstrate when dealing with the ending of the Holocaust is the idea that the Nazis ran out of Jews to kill; the Nazis had a change of heart and stopped the killing; or that they made a peace deal with the Allies. Such a wide range of preconceptions in this area emphasises the great need for teachers to ensure that they deal with how the Holocaust ended.

Many students are not familiar with the brutal death marches which took place at the end of the war, when Nazis forced inmates towards Germany to flee the advances of the Allied forces. By being presented with this aspect of the Holocaust, students realise the importance of the war in determining policy, and see how the Nazis were anxious to conceal their crimes even when they knew that the war had been lost.

If possible, practitioners should spend some time on what happened to survivors after they were liberated from the camps. Common perceptions such as 'they would go home' or 'they would look for their family' can be effectively responded to by asking learners what survivors did when their entire family had been murdered and their homes stolen or destroyed. When this is combined with the physical and psychological state of survivors, it helps students to see the bleakness of the situation which existed in 1945.

Conclusion

While the examples above demonstrate some of the most common preconceptions that exist, there will always be a wide range of ideas, beliefs and myths in any classroom. The key to dismantling misconceptions and building on existing knowledge is to take the time to explore the various preconceptions which exist within the class and to integrate effective strategies into the syllabus which allow them to be addressed. Some familiarity with the sources of students' ideas about the Holocaust will also help to clarify why students may hold certain views, and to pre-empt their thinking on the subject. Certainly, this is an important and often overlooked area of Holocaust education which has meaningful effects on so many other parts of teaching.

Recommended reading

Edwards, C. and O'Dowd, S. (2010) 'The Edge of Knowing: Investigating Students' Prior Conceptions of the Holocaust', *Teaching History*, 141: 20–26.

Gray, M. (2011) 'Understanding Pupil Preconceptions of the Holocaust in English Schools', *Holocaust Studies: A Journal of Culture and History*, 17, no. 1: 1–28.

Gray, M. and Foster, S. (2014) 'What Do Thirteen and Fourteen Year-Olds Know about the Holocaust before They Study It?' *International Journal of Historical Learning, Teaching and Research*, 12, no. 2.

Chapter 5

Using literature in the classroom

When teaching the Holocaust, practitioners often state that helping students to comprehend the nature and scale of what happened is one of their biggest challenges. To grasp 6 million of anything can be extremely difficult, and so how much more so when the subject is human lives and when we make such a demand of adolescents. Literature can thus be a very helpful entry point into the subject of the Holocaust; it can enable learners to approach the topic from the shelter of the author's sensitivities and to begin to see the impact of the Holocaust on one individual, family or community.

With so many poems and stories written about the Holocaust, it can be very overwhelming for the modern-day teacher to choose something that is engaging, appropriate and likely to prove educationally beneficial. What criteria ought one to apply when choosing a text? How should one then teach the text and what are the learning outcomes that are being worked towards? Holocaust literature is a large and potentially complex field, and great wisdom and care is needed.

Why should Holocaust literature be used at all?

A common criticism that is raised against the use of Holocaust literature in the classroom is that it only offers one perspective; that it might tell the story of a Jewish family in Germany or a Roma community in Poland but it cannot provide a holistic understanding of the Holocaust. While this may be true, it ought to be remembered that texts are not written with such an aim in mind. History lessons can provide the important holistic approach; literature can help to shed light on individual stories and demonstrate an individual or group's particular and sometimes unique experiences, which help to make up the bigger picture.

A second objection to the use of literature is that irrespective of ability or talent, it is impossible to record, narrate or describe the Holocaust. The horrors are too detached from our conceptualisation of them. Whether or not this is so is subject to debate, but surely in any case, an attempt to best understand it through conceptualisation and representation is commendable. Others suggest that literature should not be used because it trivialises the Holocaust. Clearly some texts can do this and these ought to be avoided.

Yet despite the various objections to Holocaust literature, there are many benefits which it offers those seeking to learn about this chapter of human history.

It enables students to develop their knowledge of the past

Students who read historical fiction ought to develop their knowledge and understanding of the past. A book which fails to do this is lacking a key ingredient and any author who chooses to set their text in the past will need to ensure historical accuracy. Students who read fiction should have an advantage over their peers when they study the same periods of history. It seems something of an injustice if an adolescent is disadvantaged because the author's historical inaccuracy has established misconceptions and generated confusion. *The Night Crossing* (1994) by Karen Ackerman for example, while obviously intended for young readers, can be misleading. The impression is given that Germany was at war with Austria in 1938 and targeting Austrians generally as well as Austrian Jews.

It generates enthusiasm and interest in the subject

Another benefit of literature on the Holocaust is that it can generate an interest and enthusiasm in the subject which is perhaps harder to produce in other educational settings. A powerfully written story can inspire the reader to want to find out more about this subject and this is likely to be beneficial to Holocaust educators in other disciplines such as history and RS. Perhaps more than anything else, *Anne Frank: The Diary of a Young Girl* has been the gateway for many adolescents into discovering something about the Holocaust and generating an interest in the subject.

It is accessible and understandable

The complexities of the Holocaust can be demanding for learners, and pitching historical content for a wide range of abilities can be very challenging. The range of Holocaust literature, written for a variety of ages, means that students who struggle to grasp aspects of it may find the subject more accessible and understandable. *Terrible Things* (1989) by Eve Bunting, for example, helps learners to appreciate the concepts of injustice and discrimination, even if the book does not explicitly educate about the Holocaust per se. Particular parts of the Holocaust which students may struggle to grasp can also be made more accessible through specific books. *Benno and the Night of Broken Glass* (2010) by Meg Wiviott helps to demonstrate the events and consequences of *Kristallnacht* in a way that is sensitive and understandable. Margaret Wild's *Let the Celebrations Begin* (1991) explains the liberation of the camps in a very clear and simple way, supported by helpful illustrations.

It enables the development of historical empathy

While students cannot empathise with those who experienced the Holocaust, their historical empathy can be developed. In other words, literature helps learners to understand and appreciate why people in the past thought, acted and spoke in the way that they did. Producing this sort of empathy in the history classroom can be very difficult and time consuming when the reasons behind why people did certain things can seem strange and detached from modern life. Literary texts which explain feelings, emotions and choices, within the specific historical context, can enable learners to better understand the reasons behind why certain decisions and courses of action were made. By reading Elie Wiesel's *Night* (1958) for example, it is possible to see how one could choose to live only for their own survival and forsake all ties of friendship.

It provides a unique perspective on the subject

The Holocaust is a vastly complex phenomenon and in order to understand it as much as possible, a multifaceted approach seems imperative. The discipline of history does not have exclusive rights to the Holocaust and the unique perspective that literature offers should be integrated into an adolescent's interaction with the subject. Bauer remarked: 'the historian's art is, after all, limited, and the writer, the poet, the artist, the dramatist, the musician, the psychologist, and, for the religious among us, the theologian have to be asked to add their insights' (Bauer 2001: 23). This is surely true, and poetry like *Butterfly* (1942) by Pavel Friedman or accounts such as *If This Is a Man* (1947) by Primo Levi provide a unique insight into the emotional and personal aspects of the subject.

Choosing the right texts

With such a large corpus of literature from which to choose, selecting the right text for a class can be something of a minefield. As is the case with all art forms, there is a measure of subjectivity and criticism that can be directed towards any piece of literature. Nevertheless, a good teacher will be able to justify and defend their choice because it will conform to pre-existent criteria. When dealing with the sensitive and emotionally charged subject of the Holocaust, these criteria should include the following:

It is age appropriate

The intellectual ability and the emotional maturity of a class are factors which should always be taken into account. A text should appear neither patronising nor inaccessible, which is likely to be the case if the author intended it for a readership either significantly below or significantly above the class for which it has been chosen. In such instances, the benefits of using literature in the classroom will be negated. While texts may push boundaries and challenge existing perceptions, students will gain little benefit if they are left in an unnecessarily uncomfortable position. It is also important to remember that within any class there is likely to be a wide range of maturity and texts should be chosen with that in mind.

The Holocaust is a disturbing subject and adolescents should not be left traumatised as a consequence of reading a text or viewing its illustrations. Students can learn about the Holocaust without graphic descriptions or explicit imagery. Accounts of emaciated corpses, sexual violence or brutal punishments are unlikely to develop an adolescent's understanding of the subject. Rather such descriptions seem superfluous and are likely to encourage justified parental complaints. There is a great deal of literature, such as *Number the Stars* (1989) or *The Devil's Arithmetic* (2004), which is engaging and informative but yet refrains from language or descriptions which are unsuitable for its intended audience.

It is historically accurate

While literature is often imaginative, it seems that any author choosing to use the Holocaust as their subject matter has a moral duty to ensure historical accuracy. Dates, events and places need to be correct. Holocaust literature should enhance and not confuse an adolescent's historical understanding. It should not be assumed that teachers of literature have specialist expertise in history and they will thus most likely assume that historical events described in the text are accurate. In the story of *The Boy in the Striped Pyjamas*

(2006) for example, most Jews deported from the Krakow ghetto went to Belzec and not Auschwitz. While poetic licence on some obscure technicalities seems only fair, in John Boyne's story the whole plot is historically inaccurate. The tale revolves around a 9-year-old at Auschwitz, which seems almost impossible as children were typically gassed upon arrival. According to the book, Shmuel was born in April 1934 and thus the story is set around 1943. By this time all four of the new crematoria were operational and yet Shmuel states that 'there are a lot of us – boys our age, I mean – on this side of the fence' (Boyne 2006: 110). This is implausible and likely to lead to various misconceptions about the nature of the camps.

In order to be historically accurate, children's literature should not avoid dealing with some of the more complex aspects of the Holocaust such as its causes and origins. While many texts revolve around Jewish characters, their persecution and maltreatment, many of them fail to explain why such hatred existed. If young children keep reading about hatred towards Jews but are not told about its historical roots, or the Nazis' racial ideology, then they are likely to assume that there must have been something wrong with Europe's Jews.

It is historically representative

In addition to being historically accurate, Holocaust literature which is used in the classroom ought also to be historically representative. In other words, the texts chosen should not tell of stories so exceptional and extraordinary that they misinform the students into thinking that such occurrences were typical and representative of broader Holocaust experiences. While stories of rescue, self-sacrifice and personal heroism on the part of the ordinary populations in Nazi-occupied Europe may make for exciting stories and compelling tales, they can provide a gloss which distorts the less romantic reality. Stories like *Schindler's Ark* (1982) and *Jacob's Rescue* (1994) were by no means typical; very few non-Jewish families helped to hide or protect Jews from the Nazis. If untypical accounts are used then they should be done so in conjunction with other books so as to demonstrate their untypical nature. At the very least, a clear contextualisation of the story and its unrepresentative character should be explicitly highlighted by the teacher.

It avoids stereotyping, generalisations and simplifications

In order to enable the reader to quickly recognise the identity of certain characters, some authors employ crude stereotyping. This is problematic. Not every Jew who was murdered in the Holocaust was religious, let alone devoutly so. Nazi perpetrators typically had families and were often gregarious, cultured and sociable creatures. Both victims and perpetrators alike had agency and were involved in making countless decisions, even if, in the case of the former, their available options were restricted. The most useful books will have characters which do not simply conform to these stereotypes but rather demonstrate a depth and dimension which transcends such simplifications.

It is engaging and thought-provoking

Holocaust literature ought to engage students with the topic by arousing their interest in the subject and making them think. Asking learners to have some say in what they select to read may help to tackle any resentment and enable certain themes which they find particularly fascinating to be discussed. After studying a text, acquiring feedback from the class regarding the aspects that they found most engaging can be beneficial for future planning.

Contextualising the literature

Before working through a Holocaust text with a class, it is important to provide context and to construct a framework to support their learning. If studying the Holocaust in literature lessons, practitioners should be aware of whether or not their class has studied the subject in other disciplines (especially history). This is likely to have a large impact on what the students know and may well influence the choice of which text is studied.

In addition to this, teachers should explore learners' existing preconceptions about the Holocaust and also their views and ideas about the various core themes which the book will generate. This will not only be helpful in highlighting misconceptions or potential prejudices but will also enable the teacher to see if the book has changed the way that students think about these issues.

If students have not studied the Holocaust in their history lessons then it is important that the class are provided with the historical context to the literature that they are about to study. This could involve asking a colleague from the history department to spend one or two lessons on the background to the text. Even if students have been taught about the Holocaust already, then a lesson or two contextualising the particular aspect of the Holocaust that is dealt with in the text is helpful. For example, if students were reading Karen Hesse's *The Cats in Krasinski Square* (2004) then some background on Poland, Nazi policies in the country and the establishment of ghettos would be helpful. If *Hana's Suitcase* (2003) by Karen Levine was being read, then some context and background of Czechoslovakia and its occupation by Nazi Germany would be beneficial.

Using Holocaust literature in the classroom

There are myriad ways that Holocaust texts can be included in a curriculum, which should not be considered as for the exclusive use of English literature teachers. Poems, short stories and extracts from books can enrich a history or religious studies course and help to illustrate a point or generate discussion. Nevertheless, it is most common for Holocaust texts to be used in literature lessons and many of the ideas below are produced with that in mind, although they could easily be adapted for use in other subject areas.

Analysis of the text

One of the most common methods of studying a text is to read it in class (setting some chapters to be read for homework) and to analyse it accordingly. This analytical study can be done systematically by working through the book in the exact order that it was written. Alternatively, a study can be conducted on particular characters and how they are depicted and how their experiences change them. Similarly, one can study the key themes which emerge such as prejudice, antisemitism, revenge, suffering and hope, to name but a few.

Book assignments

Another way of using Holocaust literature (and expanding the class's knowledge of the existing corpus of it) is to set a book assignment. Each student is asked to choose a book of fiction that has been written about the Holocaust. Teachers may want to provide a list of suitable texts or ensure that the title is approved before the student starts their assignment. Once each member of the class has selected their book then they are given a set period of time to read it. If a class has a timetabled reading lesson each week then they could use this to continue reading their text. During the allotted time that they have to read the book, certain activities could be set which will help to ensure they are engaging sufficiently with it. This might include writing a description of one of the main characters or discussing a key theme that appears. The culmination of the book assignment will be each student giving a five-minute presentation to the rest of the class about their particular book. Teachers should ensure that students follow a set structure for their review, which might include a brief description of the book and the author, their favourite character and why, the key themes that appeared, its historical accuracy, and whether or not the student enjoyed the book.

Journaling

One of the purposes of literature is to develop affective learning. The Holocaust is an emotive subject and it is likely that students will experience a wide range of feelings as they read certain texts. It can be helpful for adolescents to keep a 'reading journal' where at the end of each chapter or section of the book they record how they felt as they read the book and why they think those emotions were generated. This activity involves some emotional maturity from a class and the willingness to reflect honestly about their feelings.

'Reading journals' do not have to simply be used to describe affective learning. They can also provide an opportunity for students to write about how their knowledge and understanding of the Holocaust has developed as a result of the literary study. Learners can also record the evolution of characters and themes as well as what stood out for them and what aspects of the book they liked and disliked.

Comparative poetry

There are many excellent anthologies of Holocaust stories and poems, such as *Art from the Ashes: A Holocaust Anthology* (1995) and *Ghosts of the Holocaust: An Anthology of Poetry from the Second Generation* (1989). There are various ways whereby literary works can be compared and contrasted. One such example is through exploring the similarities and differences between poems written by those during the Holocaust and those written after the event. Alternatively, one might juxtapose select literary works of those who survived the Holocaust with those who had no immediate or direct relationship to it. Such approaches allow students to explore a wide range of work, to learn about the poets themselves, and to reflect on the emotions and motivations of those who produced the texts.

Comparative stories

Literary comparisons can also be made with other texts such as testimonies, stories or additional works. There is a range of comparative options which might include comparing a work of non-fiction with a piece of fiction and making an assessment of the portrayal of the Holocaust, the level of detail provided and the historical accuracy of the authors. Alternatively, character studies could be conducted between protagonists in two or even three different texts. Comparisons and contrasts can also be made between different authors and the context of, and influences on, their writing. Care and sensitivity is needed when engaging in any comparative activities. It is generally irresponsible and unnecessary to compare suffering, and largely impossible for others to judge it. It is also facile to compare the suffering or experiences of a real Holocaust victim with a fictional character.

Survivor depth studies

After reading the testimony or work of a Holocaust survivor, students could engage in a research project on the life of the author. This could be conducted as a cross-curricular project with the history department. A class could be divided into groups and asked to make a large poster presentation on the survivor's life. Examples could include Primo Levi, Elie Wiesel or Simon Wiesenthal among many others.

Examples of how to use literature in lessons

The Boy in the Striped Pyjamas (2006)

While in many senses, John Boyne's novel *The Boy in the Striped Pyjamas* can be a problematic text for classes to study due to the potential misconceptions that it can generate, its popularity as a text means that many schools do choose to study it. In such cases, practitioners should apply the principles discussed above.

One of the most useful chapters to study in Boyne's book is Chapter 12. In it, one of the key themes that appears is the journey that Shmuel took from Krakow to Auschwitz, via the Krakow ghetto. This provides a very helpful opportunity to explore the radical policies that the Nazis implemented towards the Jews, including the directive sent by Reinhard Heydrich in September 1939 to move Jews into larger cities leading to the creation of ghettos. The Krakow ghetto was established in 1941 and according to the story, Shmuel lived there with his family. Shmuel briefly describes the journey from the ghetto to Auschwitz, and this enables discussion and research on the awful conditions that existed aboard the transportations to the camps.

Key questions to explore:

1 In what ways were Shmuel and his family persecuted by the Nazis?
    (E.g. confiscation of property and belongings; forced to wear Star of David armband; forced re-location into ghetto; crowded and awful conditions; forced transportation to camps in horrific conditions, etc.)
2 What symbol was Shmuel and his family forced to wear?
    (a) Who had to wear this symbol in Nazi-occupied Poland?
    (b) Why did the Nazis introduce it?
    (c) When did the Nazis introduce this policy? (The policy was introduced for the General Government (the part of Poland that included Krakow) in November 1939.)
3 Describe the conditions in the ghetto according to Shmuel's remarks.
4 What can you learn from this chapter about the difficulties faced by Shmuel in the camp?
    (E.g. he was underfed, as he asks for food. Also Bruno noticed that he was 'small and skinny'. The weather, as Shmuel says that it was a 'very cold place'.)
5 Contrast the experiences of Bruno and Shmuel in their journeys to Auschwitz.
6 Why does Bruno fail to understand Shmuel's experiences?
7 Is Bruno innocent, naive or stupid?

8   Shmuel states that there are hundreds of other boys in the camp. Why might that have been unlikely in reality?
9   Research the experiences of Polish Jews during the war. Do you think that this account is accurate or not? Explain your answer.

Number the Stars (1989)

This book tells the story of a Jewish family's escape from occupied Copenhagen in 1943. It is important that learners are provided with a sense of context and one or two lessons ought to be spent prior to the study of the book looking at the experience of Denmark and Danish Jewry during the Second World War.

There are many historical themes that can be explored with students through this book, as well as a study of literary techniques. The ideas below show how the subjects can be approached.

1   What does chapter 1 tell us about life in Denmark during this stage of the Second World War?
    (E.g. it was under Nazi occupation; there was an illegal resistance newspaper called *De Frie Danske*; there was the rationing of food, etc.)
2   How do you think Ellen felt during the events of chapters 4–5?
3   Using the novel and what you know about Ellen, write a diary account reflecting on the experiences of the last 24 hours.
4   What was Ellen supposed to be doing rather than staying with the Johansens?
5   According to the story, what do Jews do at Rosh Hashanah?
    (E.g. attend synagogue in their best clothes; have a celebration at home; light the *Shabbat* candles; pray in Hebrew).

After the book has been read, one can reflect on its key themes (many of which will have been discussed throughout the reading and studying of the text) by completing the following activity.

1   Ask the students what is meant by a theme in a book. (Answer: an important message which recurs throughout the story.) Ask the students to list subjects which they think might be themes in *Number the Stars*. (Possible suggestions: bravery, prejudice, resistance, selfless giving to others, survival.) Write answers on individual sheets of A3 paper. Explain that what the class has just done is brainstorm a topic.
2   Divide the class into groups. They will have approximately five minutes at each A3 sheet which have been placed conveniently around the room. They will be brainstorming each subject, asking key questions about the theme, finding examples of the theme from the book, etc. Encourage students not to repeat answers and to be as creative as possible in their use of vocabulary.
3   Discuss as a class the varying responses put against each question.

Night (1958)

The powerful account of Elie Wiesel's experiences in Auschwitz and Buchenwald should be treated differently from fictional texts. Yet students should recognise that this was the story of one individual, which was not only untypical because he survived, but was very different from those of the countless Jews in Nazi-occupied Europe who never entered a camp and were murdered by the *Einsatzgruppen*.

The following questions and discussion points are based on chapter 5 of *Night*.

1   Describe how Rosh Hashanah was celebrated in the camp.
2   Use examples to explain why and how Elie Wiesel rebelled against his religious beliefs.
3   Why did the Nazis conduct selections in the camps?
    (a) Who were kapos?
    (b) Who was Dr Mengele?
4   Why was the knife and spoon such a powerful symbol in the context of Elie's relationship with his father?
        (E.g. they are everyday items of no financial value yet of great significance within the camp; they represented Elie's inheritance and their restoration to Elie's father shows his continued existence after the second selection.)

Suggested reading

Gray, M. (2014) '*The Boy in the Striped Pyjamas*: A Blessing or Curse for Holocaust Educators?' *Holocaust Studies: A Journal of Culture and History* (forthcoming).

Rosen, A. (ed.) (2013) *Literature of the Holocaust* (Cambridge: Cambridge University Press).

Totten, S. (2001) 'Incorporating Fiction and Poetry into a Study of the Holocaust at the Secondary Level', in Totten, S. and Feinberg, S. (eds), *Teaching and Studying the Holocaust* (Boston: Allyn & Bacon), pp. 156–93.

Chapter 6

Using film in the classroom

'Film is rapidly supplanting both literature and academic texts as the main purveyor of historical knowledge for the general public' (Doneson 2001: 194). If this is the case, then how film is used within the classroom is one of the most important issues in contemporary Holocaust pedagogy. Teachers of the Holocaust must therefore appreciate the significance of film to students' learning and how best to harness its influence as a positive and beneficial force, rather than one which undermines and contradicts the majority of work that is done in the classroom.

Film has played a very influential role in the development of Holocaust consciousness in the West and thus in Holocaust education. This has been particularly through the release of Steven Spielberg's *Schindler's List* (1993), which brought an awareness of the subject to a new generation and had a huge educational impact all around the world. In research conducted by the HEDP in 2009, it was found that *Schindler's List* was the most commonly cited resource for teaching about the Holocaust among teachers in English schools. In addition, the study found that 76 per cent (n = 765) of practitioners 'said they were likely to use feature films about the Holocaust' in their teaching (Pettigrew et al. 2009: 43). Yet *Schindler's List* has not been without its critics. Michael Bernstein described it as 'flawed', 'simplistic', 'inappropriate' and a film that 'manipulates the emotions' although he acknowledged its huge global impact by referring to the '*Schindler's List* effect' (1994: 42).

Yet since its release, a number of other important films about the Holocaust have been released such as *The Pianist* (2002), *Defiance* (2008) and perhaps most influentially *The Boy in the Striped Pyjamas* (2008). According to a study conducted by Gray in 2014 on 298 13 and 14-year-olds in England, over 75 per cent of the respondents had either read the book or watched the film of *The Boy in the Striped Pyjamas*. By contrast, fewer than 10 per cent had watched *Schindler's List*. Gray found that *The Boy in the Striped Pyjamas* had a huge impact on children's preconceptions of the Holocaust; that it led to a number of erroneous assumptions being drawn, and that in the majority of cases, children struggled to distinguish between fact and fiction (2014: 170–76). It certainly seems that one of the primary sources of students' initial ideas about the Holocaust is popular films. This means that if practitioners want to understand how many of their learners are thinking and why they are thinking that way, then familiarity with films like *Schindler's List* and *The Boy in the Striped Pyjamas* seems very important and worthwhile.

The benefits of film in the classroom

There are many pedagogic benefits which film can offer the Holocaust educator, unavailable through other forms. As Michalczyk and Cohen correctly note:

> The medium provides access to not only the historical events of the Holocaust, but to the psychology and behaviour of both victim and victimizer. With its graphic power, it stands as a cultural, socio-political witness to the values of the period which the films depict ... With a proper integration of the film into the curriculum, it can be an effective educational tool.
>
> (Michalczyk and Cohen 2001: 203)

One of the key benefits of using film when teaching the Holocaust therefore is the emotional power than can be generated. Whether or not this is an appropriate objective is likely to depend both on the aims of the practitioner and the discipline in which they are teaching the Holocaust. Nevertheless, the power of film to stir the emotions of the viewer should not be forgotten and undermined. Yet when employing such emotional power, this must be appropriately channelled. There is minimal pedagogic benefit in creating emotion for its own sake. Instead, it must be directed towards helping students to recognise the criminality of the Holocaust, the devastating impact that it had on individuals, families and communities, as well as the importance of preventing its re-occurrence. A number of Holocaust films which generate emotion do not necessarily help to foster sentiments to those ends. One might argue for example, that the emotional ending to *The Boy in the Striped Pyjamas* is such that viewers come away lamenting the death of Bruno (the commandant's son) with no real concern for the 6 million Jewish deaths. The harnessing of this emotion seems to have no benefit for students of the Holocaust.

In addition to touching emotions, films can enable students to imagine the past in a much clearer and more vivid fashion. Many learners lack the knowledge or mental imagery to conceive of a ghetto, a camp or a gas chamber. Finding accurate representations of these in Holocaust films can be helpful to ensuring that students have an accurate framework of reference in their minds. At the same time, it is important for teachers to emphasise the differences that existed between each of the camps or each of the ghettos so that students do not think that the image they have witnessed through a film is the only accurate form.

It is often the case that learners engage with films more effectively and easily than they do many other forms of learning. It seems that their impact on students' preconceptions is testament to this. Consequently, extracts from films can effectively illustrate or reinforce an aspect of learning, while documentary films can help to establish key knowledge.

The dangers of film in the classroom

While film offers a great number of educational benefits, the problems and dangers of using it as a teaching resource ought not to be overlooked. Children often look at media forms uncritically, and can thus assume that everything that they observe in a Holocaust film took place in exactly that fashion. Consequently, a number of misconceptions and inaccurate information can be established in children's thinking. Learners can also make generalisations from various forms of Holocaust representation. Gray found for example that many students emphasised Jews hiding during the Holocaust as a consequence of being influenced by the story of Anne Frank (2014: 176).

Another problem with using film in the classroom is that unless it is used carefully, students can choose to 'zone out'. While for many students, as discussed above, film can be particularly engaging, for others it can provide an opportunity to disengage, something which is often harder to hide when learning in other ways. There are many additional potential problems with using film in the classroom. These include the stigma in some quarters that film is a lazy or bad method of teaching, or parental objections about the content of a film. Watching a film can also take up a large proportion of a lesson or lessons, when time dedicated to teaching the Holocaust is likely to be very limited already.

Successfully using film to teach the Holocaust

The most successful way of using film to teach the Holocaust involves maximising the benefits and avoiding the various dangers and problems associated with the employment of the medium within the classroom. This can be done through a number of ways:

Do not play a film in its entirety but use carefully selected extracts

With limited curriculum time it is unlikely that spending 3 hours and 7 minutes showing *Schindler's List* or 2 hours and 24 minutes running *The Pianist* or *Sophie's Choice* is a good use of it, which is a sentiment that is likely to be shared by one's head of department or director of learning. If, however, one feels that the entirety of a film should be seen, then it is often better to encourage students to watch it during their holidays (with parental permission). It is thoroughly inappropriate to simply show students a film like *Schindler's List* or *The Pianist* and to then assume that the Holocaust has been taught. Instead, a particular extract, which has been carefully chosen beforehand, might be shown for a specific purpose. Films ought never to be used to fill the time or as an easy option on a wet Friday afternoon in the winter term. Instead, every extract that is shown must be done for a specific educational purpose; used in order to support a learning objective, illustrate a point or introduce a topic. Such extracts should be prepared in advance of the lesson so that time is not wasted finding the exact point.

Film extracts should be analysed

It would be very untypical for a teacher to provide students with a pictorial or written source but to not analyse or evaluate it in some way. Filmic representations of the Holocaust ought to be analysed with the same method that is afforded to other sources. This means assessing the historical accuracy of the content, asking and answering questions about the moral values that the film is putting across or the political message that is being communicated. If an extract featuring a ghetto is shown then the teacher needs to draw out what students think about the geographical location and size of ghettos, the conditions that existed, etc. Lines of enquiry might then go well beyond the film extract and lead on to issues regarding who was put into ghettos and why such a policy was introduced. In such an instance, the extract has acted as a visual stimulus to drive the lesson forward and to help students engage with the topic and imagine what a ghetto looked like.

Approach film extracts critically

Students often make the mistake of watching films without adopting a critical perspective. They can easily become so engrossed in the storyline that they forget to assess the plausibility, historicity or reliability of the representation that they are viewing. A broad education will help students to be able to reflect critically on sources and teachers should show their learners how to do this and why it is so important. It is far easier to adopt a critical perspective when one is using a short extract because that critical focus can more easily operate during 4 minutes than 2 hours and 4 minutes. It is often helpful to ask students to think about who produced the film, why was it made and whether it is a fair and accurate representation of the past. Encourage learners to reflect on the sources that have been used to make the film and whether or not simplifications, embellishments or omissions exist in order to suit the needs of the filmmaker.

Provide context

If learners are to maximise the benefits of watching extracts from films then they need to understand the context. This includes the historical setting. Is the film set in 1938 Germany, 1940 Poland or 1942 Lithuania? What was happening at this stage of the war and at this stage of the Holocaust? Learners need to be able to understand the film extract within the broader context of the period of history that they are studying and recognise how it relates to what they already know. Consequently, choosing the right point in the curriculum to show a particular film extract is very important. It should build on existing knowledge but look to expand and develop that further. If, for example, they are watching an extract from *The Grey Zone* (2001) then they should already know something about the function of the camps or have already discussed concepts of resistance.

In addition to providing historical context, it is often helpful to provide them with the setting of the particular story. If it is an extract from, say, *Defiance* (2008) then it is helpful to explain that this is the story of three Jewish brothers whose parents were murdered by the Nazis and who seek to avenge their deaths. This will help students to engage with the themes and messages of the film more effectively.

Ensure active learning

Rather than watching a film passively, students should engage with the medium in an active fashion. This means that learners understand why they are being shown the extract from the film and the specific subject-related educational benefits. To ensure active learning, teachers should ask students to look out for particular things or to answer pre-prepared questions which specifically relate to the extract that they are about to see. This means that if students are watching an extract about Jewish persecution for example, while they are watching the extract they may have to write down all of the different ways in which the Nazis exerted control.

Ultimately the worst use of films within the classroom is when they are simply shown from start to finish without critical engagement, analysis, context or active learning. In contrast, when they are used thoughtfully and critically with careful reflection on how they may enhance learning, then they can be a medium of great value for the Holocaust educator.

Other types of films

The discussions so far have all referred to Hollywood-style feature films which have the Holocaust as their subject. However, the use of film within the classroom goes far beyond this. The USC Shoah Foundation has made video recordings of 52,000 Holocaust survivors and the following chapter discusses how their IWitness computer program can enable students to actively engage with these films.

A production that is often very difficult to categorise or define is Claude Lanzmann's powerful and controversial film *Shoah* (1985). Lasting over 9 hours and over 10 years in the making, it includes interviews with survivors and perpetrators (often recorded clandestinely in the case of the latter) as well as visits to various Holocaust sites in modern day Poland. This film is particularly pertinent for exploring how the history of the Holocaust should be recorded and remembered as well as the treatment of perpetrators.

A similar sort of production is *KZ* (2005) which was made by Rex Bloomstein and has been described as the first ever postmodern Holocaust movie. Like *Shoah* it considers how the Holocaust is to be remembered in the modern world and thus refrains from documentary footage and even the use of survivor testimonies. The two-disc special edition version of *KZ* includes an additional disc of over 2 hours of extra material for use in schools, and is divided into six topics including a section on 'survivors', 'bystanders and perpetrators' and 'the problem of evil'.

More traditional ways of telling the story of the Holocaust through film have been through documentaries, which include a narrative of what happened and make use of historical footage and eye-witness accounts. One of the most famous of these is 'Genocide', which is episode 20 of *The World at War* (1973). A more recent documentary series is the 1997 BBC production *The Nazis: A Warning from History*. Produced by Lawrence Rees, it includes six programmes of approximately 1 hour in length. While all of the programmes highlight the development of Nazi antisemitism, programmes 4 and 5 ('The Wild East' and 'The Road to Treblinka') particularly deal with aspects of the Holocaust. Another BBC documentary series, also produced by Lawrence Rees, is *Auschwitz: The Nazis and the Final Solution*, which consists of six programmes covering the history, operations and eventual liberation of Auschwitz, placed within the wider context of the Holocaust.

While there is no doubt much educational value in watching these films and documentaries from start to finish, this is not practical, possible nor ideal within a classroom setting and carefully selected extracts are much more appropriate. For students who are particularly interested in the subject, however, such films could be recommended for viewing outside of school time.

While documentaries make use of original film footage, some of that is also available for use by teachers. Much of this, such as the footage shot at the liberation of Buchenwald and Bergen-Belsen is thoroughly inappropriate for use in schools and the disturbing scenes of piles of emaciated corpses offers little, if any, educational benefit while possibly doing considerable harm. Great care is thus needed in selecting what film footage to use, and it should always be carefully considered before being employed in class. Among the wealth of original film footage is Nazi propaganda material, which must also be used extremely cautiously, critically and carefully. While it is often helpful to show students the sort of propaganda that was being produced, great pains should be taken to ensure that every learner appreciates why the film was constructed and its divergence from historical reality. Students should learn the vulgarity and extremity of Nazi antisemitism from films like *Der Ewige Jude* (1940) or the subtlety and craft of Nazi deception from *The Führer Gives the Jews a City* (1944). They should understand when these films were made and appreciate their intended audience. Discretion and wisdom is needed to appreciate what material is appropriate for an individual class. Erring on the side of caution is always advisable if potential problems are likely.

Drawing together many of the ideas discussed in this chapter is the DVD *Thinking Film*, which was released in 2012 through collaboration between the Film Distributors' Association, the Holocaust Educational Trust and Film Education. This two-disc DVD includes carefully selected film extracts from twelve Holocaust-related films such as *Cabaret* (1972), *Night and Fog* (1955) and *Judgement at Nuremberg* (1961), along with activities and teachers' notes to help critically analyse the extracts. It is a very helpful resource for practitioners wishing to use film in their teaching of the Holocaust.

Examples of how to use films in Holocaust lessons

Some of the extracts described below contain disturbing scenes, offensive language and acts of extreme violence. Teachers must ensure that they respect the age certification of the film and do not show material which is inappropriate for the age or maturity of their class. All extracts should be viewed by the teacher before showing them to a class to ensure they are appropriate.

Schindler's List – 'Moving into the ghetto'

Extract: 16:46–23:52

This 7-minute extract from *Schindler's List* can be effectively used when teaching about the Nazis' policies towards the Jews in occupied Poland throughout 1939 and 1940. The extract begins with the Jews of Krakow moving into the newly established ghetto and an explanation of the edict which the Nazis decreed. Throughout the subsequent scenes the viewer sees a Jewish family being evicted from their property in order for a German (Oskar Schindler) to move in. Schindler subsequently strikes a hard deal with local Jewish businessmen and establishes an enamelware factory, employing Jewish labourers due to the fact that they are the cheapest workers that he can employ.

Before showing the class this extract from *Schindler's List*, ask them to answer the following question as they watch it:

1   Give examples of how the Nazis were treating Polish Jews.
   (E.g. Jews forced into ghettos; Jews evicted from their homes; Jews made to wear Star of David armbands; Jews living in crowded conditions with other families, etc.)

Once students have watched the extract, discuss the following questions:

1   Why were Jews offered a role policing the ghetto?
2   Did the Nazis' policies against the Jews seem popular?
   (a)   How might non-Jews have benefited from Jews living in the ghetto?
3   Why did Schindler want to employ Jews?
   (a)   What happened to their wages?
   (b)   Why did Jews want to work outside of the ghetto?

4   Describe the conditions that Jews would endure in the ghetto.
5   Do you think that this film is an accurate depiction of what really happened?

To help answer question 5, there are later scenes in *Schindler's List* which show the deteriorated conditions in which Jews were living.

The Pianist – 'Life in the ghetto'

Extracts: 15:12–19:38 and 32:32–33:49

There are two particularly powerful scenes in *The Pianist* which show something of what life was like in the ghetto. In some senses these scenes are similar to the extract above from *Schindler's List* but refer to the Warsaw ghetto rather than the Krakow ghetto. It shows Jews moving into the ghetto and the crowded conditions. It is often difficult for students to imagine the ghettos, whereas many have some conception of what a concentration camp looked like. Showing extracts such as these two scenes from *The Pianist* helps students to appreciate this aspect of the Holocaust. Before they watch the extracts ask them the following question:

What was life like for Jews in the ghettos?

After watching the second scene, the following questions could be discussed:

1   Why did the man steal the food?
2   Why did no one intervene?

If students have seen the extract from *Schindler's List* then they might be able to talk about the similarities and differences in the portrayal of the ghettos. There could also be a discussion regarding the historical accuracy of the film.

Defiance – 'Resistance'

Extract: 1.05:05–1.09:30

Before playing the extract, explain to the class that the film is about three brothers (the Bielskis) in Belorussia whose parents have been murdered by the Nazis and who seek to avenge their deaths. Students should know that the Nazis were conducting a systematic programme to murder all Jews in the country. One brother leaves the other two to join a Russian partisan group who use sabotage and violence to resist the Nazi occupation. The other brothers continue to live in the forest with a number of Jews who have avoided capture or death.

In the extract, one of the Bielski brothers is getting married and the rest of the Jewish community hiding in the forest is celebrating with the young couple. By contrast, the groom's brother has joined a Russian partisan group which is ambushing a Nazi truck. After these events the harsh realities of winter in the forest are shown, such as the lack of food, the low morale and the freezing conditions.

While students are watching the extract, ask them to think about the meaning of resistance within the context of the Holocaust. After watching the extract, discuss the following questions:

1   Are the partisans in the forest resisting the Nazis?
2   Does resistance always need to involve violence?
3   Why was it so difficult for partisans to survive in the forests?
4   As a consequence of the Bielski partisans over 1,000 Jews survived the Holocaust. Is
     their survival a form of resistance?

Sophie's Choice – 'Morality'

Extract: 2.07:15–2.13:15

The story of *Sophie's Choice* climaxes around a particular scene near the end of the film
where Sophie reminisces her arrival at Auschwitz when she is forced to choose between
her two children. This powerful scene is particularly helpful for showing students the
moral dilemmas that the Holocaust could generate. This extract could be used effectively
in RS lessons. While the students are watching the extract, ask them to think about the
following questions:

1   Where is Sophie?
2   Why is she there?

   After watching the harrowing scene, discuss with the class whether or not Sophie
made the 'right' choice and the impossibility of her situation.

The Boy in the Striped Pyjamas – 'Auschwitz'

Extract: 30:43–33: 52

Before showing this extract from *The Boy in the Striped Pyjamas*, students should be
informed that Bruno is a German boy who is the son of the commandant of Auschwitz.
They should also know that unlike *Schindler's List*, *The Pianist* and *Defiance*, it is not based
on a true story. According to this fictional tale, Bruno is bored in his house and goes out
to explore.
   The scene shows Bruno meeting Shmuel for the first time and the viewer sees a
somewhat peculiar conversation unfold between two boys of the same age with very
different understandings and experiences. Before watching this scene, students should be
asked to consider the following two questions:

1   How is Auschwitz portrayed in this film?
2   How is life in Auschwitz portrayed in this film?

   As research to date suggests that many learners struggle to approach this story critically,
it is particularly important to reflect on the historical accuracy of this scene. Subsequently,
the following questions could be discussed:

1   Do you think that the film portrays Auschwitz in an accurate way?
           (E.g. sparsely populated, containing children, no/very few guards)
2   How old is Shmuel?
3   What is he working on according to this scene?
4   Would an 8-year-old be doing this within the camp?

5   Should films about the Holocaust try to be as accurate as possible?
    (a) Why or why not?

Eichmann – 'Post-war justice'

Extract: 06:12–09:28

The film *Eichmann* tells the story of Eichmann's interrogation in Israel and is based on the original manuscripts. The film draws out many important themes regarding post-Holocaust justice and the complex moral questions which emerged for those who sought to capture and try Nazi perpetrators. This scene would be especially useful in an RS lesson or in a history class which is looking at what happened to perpetrators after the war. This extract shows Eichmann in jail after his capture in 1960. It then shows Captain Avner Less (the man charged with interrogating him) and his family discussing what they think should happen to Eichmann.

Before watching this extract students should find out the answers to the following questions:

1   Who was Adolf Eichmann?
2   What was his role in the Holocaust?
3   What happened to him after the war?
4   How was he brought to Jerusalem?

After watching the extract the following questions could be discussed:

1   Do you think it was right or wrong for Israeli agents to capture Eichmann and bring him to Jerusalem?
2   Do Nazi perpetrators deserve a fair trial?
3   Is it wrong to execute them?
4   How important was the trial of Eichmann in raising global awareness of the Holocaust?

Suggested reading

Kerner, A. (2011) *Film and the Holocaust: New Perspectives on Dramas, Documentaries, and Experimental Films* (New York: Continuum).

Michalczyk, J. and Cohen, S. (2001) 'Expressing the Inexpressible through Film', in Totten, S. and Feinberg, S. (eds), *Teaching and Studying the Holocaust* (Boston: Allyn & Bacon), pp. 203–22.

Rosenberg, B. H. (2014) *The Holocaust As Seen Through Film: A Teachers' Guide to Movies, Documentaries, and Short Films that will Impact your Students and Spark Dynamic Classroom Discussion* (Hamburg: BEHR Publishing).

Chapter 7

Digital learning and new technologies

The digital revolution of recent years has affected almost every sphere of learning and Holocaust education is certainly no exception. The ubiquity of information and ideas; the ease with which they are accessed and the nature of social media, has brought a combination of opportunities and challenges to the classroom and beyond. Contemporary teachers of the Holocaust need to reflect on how technology can enhance their pedagogy, as well as appreciating the new difficulties with which practitioners and learners are faced.

In what ways are new technologies relevant to Holocaust education?

The technological revolution, which has affected both teaching generally and specifically Holocaust education, offers myriad pedagogic opportunities. As Symer astutely remarked:

> Computers can facilitate boundless educational and research opportunities for all levels of students. They can then explore the history inside or outside of the traditional classroom setting. Although computers should not make studying the Holocaust 'fun' per se, they can assist in making this topic more tangible, more immediate, and more accessible for many students.
>
> (Symer 2001: 224)

Yet since 2001, the pace at which technology has advanced has been profound and its integration into adolescents' lives has been significant. This naturally impacts on their knowledge and understanding of the Holocaust.

Instant access about any aspect of the Holocaust is now available to most young people

For most individuals in the developed world, the internet has probably become the primary source of information. The speed and efficiency of leading search engines makes access to information both instantaneous and easily accessible. This means that if a student wants to find something out about the Holocaust then they will most likely use the internet to do so. This obviously has a number of implications (both positive and negative) for teachers which will be discussed throughout the chapter.

Learners' preconceptions of the Holocaust are influenced by online sources

To date, there has been a lack of research into the sources of students' prior knowledge and understanding of the Holocaust. While books, films, parents and museums clearly have a very significant impact, the influence of the internet should not be undermined or marginalised. As discussed in Chapter 4, teachers have to discover students' initial ideas and challenge their misconceptions. If contemporary learners have unprecedented access to a whole world of information then it is possible that they are increasingly approaching their studies with more entrenched views and with a wide range of preconceived ideas.

Many adolescents are not capable of approaching online information critically

Understandably, many adolescents have not developed the skills and abilities to critically approach the multiplicity of websites which purport to provide accurate information on the Holocaust. This means that they may be unable to distinguish between the website of a major Holocaust museum and that of a Holocaust denier or distorter. When information was principally gleaned from books, market forces typically determined the supply of such publications, making adolescent access to extreme Holocaust literature very unlikely. The ease with which learners can innocuously and unintentionally stumble across Holocaust distortion and denial websites without realising it, means that teachers cannot afford to ignore the importance of the internet to Holocaust education.

There is a wealth of online information about the Holocaust

While this may seem a very axiomatic point, it should not be overlooked. There are far more websites dedicated to the Holocaust (and also Holocaust education) than perhaps any other chapter of human history. Unsurprisingly therefore, there is a wide spectrum of quality, and reliability in terms of the information provided, the resources available and the ideas offered. Teachers need to think very carefully about the suitability and applicability of what they use from the internet. While on the one hand, some teachers do not make as much use as they could of the myriad first class resources available, others, it seems, fail to discriminate sufficiently and depend too heavily upon online resources.

What challenges can digital learning and new technologies bring to Holocaust education?

Holocaust distortion and denial websites

The ease with which distortion and denial websites can be stumbled upon is quite remarkable. When typing 'Holocaust' into YouTube, the dropdown suggestions include 'Holocaust denial' and 'Holocaust hoax'. Similarly, dropdown suggestions can also appear on leading search engines. Perhaps equally concerning is the way that these websites give the appearance of legitimacy and the facade of scholarship. Their careful designs and subtle rhetorical devices make it very difficult for students to discern whether or not they are reliable and dependable sources of information. The consequences of students accessing such sites are severe. Adolescents may embrace their ideas because they want to rebel against established knowledge or defy the social status quo. Conversely, they may embrace their ideas because they are not intellectually equipped to refute the claims and arguments which they read, which supports the argument that practitioners should teach about Holocaust distortion and denial. It is also possible that students will integrate the arguments or teaching of such websites into their existing corpus of Holocaust knowledge without realising the fallacious nature of these online sources. For example, when learning about the 'Final Solution', a student might innocently remark that they read that the gas chambers had been built after the war or that gassing had not been used by the Nazis as a means of killing. This suggests that they have encountered Holocaust distortion and denial websites without necessarily realising so and have accepted their ideas alongside their existing knowledge and understanding.

While it is perhaps impossible to prevent learners from accessing problematic Holocaust websites, there are certainly a number of ways whereby the appeal of doing so, the likelihood of accidentally stumbling onto one and the impact that they have on adolescents' thinking can be severely reduced. By teaching about the motives and work of those who distort and deny the Holocaust, as well as equipping students with the evidence against their spurious claims, students will be better able to assess the reliability of websites and the appeal of accessing them is likely to be significantly diminished. In addition to this, it is also helpful to avoid setting generic research projects which may encourage students to stumble across Holocaust distortion and denial websites. Instead, research projects should be specific and precise. It is often very useful to provide a series of reputable and trustworthy web links for students to use. If they become familiar with these websites then it is likely that they will continue to use them in the future as a dependable source of information and knowledge.

Closely linked with the Holocaust distortion and denial movement is antisemitism and militant anti-Zionism. The access that students have to this hate propaganda should not be ignored and can influence learners' ideas and attitudes or reinforce existing prejudices and misconceptions. In a similar way to minimalising access to Holocaust denial and distortion websites, providing specific web links can reduce the likelihood of visiting antisemitic websites.

Trivialising the Holocaust

The amount of Holocaust-related references, content and imagery online threatens to trivialise the subject. In its worst form, this includes Holocaust 'jokes', which are easily accessible online and which circulate through social media, chat rooms and websites specifically dedicated to offensive 'jokes'.

Searching for the Holocaust on the internet can also lead to students accessing a wide range of very graphic images from the Holocaust. This can be problematic for a number of reasons, not least of all because it dehumanises the victims and seldom benefits the learners' understanding of the subject. Discouraging students from conducting generic searches and providing them with specific websites to visit can help prevent this.

The use of social media has arguably led to the trivialisation of the Holocaust through the likes of YouTube videos which are intended to satirise Hitler or the Third Reich. Hansen, who argues to this effect, provides various examples (Hansen 2013). One of these is the common parody of Hitler from the 2004 German film *Downfall* where the scene of his angry outburst in the Berlin bunker has been given different subtitles about incidents as varied as Hitler being banned from the X-Box and plans to murder Justin Bieber. Many of these videos have received several million downloads and led to users' comments which suggest that the severity of Hitler's policies is not considered. One comment for example, in response to the *Downfall* parody of Hitler plotting to murder

Justin Bieber stated, 'Hitler is my hero now'. Other examples of trivialising the Holocaust include Lego models of Auschwitz and 'Darth Vader vs. Hitler – Epic Rap Battles of History 2', the latter of which had over 84 million downloads and over 361,000 user comments. While such examples may be disregarded by some as harmless, it does seem to be the case that aspects of social media have helped to trivialise the horrors of the Holocaust or at the very least, the historical context in which it was perpetrated.

Social media can of course have the opposite effect and can reinforce the seriousness of what happened and the impact of the Holocaust on individuals, families and communities. The USC Shoah Foundation, for example, have uploaded several survivor testimonies from their video archives which give harrowing and sobering accounts of the atrocities that took place. The Twitter accounts of key Holocaust organisations such as the USHMM and the Holocaust Educational Trust frequently tweet about Holocaust anniversaries, contemporary antisemitism or new work that they are conducting in the field.

Misleading information

Another problem that the internet can generate for adolescents is that it can provide them with incorrect or misleading information about the Holocaust. Many Holocaust websites have been constructed by well-meaning individuals who nevertheless lack the expertise or historical knowledge to provide sufficient depth or clarity. In order to help avoid this, it is important that teachers familiarise themselves with the various websites that exist and recommend those that they think are particularly beneficial and accurate.

Some of the ways that individuals have used social media to commemorate or represent the Holocaust have also led to confusion. One particularly controversial method was the creating of Facebook pages for certain Holocaust victims. This included a page for Anne Frank, which led to some Facebook users posting comments with the apparent belief that they were contacting Anne directly and remarking how pleased they were that she was still alive after all. Similarly, until 2010 it was possible for Facebook users to become 'friends' with Henio Zytomirski, a 6-year-old Polish boy who was murdered at Majdanek in 1942. While some may feel that this enables social media to perform as a meaningful and relevant educational platform, others may feel it is misleading, unethical and inappropriate.

Research conducted by Lazar and Litvak Hirsch explored how students use online question-and-answer discussion boards to research their homework on the Holocaust. They specifically investigated the Yahoo! Answers community and concluded that 'educators should take into consideration this aspect of Internet activity available to their students and the results it provides' (2013: 13). They also remarked on the nature of responses and noted that the answers were seldom provided by anyone with expertise in the subject and that they frequently reflected common Holocaust perceptions. One way of combating this problem, as Lazar and Litvak Hirsch point out, is to spend time in class comparing and contrasting the answers from such question-and-answer communities with a detailed and historically accurate response.

How can practitioners make best use of new technologies in their teaching?

Become familiar with the technology

While it is difficult to control how learners make educational use of new technologies outside of the classroom, the expansion of digital learning has opened up myriad opportunities for teachers to introduce it into their lessons. It will, however, be impossible for teachers to feel comfortable using online learning techniques or to facilitate the learning effectively if they themselves are not sufficiently comfortable with it in the first place. Consequently, teachers should explore how social media sites, for example, can become a useful pedagogic tool. Practitioners should spend time exploring new programmes, applications and innovations which are geared towards improving Holocaust education.

One example is the use of live tweeting as was used by Yad Vashem when Barack Obama paid the Museum and Memorial a visit in March 2013. Similarly, various Holocaust organisations such as the Holocaust Educational Trust frequently conduct interviews with Holocaust survivors where users are encouraged to tweet questions which they would like to have answered. This could easily be used effectively in a lesson or projected while other activities were taking place. While use of digital and new technologies by no means equates to good pedagogy in its own right, it can be a very useful medium for helping learners to engage with the Holocaust and to recognise its relevance to modern life and society. It helps to teach them about the Holocaust by using the principal media through which they interact and view the world. An effect of this is that new technologies may help students to develop an interest in the subject and to explore their enthusiasm outside of the classroom. If young people choose to do this, then they are most likely to do so through social media and smartphone technology. While adolescents may be perceived to be very technologically savvy, practitioners should not forget that most young people have minimal knowledge of how to harness the power of new technology and social media for educational purposes. Teaching them how to do this and showing the countless opportunities that exist within the field of Holocaust education will open up new dimensions for them. Most learners see technological advancement as socially useful rather than educationally useful. If teachers can familiarise themselves with the capabilities and opportunities offered by new means of learning, then they will be able to help students also recognise the broader potentials of their smartphone devices and technological interests.

Be flexible in its use

There are many times when things don't go exactly to plan with a lesson activity. Sometimes this is due to technological failure, sometimes because of the way that the activity was delivered and other times because of the dynamics and composition of a class. Spending time thinking about how students will react to innovative (or just different) teaching methods is important and will be helped by how well the teacher knows their class and the rapport that they have with them. Yet even the most experienced practitioners often find things don't work as well as they hoped. Flexibility is crucial here, as well as a contingency plan which can be called upon if necessary. Reflection is also important, and teachers should consider the pedagogic value of the exercise or activity, the engagement of the class, and how its use could be built upon or improved if used in the future.

Be sensitive about the subject

There are various web-based programmes which allow for exciting games and fun activities which help students to either develop their thinking or consolidate their learning, yet these seem inappropriate when teaching about the Holocaust. Practitioners should bear in mind the seriousness of the topic and seek to prevent diminishing its importance or solemnity. Technologies should thus be used to enhance and further the learning of the subject and not for its own sake. If one wants to use technology to help generate engagement, then there are many sensitive and pedagogically beneficial ways of doing so. For example, an appropriate homework might be to ask students to download a podcast about the Holocaust and to answer a series of questions on it.

Be imaginative

While sensitivity to the subject is important, this does not prevent imaginative use of technology in lessons. If, for example, one is teaching about Auschwitz-Birkenau or the size and scale of the Nazi killing programme, then using Google Earth to show students the size of Birkenau can be very helpful. By zooming in, one can see the remains of the crematoria and underground gas chambers, which the Nazis sought to destroy as they fled from the advancing Soviet forces. It is also possible to have 'street views' of various points of Birkenau by dropping 'Pegman' into various available places in the camp. While it is seldom possible to take a whole class to Auschwitz-Birkenau, experiencing it through Google Maps is often very insightful. Similar experiences can be had at Auschwitz I, where 'Pegman' can be dropped at various key points in the original camp, such as the wall of execution between blocks 10 and 11, as well as the reconstructed gallows and other areas. By using technology in this way, the reality, scale and horrors of places like Auschwitz-Birkenau are made much more real to learners and will most likely increase their engagement and understanding of the subject. Google Earth can be used just as effectively with a wide range of other Holocaust sites including Dachau, Mauthausen or Treblinka. By zooming out from Treblinka for example, students can also see how rural the surrounding area is, which hints at the secrecy of the murderous programme that was conducted there.

Other imaginative ways of using technology in the classroom could be by taking virtual tours of Holocaust museums or using the various online exhibitions. Many museum websites provide online access to various artefacts and explain the history and relevance of them. The USHMM website, for example, has online exhibitions and collection highlights which are arranged by theme. This enables practitioners who are teaching a particular subject to explore individual case studies and to integrate primary source work into their teaching. The wealth of written or printed documents, photographs and other artefacts that have been digitised and made available online should not be ignored by teachers. These include items such as the June 1933 Concordat with Nazi Germany, the full minutes taken at the Wannsee Conference, or various documents relating to the Nuremberg Trials. Enabling students to access these documents and read them for themselves helps the subject to become much more meaningful and interesting to them.

Keep up to date with new developments

With the multiple demands that teachers face, it is often difficult to keep abreast of the new developments in the field. Nevertheless, if one can find time to keep track of these then they can often be used effectively in lessons. What new documents or artefacts have recently been digitised? What new temporary exhibitions have just opened? Following key organisations on Twitter or subscribing to e-updates can be one simple way of doing this. It can also keep you informed on what activities are happening near you, for example a talk by a Holocaust survivor.

New opportunities in Holocaust education

There are a number of exciting innovations where new technology and Holocaust education have been combined.

IWitness

After Steven Spielberg made *Schindler's List* in 1993, he formed the 'Survivors of the Shoah Visual History Foundation', which recorded over 50,000 survivor testimonies. In 2005, this joined with the University of Southern California to form the USC Shoah Foundation. Since then, a great deal of the pioneering work with Holocaust testimonies has taken place and one of the most useful for teachers is the IWitness program. This provides access to over 1,300 testimonies from survivors and others, which students can search through and access. Yet this program offers more than simply watching videos. Teachers can use the video testimonies and the activity builder function of the program to construct specific assignments that they want their students to complete. In addition to this, teachers can monitor and moderate the work that their learners are completing through the program, with their students' work not accessible to anyone else.

The IWitness program offers teachers the opportunity to integrate testimony into the curriculum in a variety of ways, not least of all in a manner that enables the students to be actively engaged in the process. Listening to a survivor's testimony can often be a passive learning experience for students. The IWitness program, however, enables students to produce their own media projects by using the built-in video editing system which is part of the program. Each testimony is divided into short clips (about 1 minute) which can be accessed through keyword searches. This means that students can engage with the medium to find out some of the answers to their questions.

In order to access all of the content, teachers need to register with the site and can then invite students to join. Students are not able to register without an invitation from a teacher. Once registered and invited, students can work on projects and access video testimonies in a variety of ways, including in lessons or at home. The program is also available through mobile devices and further development in this area is currently taking place.

New dimensions in testimony

The work of the USC Shoah Foundation in combining technological and pedagogical innovation with Holocaust survivor testimonies is also evident through their more controversial program 'New Dimensions in Testimony' (in collaboration with the 'USC Institute for Creative Technologies' and 'Conscience Display'). With the imminent passing of all Holocaust survivors, this project aims to maintain the connection between survivor and student and to preserve the dynamic and interactive process of storytelling, questioning and answering. To that end, 'New Dimensions in Testimony' has recorded various survivor testimonies in a 26-foot spherical stage, lit by over 6,000 LED lights which produce a hologram-like projection. Survivors answer the typical questions that students ask and a program called 'Natural Language Understanding' generates the most appropriate answer to a student's question, when the hologram projection is used in the classroom. In other words, interaction between a survivor and a student is able to continue so far as it is possible, even after the survivor has passed away. The aim of the project is to create

> an environment in which an individual or an entire class can have a survivor sit with them to tell his or her story, via video or projector; they will be able to ask questions, and the survivor will answer from the testimony as if he or she were in the room.
>
> (Maio et al. 2012: 24)

Whether or not students will take such an experience as seriously as they would a survivor visit to their school remains to be seen. Moreover, its success is dependent on the range and nature of the questions that students ask. There are also ethical issues with this. While many feel that this is an important step to take in order to ensure the continuation of survivor–student interactions, others feel that this could undermine the power of testimony. Examples of this programme in use are available to watch online and may help practitioners to decide whether or not this is something which they might want to use in their classrooms at some point in the future.

Although separate from 'New Dimensions in Technology', the USC Shoah Foundation has collaborated with Broadcastr, which is a smartphone app that provides people with content based on their current location. For example, if someone was visiting New York, the app could provide local news or information, based on a user's preference settings. Regarding Holocaust education, the app enables students to listen to Holocaust testimonies from the USC Shoah Foundation's testimony collection, which directly relate to the location of the user. For example, if a student is visiting Budapest, Prague or Krakow, testimonies where the individual spent time in that place can be downloaded. While this may be of limited use in a classroom setting, it is a pioneering experience for Holocaust-related school trips.

'Geo-Immersion'

While 'New Dimensions in Testimony' helps to preserve survivor testimonies in 3D, the work of 'Geo-Immersion' is working on a fourth dimension. Buildings, sites, and other locations can be changed to show how they have undergone transition over time by creating computer-generated virtual spaces. This essentially adds another dimension. Regarding Holocaust education, with further development, students can see how sites like Auschwitz, the Warsaw ghetto or even a particular street changed during the course of the Second World War. Their knowledge of a particular place can be enhanced by analysing the computer-generated changes that took place there over a particular time.

Conclusion

Technology within the classroom ought to be used to enhance learning, to help students engage with the subject in hand. Holocaust education, unlike many other subjects, is blessed with a great deal of available resources which have been carefully produced and have often been well funded. Reflecting on how these might be best used is important.

This ultimately means working out the learning objectives and choosing the best available means to achieve them. Using technological advancements, pioneering programs and even social media within the classroom can work effectively if these are carefully and judiciously integrated into Holocaust education programmes.

Suggested reading

Gray, M. (2014) 'The Digital Era of Holocaust Education', in Gray, M., *Contemporary Debates in Holocaust Education* (Basingstoke: Palgrave Macmillan).

Lazar, A. and Litvak Hirsch, T. (2013) 'An Online Partner for Holocaust Remembrance Education: Students Approaching the Yahoo! Answers Community', *Educational Review*, DOI: 10.1080/00131911.2013.839545. Available at: www.tandfonline.com/doi/full/10.1080/0013 1911.2013.839545#.VGzyODSM1n0.

Manfra, M. M. and Stoddard, J. (2008) 'Powerful and Authentic Digital Media and Strategies for Teaching about Genocide and the Holocaust', *The Social Studies*, 99, no. 6: 260–64.

Chapter 8

Visiting Holocaust sites

After discovering that a number of girls had been making antisemitic comments in her school, a distressed teacher remarked to me recently, 'I wish I could take them on a school trip to Auschwitz so that they could see where antisemitism leads.' Clearly, there are countless reasons why educators choose to take their students on school trips to Holocaust sites. Some opt to do so in an attempt to combat prejudice and intolerance, others to press upon their learners the true extent and nature of the Nazis' crimes, while many practitioners see such excursions as a valuable way of increasing their class's knowledge and understanding of such a complex topic. Experience suggests that the majority of students will be simultaneously affected in a number of ways. As they learn more about the horrors of the Holocaust and visit the actual place where such atrocities occurred, they are likely to recognise the danger of antisemitism and feel the emotional impact.

Yet educators should not assume that Auschwitz, or any other Holocaust site for that matter, possesses some intrinsic ability to radically alter every adolescent's mind-set and worldview. Instead the value of such a visit needs to be thoughtfully developed through careful pre- and post-trip work, as well as the sensitive and effective implementing of the trip itself. Too many teachers, I fear, spend large amounts of time and money in organising visits to Holocaust sites without giving sufficient thought to how the learners are to be prepared for their experiences and how those same experiences can be followed up and articulated. Consequently, this chapter, among other things, attempts to present a number of both pedagogic and practical ideas about planning and preparing for an excursion, ensuring it occurs smoothly and that it achieves the initial aims which were laid out.

Is it morally acceptable to visit Holocaust sites?

In recent years there has undoubtedly been a significant increase in what is known as 'dark tourism': the visiting of historical sites which are connected to death and destruction. Sites such as Auschwitz have been at the forefront of such developments, with the former camp now being recognised as a UNESCO heritage site and attracting well over 1 million visitors each year. As one walks around the museum in Auschwitz I, the number of photograph-snapping tourists is somewhat disconcerting, made no less so by the refreshment stands and shops which are by the parking facilities. While the sheer size and scale of Birkenau (Auschwitz II) makes it feel infinitely less commercialised, one is forced to ask whether such visits are morally responsible or reprehensible. Is this visit about remembrance and learning or about satisfying morbid curiosity as visitors walk, talk and photograph their way past blown-up crematoria and along the railway lines which transported around 1 million Jews from the ghettos to this centre of extermination and murder?

While it is always painful to see a minority of visitors failing to act with the reverence and appropriateness that Auschwitz both demands and deserves, this does not prevent a school trip there from being an important and beneficial experience. It seems that standing in the spot where the selections were made or where inmates lived, provides a new dimension on students' learning, which neither the textbook nor the teacher in the classroom can adequately provide. If such visits ensure that the Holocaust remains within the consciousness of the next generation and that they develop an even greater historically grounded understanding, then it seems difficult to argue that they are morally unacceptable.

Almost universally, students understand what is deemed correct behaviour when they are standing outside a gas chamber or next to a mass grave, and with right motives and conduct, school trips can offer learners a unique insight into the past and a valuable chance to remember what took place. It is also possible that if deprived of the opportunity to visit such sites at school, they may never do so in adult life. Moreover, learning outside of the classroom can be one of the most effective means of preparing students for the future.

Sites to visit

Deciding where to go on a Holocaust-related trip can be both exciting and daunting. A well chosen place and a thoughtfully designed itinerary can provide students with a valuable cultural experience as well as an opportunity to learn and remember. In making a decision, one ought to be guided by the aims of the trip, although undoubtedly practical considerations such as cost and time cannot be downplayed. Therefore, if the aim of the visit is to tackle antisemitism and develop students' knowledge and understanding of Jewish life, then it may be beneficial to ensure that the trip includes a guided tour of a synagogue, a Jewish cultural centre or a Jewish quarter. This can easily be integrated into a visit to a camp. For example, one might spend a whole day at Auschwitz, but also spend time in Kazimierz, the former Jewish quarter in Krakow, visiting the Judaica Foundation's Center for Jewish Culture, Old Synagogue or go outside the city to Oskar Schindler's enamel factory which is now a museum. Yet Holocaust-related sites do not need to revolve around Auschwitz-Birkenau. There is much to see and learn in Warsaw, while older students in particular may also acquire understanding by visiting the site of one of the other extermination camps in modern day Poland such as Treblinka or Belzec. Conversely, one might rather go somewhere like Prague, from where Theresienstadt is easily accessible and where students can visit synagogues such as Pinkas Synagogue which is now a memorial to Holocaust victims in the former Jewish quarter of Josefov, which was previously the Jewish ghetto. Moreover, Vienna is a good base for visiting Mauthausen (approximately a 2-hour journey), Munich for Dachau (approximately a 30-minute journey) and Berlin for Sachsenhausen (approximately a 40-minute journey). Conversely, one can conduct a very effective Holocaust-related trip without visiting a camp at all. The fascinating Jewish quarter, vast synagogues, enlightening museums, poignant memorials and former ghetto in Budapest tell the untypical story of Hungary's Jews.

In many senses there is no right or wrong place to visit and practical consideration can often help with the decision-making process. For example, if the trip was to take place during term time, it may be easier to justify to senior management the children missing a couple of days of school if the trip was in collaboration with the modern foreign languages department. In which case, a visit to Munich and Dachau may be the best option, or to Paris, Drancy and the *Memorial de la Shoah*. Similarly, a partnership between the history and religious studies department would work effectively if the destination was somewhere like Prague or Budapest. Working with another department brings with it many advantages, not least because it divides the workload and the responsibility, which is very important for new practitioners or those who do not have experience in organising and running foreign excursions. Furthermore, partnership with another subject, especially in year 10 or above, by which time students have chosen their GCSE subjects, helps increase the chances of having enough uptake for the trip to be financially viable. Working with another department does often involve making compromises on the itinerary so that it fairly reflects the dual nature of the trip, although this is often beneficial for the learners.

Deciding where to go should also be determined by the time that is available. If both the teachers and a sufficient number of students are happy giving up four or five days of their half term or summer holiday, then one can comfortably cover the key sites in any European city. A short trip of only one or two nights does of course reduce the cost, which increases both the likelihood of having enough students signed up as well as opening up the opportunity to a broader range of socio-economic backgrounds. If the trip is permitted only one day in the middle of term, then options are much more limited. With an early start and late return it is possible to visit Auschwitz in a single day, although this would provide no time to visit Krakow and runs the risk of students feeling sleep-deprived and irritable.

Choosing the location is also likely to be determined by the age of the students who will be going. The distress of visiting somewhere like Auschwitz or Dachau may be considered too great for younger adolescents and thus somewhere like Budapest may be more suitable.

Box 8.1 Practical tips in planning

- Be meticulous in working out every cost of the trip. Asking the parents for more money or running into debt will not be well received. Ensure you include staff costs in your budgeting.
- Justify the benefits of the trip to senior management and to parents. Explain how it will broaden both their knowledge and understanding of your course, but also their personal and cultural horizons.
- Promote your proposed trip enthusiastically but be sensitive to the fact that some students may love to go but be unable to afford it.
- Do not book flights until deposits have been paid. Otherwise if a student pulls out you may incur large costs to change the passenger names and run the trip into debt.
- Ensure that you have all the appropriate consent forms, necessary (and up to date) medical details, and that the completed risk assessment is as comprehensive as possible. Think about things you can do to minimise any risks.
- Keep a file containing print-outs of all your bookings, contact details and arrangements. This will be particularly useful if you repeat the trip in the future.

How should I prepare my students for the trip?

The extent of your preparatory work very much depends on the age and maturity levels of those who will be going. Yet, irrespective of this, it is important that one covers the following three areas:

- Intellectual issues
- Emotional issues
- Practical issues.

Intellectual issues

Although one of the purposes of visiting a Holocaust-related site is to increase students' levels of knowledge and understanding, the likelihood of this happening as effectively as possible will be significantly enhanced if they have already acquired a sound foundation. Consequently, any visit ought to be preceded by teaching on the Holocaust, which should include: pre-war Jewish life and culture; Nazi antisemitism; the evolution of the Nazis' Jewish policies; the ghettos, *Einsatzgruppen* and the camps; the liberation of the camps and the struggle of survivors. By providing students with as detailed a framework as possible, they will be able to fit new knowledge into their existing thinking and maximise the learning opportunities which are offered on the visit.

If such knowledge and understanding is absent, it seems probable that the intellectual usefulness of the trip will be severely reduced. Ideally therefore, a Holocaust-related visit should take place *after* students have completed their study of the subject in history classes.

Part of the intellectual preparation for the trip should involve encouraging students to pursue an increase in their knowledge and understanding of the subject. To that end, it is often very helpful to ask the students to list five things that they want to find out about during their visit. Students should ensure that they take these questions with them and look for the answers in the museums or by asking their guide.

Emotional issues

Preparing adolescents for the emotional impact of their trip is an important and often overlooked responsibility. It is impossible to know how individual students will respond as they stand in the very place that so many people were murdered and as they listen to the chilling stories that are told by the guides. If students have already studied the Holocaust by the time that they make the trip, then it is possible that they will have already begun to engage with the emotional aspect of the subject, although it is important to explain to adolescents that actually visiting Holocaust-related sites is quite different again. One way of potentially reducing the emotional impact of the trip is to show photographs to the students of what they will be seeing when they make their visit. However, by doing this, the trip itself becomes less about discovering new things and simply seeing something in real life. It also leads to the danger that students become emotionally anaesthetised when visiting the site because they have already seen the artefacts or buildings which they are visiting. It seems a more sensible solution is to inform the pupils of some of the things that they may see without showing them any pictures. This not only helps to prepare them emotionally but engages them during their visit as the things that they observe relate back to what they heard and learnt about in the classroom.

One way of helping students to become both emotionally prepared and engaged in the topic is to ask them to produce a spider diagram on how they think they will feel as they visit the sites. What thoughts might go through their heads? What emotions will they feel? Will it be anger, sadness, confusion or a combination of several different feelings?

Practical issues

There are a number of things which are simply good practice when it comes to running a school trip and it is important that these are done effectively. The list below is not exhaustive but serves as a useful starting point.

- Provide the students with a list of essential items that they will need to bring. Only include what is necessary as parents will not want to incur costs purchasing unnecessary products. Yet, if you are visiting Poland in the winter for example, students will need as warm a set of clothes as possible and a good pair of shoes to walk in.
- Ensure students and their parents know the extent of their baggage allowance. You do not want to incur additional costs at the airport and potentially run the trip into debt.
- Inform students and their parents of the currency of the country you are visiting. Poland for example, currently uses the złoty and not the euro. How much will the students need to bring with them? Are all meals provided? It is helpful to suggest an approximate amount of money which students may want to bring. You may wish to set a maximum amount allowed to prevent any students from bringing too much.
- Make sure that all the students and their parents are absolutely clear about when and where they need to meet for departure to the airport. It will cause no end of problems if a student is left behind because of ambiguity in the information that was provided or if the flight is missed because people are late. It is better to tell the students and their parents an earlier time than is absolutely necessary to allow for a lack of punctuality.
- Give a briefing to the group about what is the expected standard of behaviour during the trip; explain how they should behave on an aeroplane, in a hotel or at a concentration camp. It can be helpful to inform the students that misbehaviour may lead to them being sent home at their parents' expense. This can be made a requisite for accepting a student on the trip. This briefing is best delivered by a senior member of staff.
- Familiarise yourself with the details of the school insurance policies. Find out what would happen if a student was unable to go on the trip, for example. Ensure that when you travel, you take the details of your insurance policy with you as well as contact details for the appropriate senior member of staff. Give a copy of all your paperwork (e.g. insurance policy, flight details, hotel booking and itinerary) to the appropriate senior member of staff.

On the trip

Itinerary

Getting the itinerary right is always difficult and it is an important balancing act to ensure that there is a sufficient number of activities built into the schedule but also enough opportunities for the students to reflect and to take in what they have experienced.

Depending on the age of the students, free time in a city can be a very enjoyable experience, although it is essential that they stay in groups, have your contact number and know where and when they need to re-convene. Conversely, free time outside the hotel could be kept to a minimum in order to reduce the likelihood of students misbehaving, getting lost or purchasing illicit products.

It can be very useful to have one or two contingency plans (and accompanying risk assessments) in case a museum is unexpectedly closed or an activity is cancelled without warning.

If the focal point of the trip is a visit to a concentration camp then how that evening is spent is particularly significant. If the group have completed a 6-hour walking tour of Auschwitz-Birkenau and sat on a coach back to Krakow for well over an hour, they are most likely to need a good hour or so to relax at the hotel before any evening activities. Typically a quiet meal in a nearby restaurant – perhaps a Jewish restaurant in Kazimierz if one is in Krakow – is the most poignant and appropriate end to what will have been a physically as well as emotionally exhausting day. This also provides students with the opportunity to reflect on what they have seen and heard and share their emotions with their peers and teachers.

Emotional reactions

One concern that is shared by teachers before they run a Holocaust-related school trip for the first time is how to cope with the emotional responses of their students. This is a very natural and correct concern. While it is impossible to know how students will react, either individually or collectively, it can be helpful to adhere to a few general principles.

- Throughout the visit, try to continually assess the emotional state of those within the group. How are they walking? How are they interacting with their peers and with the guide? What is their facial expression? Do they seem upset?
- Without jumping to conclusions or making assumptions, think about which students may be particularly emotionally vulnerable. Has a member of the group recently suffered a bereavement? Has a student fled from a war-torn country? Did an individual lose members of her family in an act of genocide or the Holocaust itself?
- Remember that each student has a unique set of circumstances and a unique character which has generated this response. The subject of the Holocaust is disturbing in the extreme and thus it is a perfectly natural and reasonable response to feel sad, confused or distressed and to express this through tears. Some students may need time to mourn and reflect and would value the opportunity to do this, rather than have their teacher pepper them with questions about whether or not they are alright – or even worse, try to cheer them up.
- It is likely that some students will not have experienced anything as emotionally challenging as their visit to a Holocaust site and may be uncomfortable with their emotions or insufficiently mature to respond appropriately. Consequently, it is possible that some students present an emotional bravado and give the impression of being unmoved in order to prevent shedding tears in public. A good practitioner will act sensitively and thoughtfully within and around a group, recognising that adolescents' emotions are not always as transparent and evident as may at first appear. Similarly, some members of the group may try to make light of the visit or minimise the seriousness of the collective experience. Such situations need to be dealt with

carefully, and dealing with inappropriate attitudes or comments on a one-to-one basis is almost always more effective that confronting them publicly in the presence of their peer group.

Follow-up work

The success of a school trip is sometimes judged by the extent of its impact upon its return. This may come in the form of a comment made by a student or a parent, by the increased fascination with the subject in lessons or by evidence of greater knowledge and understanding in their work. Such indicators can be very rewarding indeed, and more than sufficient compensation for the labour and energies which have been exerted in making the trip a reality.

Yet despite such inferential examples, it is often beneficial to explicitly work with students in order to build upon their experiences and help to fulfil the original aims of the trip. If students have completed the pre-trip material whereby they predicted how they would feel and what they hoped to learn, then this material should be revisited. It may be appropriate to ask students to reflect on how they felt in the evening after their visit to the camp, or it could be left until students return to class. If the entire class did not go on the trip, then it may be helpful for individual students who are happy to do so, to share with the rest of their peer group how they imagined they would feel and how they actually felt, as well as what they wanted to learn and some of the things that they did find out during their visit.

Effective dissemination of the success of the trip can help to cement the visit as an annual or biennial event in the school calendar. It will also encourage younger students to enthusiastically anticipate their opportunity to do something similar. With that in mind teachers may want to construct a video of students' comments about the trip; what they found fascinating, upsetting or poignant. Moreover, students may want to share their experiences in a year-group or even whole-school assembly. Students' experiences could also be published on the school website and the local media could be contacted to run a story, although permission from senior management for such things would be needed. This would enable the positive effects of the trip to spread much more widely and throughout the community.

Conclusion

There is no doubt that organising a school trip – especially one of this nature – can be daunting and laborious. During the planning and preparation it is easy to wonder whether the benefits will be commensurate with the effort made. Nevertheless, it is typically these experiences which students remember more than almost anything else when they look back on their schooling. The impacts that such visits can have upon their social, personal, moral and educational development are difficult to quantify but ought not to be marginalised or forgotten.

Recommended reading

Andrews, K. (2010) 'Finding a Place for the Victim: Building a Rationale for Educational Visits to Holocaust-Related Sites', *Teaching History*, 141, December: 42–49.

Gilbert, M. (1997) *Holocaust Journey: Travelling in Search of the Past* (London: Weidenfeld and Nicolson).

Winstone, M. (2010) *The Holocaust Sites of Europe* (London: I. B. Tauris).

Chapter 9

Comparing the Holocaust to other genocides

Whether or not the Holocaust either can or should be compared with other genocides is a controversial issue. Scholars in this field have disagreed vociferously and both sides have put forward compelling cases to support their position. As far as teaching the subject in the classroom goes, it seems important that practitioners who choose to compare the Holocaust with other genocides should, at the very least, be aware that there is a debate about the legitimacy of so doing and, ideally, be familiar with the arguments of both sides. This chapter attempts to summarise the divergences, highlight the pedagogic pros and cons, expose the pitfalls and explain how this can fit into a scheme of work.

The debate

The word 'genocide' was first used by Raphael Lemkin in 1944 and through his diligent and concerted efforts, the United Nations approved the *Convention on the Prevention and Punishment of the Crime of Genocide* in 1948. The term, which has a specific and legal meaning, is defined as:

> any of the following acts committed with intent to destroy, in whole or in part, a national, ethnical, racial or religious group, as such:
>
> (a) Killing members of the group;
> (b) Causing serious bodily or mental harm to members of the group;
> (c) Deliberately inflicting on the group conditions of life calculated to bring about its physical destruction in whole or in part;
> (d) Imposing measures intent to prevent births within the group;
> (e) Forcibly transferring children of the group to another group.
>   (UN Convention on the Prevention and Punishment of the Crime of Genocide)

Tragically, since 1948 genocide has occurred in various countries, perhaps most notably in Cambodia (1975–79) and Rwanda (1994). Is it possible to draw parallels between what happened in these cases and the Holocaust? A number of historians, most notably Steven Katz and Deborah Lipstadt, have asserted the uniqueness of the Holocaust, with the latter controversially describing comparisons as 'immoral equivalences' (Lipstadt 1993: 215). Some of the arguments that have been put forward in defence of this position are summarised in Box 9.1.

Box 9.1 Arguments supporting Holocaust uniqueness

- It was the first time that a state had intended to exterminate – and made it a policy to do so – every man woman and child of a particular people group.
- There was no economic or political justification for murdering the Jews.
- Jews were the only group murdered simply for existing.
- It was the first case of mass murder on an industrialised scale.

It is certainly possible to refute many of these historical arguments, as Kinloch does most succinctly in his article in the 'Recommended reading' section at the end of this chapter. Despite this, philosophers and theologians have asserted the absolute uniqueness of the Holocaust in a paradigmatic and almost 'mystical' sense. This shows the distinction between two related, but separate arguments. One of these is that the Holocaust cannot be compared with anything else and the other is that the Holocaust should not be compared. Both are relevant issues when teaching the subject in relation to other genocides.

Conversely however, there are a number of historical arguments as to why the Holocaust was not unique, articulated by the likes of Bloxham (2009) and Levene (2008) among others. Some of the arguments are summarised in Box 9.2.

Box 9.2 Arguments opposing Holocaust uniqueness

- In terms of individual suffering, Jewish experiences are comparable with other victim groups such as socialists, homosexuals or prisoners of war.
- Proportionately, the Roma population of Europe was devastated as much as the Jews. They too were murdered for simply existing.
- Cases can be made for other genocides lacking in economic or political motivation.

In recent years, the debate about uniqueness has moved on and as Bloxham points out, 'the genocide of the Jews had both specific and more general characteristics' (Bloxham 2009: 1). Teachers need to emphasise this when they teach comparative genocides. Extermination camps were unique to the Holocaust, but it seems unlikely that the extent of the Nazis' hatred of the Jews was more ferocious than that of the Hutu extremists against the Tutsis in Rwanda. Moreover, in one very obvious sense, every historical phenomenon, including the Holocaust, is unique in that it has a specific set of antecedents, events and characters. Yet, it seems difficult to assert the Holocaust's uniqueness however, if the term 'unique' is being employed in the sense that it is unparalleled or has no equal. When teaching about the Holocaust and other genocides, the choice of words and the meaning attached to them can be very significant indeed.

Why compare the Holocaust to other genocides?

There are many reasons why comparing the Holocaust to other genocides can prove to be very beneficial and can help students to engage with the topic more readily.

1. It enables students to understand both the legacy of the Holocaust and the origins of genocide as a concept.   Without either Lemkin or the 1948 Genocide Convention, the term 'genocide' would neither exist nor have its prized status in international law. The Holocaust is therefore the natural starting point for any study of genocide, even though the term can be applied to atrocities before the Holocaust, such as the Armenian Genocide (1915).

2. Relating the Holocaust to other genocides helps to justify its inclusion in the curriculum.   In multicultural classrooms throughout Europe or in countries which have no immediate connection to the Holocaust, it seems reasonable to ask why the Holocaust is studied at the expense of events in Cambodia or Rwanda. By including comparative elements into a Holocaust curriculum, it can be more readily defended.

3. Many students would never learn of other genocides were they not compared to the Holocaust.   The ubiquity of the Holocaust within popular consciousness and national discourse means that there seems little chance of students not encountering the subject in their schooling. Conversely, many students appear to leave school having never even heard of other genocides. Research indicates that at present there is significant ignorance about genocides which have occurred since the Holocaust. In a study conducted in 2013 on 2,304 adults in the UK, over 80 per cent of 16–24-year-olds could not name a single genocide that has taken place since 1945, while only 33 per cent were able to identify the correct definition of genocide (*Huffington Post* 2014). If students do not find out about such atrocities when studying the Holocaust, they may leave education without such knowledge.

4. Many students want to learn about other genocides.   Despite the apparent lack of knowledge regarding other genocides, the 2013 survey mentioned above also found that nine out of ten 16–24-year-olds think that they should learn more about genocide (*Huffington Post* 2014). If students are keen to learn about such historical phenomena then it seems only appropriate and correct that they have the opportunity to do so while they are in education.

5. Aspects of the Holocaust share similarities with aspects of other genocides.   The gradual erosion of basic rights, the marginalisation from society and the virulent nature of hateful propaganda were antecedents to both the Holocaust and other genocides. Studying these overlapping themes (and their differences) therefore seems logical and scholarly. Students should be taught how to make such links in a meaningful and sophisticated way.

6. Emerging trends in the history of genocide may help to prevent its reoccurrence.   While every occasion of genocide has its own very specific set of circumstances it seems that most, if not all genocides have defining characteristics. If students can understand what these are, then they are likely to be better placed to discern them in contemporary crises. Students who are capable of recognising the common antecedents of genocide and who are familiar with the horrors of the past are more likely to be active in pressurising governments to prevent genocide's reoccurrence.

7. Comparative genocide may generate interest in the subject and awareness of its contemporary relevance.   Students may find it more interesting to draw comparisons and contrasts between the Holocaust and other genocides. They are also more likely to understand that similar atrocities have been repeated and be more conscientious in trying to prevent its repetition in the world.

8. A comparative approach will enrich students' understanding of the Holocaust.   By studying other genocides, students will inevitably come across issues which are less likely to emerge in their study of the Holocaust. For example, when studying the Rwandan Genocide, students may encounter the sexualised nature of the violence or the post-genocide relations between survivors and perpetrators. This may lead them to enquire about under-researched or marginalised aspects of Holocaust studies such as the experiences of women in the Holocaust or the fate of Holocaust survivors.

Mistakes to avoid

While there are many potential advantages of comparing the Holocaust with other genocides, if this is done badly then it is far better that it not be done at all. Consequently, sensitivity, thoughtfulness and clarity are all essential ingredients.

Avoid only making comparisons

The term 'comparative genocide' in its proper and fullest sense, means drawing out contrasts as well as similarities. It is essential that the differences as well as the similarities between the Holocaust and other genocides are highlighted. There were many aspects of the Holocaust which were unique and these should be articulated clearly. This will help students to recognise the complexities involved with making comparisons and help to avoid generalisations.

Avoid trivialising either the Holocaust or that to which it is compared

While the Holocaust can legitimately be compared with certain historical phenomena such as the Rwandan Genocide, there are some comparisons which appear to undermine and trivialise the Holocaust. People for the Ethical Treatment of Animals (PETA) for example, controversially juxtaposed images of cruelty towards animals with photographs from the Holocaust in a notorious campaign called 'Holocaust on the Plate' which was banned in Germany (PETA 2014). Conversely, comparisons can trivialise or undermine the subject that is being compared with the Holocaust. South African Holocaust educators have reported such problems when making comparisons with apartheid (Nates 2010).

Avoid comparing or measuring suffering

Related to the problem of trivialising the Holocaust is the equally problematic occurrence of comparing or measuring suffering. It is impossible to judge individual suffering whether on a slave ship in the Atlantic, in a church in Kigali or in a concentration camp in Poland. Moreover, it seems facile to arbitrate who endured the most collective suffering as a people group. Such endeavours are far removed from the objectives or aims of comparative studies, which seek to draw out historical themes and thematic links which are justified and supported by precise and detailed evidence.

Avoid de-Judaising the Holocaust

While the Holocaust had important ramifications for both Europe and the whole of humanity, its specifically Jewish nature should not be undermined or marginalised. Historical and Nazi antisemitism should not be glossed over by comparing it with conventional ethnic or geo-political tensions. The Holocaust needs to be understood within its Jewish context and when making connections with other genocides it is important to remember this.

Avoid politically or ideologically driven comparisons

Whilst recognising the legitimacy of appropriately contextualised and historically grounded comparisons, teachers must avoid attempts to undermine the Holocaust or the State of Israel by accepting ideologically driven comparisons. Some students, for example, may wish to compare the Holocaust to the *Nakba* (the displacement of Palestinians in 1948) for political ends. The contemporary weight and significance that is attached to the word 'Holocaust' is also such that some may wish to advance their cause by making comparisons with it.

Avoid de-contextualising

The Holocaust, as well as the events to which it is sometimes compared, need to be carefully understood within their historical context. It seems impossible that effective or meaningful comparisons can occur without students having a firm understanding of both topics. Consequently, any parallels which are drawn ought to occur only after sufficient contextual depth has been established. It is questionable whether the level of depth needed can be found among classes of younger students or among those who have not been studying the subject for some time.

Integrating comparative genocide into the curriculum

While there may be benefits to teaching comparative genocide, it is not always easy to integrate it into the curriculum and clearly the task is easier in some subjects than in others. Certainly the history classroom allows for evidence-based parallels to be made, which might occur at the end of a Holocaust unit. While it is possible to teach history thematically, looking at colonialism, nationalism or war, it seems that such an approach will only be successful if care is taken to provide sufficient depth to each case study and if the comparisons which are made are not de-contextualised and considered within a historical vacuum.

Such thematic approaches can work well in citizenship studies, where similarities and differences can be drawn out between the treatment of the Jews in Germany during the 1930s, Christians living in Stalinist Russia before the Second World War or blacks in America in the 1950s and 1960s. Studies can consider these groups' legal status, how this changed over time and the conditions and attitudes that they faced.

Within religious education, thematic and conceptual comparisons can also be drawn by looking at the ethical complexities involved with terms such as 'bystander' and 'collaborator'. This enables a detailed study of the context in which decision-making took place and what factors would determine the choices that were made. The Holocaust and every subsequent genocide has generated countless moral dilemmas, and studies of sub-topics such as the *Judenrate* (Jewish Councils within the ghettos), the Kastner Trial (1955) or the *Gacaca* courts (the community justice system used in Rwanda) provide a wealth of material which relates to the salient issues of acquiescence, collaboration, justice and retribution.

In English literature a teacher may want to compare two books, one set in the Holocaust and the other in a more recent genocide. Parallel themes could be drawn out and historical background provided which explicitly highlight both the similarities and differences in the contexts of the stories. If fictional texts were being studied, examples might include a comparison between Gil Courtemanche's *A Sunday at the Pool in Kigali* (2000) and *Jacob's Courage* (2007) by Charles Weinblatt. While the overarching theme in both novels is love amidst impossible situations, the former is set in Rwanda, while the latter finds the characters in Theresienstadt ghetto and then Auschwitz. Such books would most likely be only suitable for sixth-form students due to their adult themes and graphic descriptions. If non-fiction books were preferred, the disturbing account of Reverien Rurangwa in *Genocide: My Stolen Rwanda* (2009) could be read alongside Primo Levi's *If This Is a Man* (1947) or Elie Wiesel's *Night* (1958).

Similarly in drama, two plays could be studied or performed which address concurrent themes, such as post-genocide justice in Erik Ehn's *Mario Kizito* (based on Rwanda) and Kitty Felde's *A Patch of Earth* which is set in a Bosnian war crimes courtroom. In *The Theatre of Genocide*, edited by Robert Skloot, there is detailed discussion of these particular plays as well as a list of plays about genocide in the English language (Skloot 2008).

Attitudes towards comparative genocide

One of the practical benefits of making comparisons between the Holocaust and other genocides is that it helps to justify its inclusion on the curriculum. While many may legitimately argue that the sheer nature and scale of the phenomenon, as well as the fact that it occurred in Europe, makes no other justification necessary, such an argument often has limited resonance among those from non-European backgrounds who point to more recent genocides, which were of equal devastation to the victim group. Eckmann highlights the problem of only focusing on the Holocaust and also describes the solution that many teachers adopt when she writes:

> Teachers also find it difficult to answer questions such as 'Why are you always speaking about Jews?' and 'Why not speak about Rwanda, about slavery or about the Roma?' Or, in post-Soviet countries they might ask, 'Why not speak about the Gulag?'. In Western European contexts, we observed that such questions lead teachers to adopt new strategies. Usually in the lower grades the Holocaust is taught within the context of World War II and the rise of Nazism. But more and more educators, especially in the upper grades, tend to teach it within the context of comparing genocides, or within the context of topics like racism, totalitarianism, and colonialism.
>
> (Eckmann 2010: 9)

The particular importance of the Holocaust is certainly suggested by its position on the UK National Curriculum, where the subject is, as Eckmann intimates, typically taught within the context of the Second World War. Consequently, it is thus often difficult to neatly include other genocides, and their marginalisation within schools may partly be due to the fact that they cannot easily be integrated into a chronological study of British or European history.

The potential difficulty of including other genocides into one's teaching does not mean that most teachers share the sentiment that the Holocaust ought to be mandatory at the exclusion of other genocides. Research conducted by the HEDP on over 2,000 teachers in 2009 found that 51 per cent of all respondents 'who have taught or currently teach about the Holocaust said they agreed or strongly agreed that, "The Holocaust is clearly very important but so are other genocides and crimes against humanity: these should get similar curriculum time attention". Fewer than 17 per cent of all those with experience of teaching in this area disagreed with this position' (Pettigrew et al. 2009: 64). In the light of these findings it certainly seems possible that although the teaching of other genocides is not among the requirements of the National Curriculum, many teachers may attempt to integrate it into their courses. This seems especially likely in academies, which do not have to follow the National Curriculum and are perhaps less likely to adopt a chronological approach.

Case study: the Holocaust and the Rwandan Genocide

Perhaps the most pertinent and appropriate comparison with the Holocaust is the Rwandan Genocide. Consequently, this is reflected in the resources which accompany the Citizenship scheme of work in Chapters 13–15. These tragic events in human history share a number of similarities and differences which consequently enable a thoughtful and sophisticated comparison.

The nature, scale and extremity of the Rwandan Genocide make it appropriate for comparison with the Holocaust. Gourevitch states that there were 'three-hundred and thirty-three and a third murders an hour – or five and a half lives terminated every minute' (Gourevitch 1998: 133).

As previously mentioned, any appropriate comparison must also recognise the differences which exist. The sections of Table 9.1 represent useful starting points for discussion and development.

Conclusion

Teaching comparative genocide offers a number of benefits but, if done poorly, can undermine and trivialise the Holocaust. Sensitivity, specificity and great care are all needed if appropriate and contextually grounded similarities and differences are to be analysed. Using the Rwandan Genocide as a parallel is by no means the only option. More contemporary examples such as Syria, South Sudan or the Central African Republic may seem more relevant. In any case, it helps to tackle the misconception that the Holocaust occurred a long time ago and could never be repeated.

Table 9.1 Comparing the Holocaust and the Rwandan Genocide

Similarities	Differences
Virulent and inflammatory propaganda existed against both the Jews and the Tutsis. In both cases this involved suggestions that the victims did not belong in the country and that they were outsiders. In the case of the Tutsis, Hutu extremists argued that they were descendants of Noah's son Ham and had come from Ethiopia. Jews were described as the descendants of Shem who were not ethnic Germans. Within the propaganda used by both the Nazis and the Hutu extremists, the victim group was portrayed as sexual predators.	Within Hutu hate propaganda, it was always Tutsi women who were targeted as sexually devious and seductive. Hutu men were warned against their lures. Conversely, it was Jewish men who were the object of sexually related accusations and German women were told to take care. Connected to this is the predominance of rape and sexual violence in the Rwandan Genocide as Hutu men sought to exert their sexual hegemony and undermine female sexuality.
Acts of mass murder had occurred by the perpetrators against the victims before the respective genocides. In Germany, *Kristallnacht* led to the deaths of over ninety Jews, while the mass murder of Tutsis had sporadically and sometimes systematically taken place between 1959 and 1994.	The Nazi regime sought to keep the Holocaust as secretive as possible and employed euphemistic terms when discussing it. Conversely the genocide was openly discussed by Hutu extremists both before and during the killings.
Both occurred within the context of war; in the case of the Holocaust, the Second World War and in Rwanda, the civil war which recommenced after the genocide began. Both genocides only failed to achieve their goals (the total annihilation of the victim group) because they were defeated by military force.	The Second World War played a key role in shaping the direction and nature of the Holocaust. Moreover, the systematic mass murder of Jews began after the commencement of war, whereas in Rwanda, the RPF invaded the country because the systematic mass murder of the Tutsis had begun. It is important to emphasise that neither the Holocaust nor the Rwandan Genocide should be seen as war crimes, but a specific and planned annihilation of a people.
The Nazis and the Hutu extremists sought to murder every Jew and Tutsi respectively who was under their political control. It mattered not whether they were men, women or children.	The Nazi regime used able-bodied Jews to work for them and sought to murder them through exhaustion. The Hutu extremists almost always murdered on the spot.
The key organisations involved in the killing were quasi-autonomous groups, connected (either directly or indirectly) to the state. The SS and the *Interhamwe* both acted with some independence and were assisted by collaborators.	The Nazi regime generally perpetrated the killing a long way from Germany, transporting Jews to specialist centres of mass murder. They employed modern and efficient techniques. Conversely, the genocide of the Tutsis occurred in Rwanda, wherever the victims were to be found. The method of killing was principally by machete which was unsophisticated and old-fashioned.
While many Nazi perpetrators fled to Latin America and Hutu killers into the Democratic Republic of Congo, various court cases were set up to try and bring about justice. The Nuremberg Trials took place in Germany and the International Criminal Tribunal for Rwanda was set up in Arusha, Tanzania.	While the Nuremberg Trials have often been viewed in a positive light, there have been suggestions that perpetrators in Rwanda have not always received justice. In 2001, *Gacaca* courts were set up to administer community justice, and these have also been considered controversial.

Recommended reading

Avraham, D. (2010) 'The Problem with Using Historical Parallels as a Method in Holocaust and Genocide Teaching', *Intercultural Education*, 21, S1: S33–S40.

Kelleway, E., Spillane, T. and Haydn, T. (2013) '"Never again"? Helping Year 9 Think about What Happened after the Holocaust and Learning Lessons from Genocides', *Teaching History*, 153: 38–44.

Kinloch, N. (2001) 'Parallel Catastrophes? Uniqueness, Redemption and the Shoah', *Teaching History*, 104: 8–14.

Task Force for International Cooperation on Holocaust Education, Remembrance and Research (2010) 'Education Working Group Paper on the Holocaust and Other Genocides'. Available at: www.un.org/en/holocaustremembrance/EWG_Holocaust_and_Other_Genocides.pdf.

Chapter 10

Teaching in a multicultural setting

Over the last two or three decades the demographic composition of the average classroom has undergone a significant transition. In England and Wales, 13 per cent of usual residents were born abroad compared with only 7 per cent in 1991. In London, only 44.9 per cent of people living there are White British, while 7 per cent of Londoners are African, 6.6 per cent are Indian and 4.2 per cent have the Caribbean as their ethnic origin (ONS 2012a: 8). Multiculturalism is a European wide phenomenon, with eight other EU states having a higher percentage of foreign born residents (ONS 2012b). The contemporary student population therefore, is ethnically, religiously and culturally diverse, which poses a wide range of opportunities and challenges for the practitioner.

What opportunities does multiculturalism offer Holocaust education?

When approaching the teaching of the Holocaust it is important to remember that there are a number of benefits to having a multicultural audience. Making full use of these is likely to improve the quality of the education delivered.

1. Increased understanding of difference

Students who live in a demographically homogeneous society may struggle to understand what it is like being a minority within a particular society. While they may be able to conceptually sympathise, they will certainly not be able to experientially empathise. Those living in a culturally diverse society are in many senses used to a range of different ethnicities, religions and cultures. Moreover, they themselves may have experienced discrimination or persecution. Consequently it seems they will be able to better appreciate the problems that Jews faced when they were presented as outsiders by the Nazi regime.

When teaching about the persecution of the Jews during the 1930s, many students ask 'Why didn't they simply leave?' While many eventually did or at least attempted to do so, a number of students – especially those who have always lived in the same place – have little sense of the difficulty and uncertainty that is attached to moving, let alone moving to another country. Teachers need to explain that if Jews decided to leave Germany then they would have to leave their home, their friends, their job and move to a foreign country, which spoke a different language and where they did not know anyone. Students who are refugees or who have fled other countries may be able to understand this far better.

2. Greater interest in the subject

While it is possible that some students, perhaps those of non-European descent, find little relevance or significance to learning about the fate of Europe's Jews in the last century, students who are learning within the context of a multicultural environment may find that many of the themes within their study of the Holocaust do resonate with them. This is not to say that the aim of teaching the subject should be to make links between the past and present, but if overlapping themes such as discrimination, prejudice and persecution exist, then students will automatically make comparisons and contrasts in their mind. This may generate greater interest and enthusiasm for studying the subject.

3. A broader awareness of the Holocaust

As a consequence of the Holocaust being central to the socio-cultural and moral psyche of the West, it is easy to forget that this is not so in many countries. An important study conducted by the USHMM and the Salzburg Global Seminar (2013) looked at trends, patterns and perspectives in Holocaust education in the countries which were not part of the IHRA – the intergovernmental body for Holocaust remembrance. It found that while Holocaust education has permeated many parts of the world, the majority of students in a number of countries in Africa and Asia are unlikely to have ever studied the Holocaust. For many students who come to the West from other countries, they develop an awareness of the subject of which otherwise they may never even have heard. If those learners decide to one day return to their country of origin, then they will be able to help develop Holocaust consciousness and increase awareness of it in those places.

4. Particular cultural insight

Teaching the Holocaust to Jewish, German, Roma or Polish children involves that fine balance of historical integrity and sensitivity. Yet experience suggests that many students – especially Jewish ones – are pleased that their own people's history and culture is being explored. In such instances, they can often provide particular insight into the relevance of certain practices and help to explain why Nazi actions were so abhorrent. For example, when non-Jewish students learn about the burning of Jewish books they are unlikely to appreciate its significance. Yet if a Jewish student can explain to his or her peers why sacred writings are of such importance within Judaism then they are more likely to appreciate and understand the gravity of the Nazis' crimes. Moreover, students from a Christian or Muslim background are also likely to be able to understand the centrality of sacred writings to a particular faith.

What challenges does multiculturalism offer Holocaust education?

Although there are many benefits to teaching the Holocaust within a multicultural setting, it can also pose a number of challenges.

I. Students can be disinterested in the subject

The main problem that teachers cite when expressing the challenges of teaching the Holocaust in a multicultural setting is the apathy and lack of engagement which students show. This is especially the case of learners from non-European backgrounds. It is important that teachers consider why this is the case and what strategies and initiatives can be put in place to remedy it (some ideas are included later in the chapter). It seems that there are various reasons why students of non-European backgrounds especially struggle to engage with the subject.

First, learning about the Holocaust seems irrelevant to them as it appears to have little connection to their own history or the history of their family. The Holocaust appears to them as a European phenomenon which was far removed from Asia or Africa. Second, students of non-European origin feel that by learning about the history of Europeans, their own stories are being marginalised. This can lead to resentment and bitterness as students sense that their own history (personally, ethnically or nationally) is perceived to be of less value by the very fact that no one is learning about it in school. This can also lead to isolation as such students are likely to be familiar with their own histories, whereas compared to their European peers, they may feel less knowledgeable and thus disadvantaged. Third, a number of students can feel that learning about a specific set of circumstances in a different continent several decades ago is very detached from the contemporary issues and problems that they face on a day-to-day basis. Avraham summed up the problems perfectly when he stated:

> While the local European students view learning about the Holocaust and WWII as part of studying their national history or European history in general, students of Turkish, Moroccan, Vietnamese, Chinese, Afghani or Indian extraction living in Europe have a hard time developing empathy or any sort of connection to the subject. To these students, the children of immigrants, the subject of the Holocaust seems irrelevant, both because of the particular past to which they feel they belong, and because of the difficulties they face in the present.
>
> (Avraham 2008: 4)

2. There can be a wider range of existing knowledge

In any class, whether it is in a multicultural setting or not, there is likely to be a range of pre-existing knowledge. Nevertheless, when there are a number of students from various backgrounds and cultures in the same class, the disparity of existing knowledge is likely to be increased. Some European students may have grown up learning about the Second World War and the Holocaust at home; they may have read books about it or seen documentaries on television. In contrast, it is perfectly possible that a student who has recently arrived in the country from a non-European country may never have heard of the Second World War, the Holocaust, Hitler, the Nazis or Jews. Trying to ensure that both sets of learners are catered for in the lesson is no easy task. The student who already has a considerable amount of knowledge will need to be stretched, while the very basics and foundational knowledge of the Holocaust will need to be taught to the other. This involves careful differentiation, and it can be very challenging to ensure that the wide range of students have their learning needs sufficiently met.

3. Students can target specific minorities

Within a multicultural classroom, it is possible that ethnic or religious tension may be higher. In some instances a culturally diverse environment leads to higher levels of tolerance amongst the learners, but this is not always the case. If a particular ethnic group features in the story of the Holocaust and if careful sensitivity is not employed by the teacher, students may use this as a means of targeting another culture.

To what extent should Holocaust education adapt for a multicultural audience?

Although the term 'multiculturalism' is commonly defined to mean cultural diversity, it also has a more precise ideological meaning. In this sense, multiculturalism refers to the *approach* that is adopted towards a culturally diverse society. Those who advocate multiculturalism as a political position seek the advancement of marginalised or disadvantaged groups by recognising and celebrating difference, taking account of it and where possible, adapting to accommodate it. In a controversial speech delivered in Munich in 2011, British prime minister David Cameron stated:

> Under the doctrine of state multiculturalism we have encouraged different cultures to live separate lives, apart from each other and apart from the mainstream. We've failed to provide a vision of society to which they feel they want to belong ... Frankly, we need a lot less passive tolerance of recent years and much more active, muscular liberalism.
>
> (Quoted from Le Petit 2011: 1)

This approach, when applied to Holocaust education, would mean that all students, irrespective of culture, religion or ethnicity should study the Holocaust and learn about the history of the Nazi persecution and mass murder of Europe's Jews. In many countries in the West, learning about the Holocaust is legally mandated, although in England and Wales for example, many schools are becoming academies which are not required to follow the National Curriculum.

It seems that there is certainly a legitimate argument that all students should learn about the Holocaust as it was a paradigm shifting phenomenon in human history. Moreover, as the subject is so culturally important within the West, students who live there should know why this is. Few, it seems, would disagree that all students studying within a secondary school in Europe should learn about the Holocaust. One might go further and say that because they are in Europe, students should therefore study European history and culture, irrespective of whether or not they want to do so or whether or not they find it relevant.

Yet if the Holocaust is and should be taught within schools, how relevant is the demographic composition of the student population? Should teachers adapt their courses and lessons because they have an ethnically diverse class? There is by no means a consensus on these questions.

Those who would advocate adjusting the lessons to suit the learners would argue that students are unlikely to benefit from their education if they see no relevance to what they are studying. By adapting Holocaust education to suit the learners, then the subject can become inclusive and be of educational benefit to all students, irrespective of their cultural background. Moreover, in schools where learners from non-European countries form the majority of the class, it seems unrealistic to be unwilling to adapt the nature of teaching accordingly. Holocaust education approaches in Germany, Israel and Poland all take into account the various sensitivities and issues which are relevant to their own national identity. In the same manner one might argue that Holocaust education for a class of students from non-European countries should be equally sensitive to the needs, attitudes and issues which relate to them. In addition to that, it might be said that in the same way that teachers adapt their lessons for students of different ages and abilities, so they must do so for those of different cultures.

While this sounds commendable in principle, critics of this view have argued that it risks watering down the Holocaust, being selective with the history and plundering the past to suit the likes and dislikes of the student population. Critics would also state that the Holocaust is the same irrespective of who is learning about it and thus the teaching of it ought also to be the same. The USHMM suggests that the nature of the class should not affect the way that the Holocaust is taught.

> Educators should avoid tailoring their Holocaust course or lesson in any way to the particular makeup of their student population. Failing to contextualize the groups targeted by the Nazis as well as the actions of those who resisted can result in the misunderstanding or trivializing of this history. Relevant connections for all learners often surface as the history is analyzed.
>
> (USHMM 2014b)

Perhaps the most important thing to remember when planning a Holocaust curriculum which is specifically aimed at a culturally diverse audience is that the historical content should not be changed to make it more palatable, convenient or accommodating. The past – not least of all the Holocaust – contains much which is unsavoury in the extreme and which may put certain groups in a very bad light. Being true to the history is crucial, and if a selective or postmodern approach is taken, then Holocaust denial and distortion, prejudice and ignorance will soon emerge. Consequently, the origins and events of the Holocaust must be covered. Students need to have a historical and contextual understanding. They need to learn about the Nazi regime and the evolution of Jewish policy; the ghettos, *Einsatzgruppen* and camps; the scale and geography of the Holocaust, how it ended and the experiences of survivors. Irrespective of the demography of a class, students cannot understand the Holocaust without knowing its history. If this is ignored they will have a superficial and artificial conception which is of very limited value. The European Agency for Fundamental Human Rights correctly states:

> Holocaust education must first be about exploring and attempting to understand and explain the historical context of the Holocaust. To be meaningful, it is vital that the past is not shaped to serve the needs of any moral, political, social or ideological agenda.
>
> (FRA 2010: 31)

In the 2009 HEDP survey of teachers of the Holocaust in England, respondents were asked whether or not they agreed with the statement, 'I find that having students from diverse cultural backgrounds influences the way that I teach about the Holocaust.' Interestingly, only 23.3 per cent of teachers agreed or strongly agreed, although many remarked that they wanted their students from different backgrounds to find the Holocaust relevant and consequently looked at other examples of prejudice, discrimination and racism alongside the Holocaust (Pettigrew et al. 2009: 88–89). Box

10.1 shows some of the reasons that teachers gave as to why they did or did not agree with the statement.

Box 10.1 Does having students from diverse cultural backgrounds affect the way I teach the Holocaust? Some responses from the HEDP survey

'The ethnic mix of a class should have absolutely no bearing on how the Holocaust is taught and nor does it affect my teaching in any way – it doesn't affect the facts in any way.'

'I do not teach it to draw explicit moral lessons or sermons and so even in a school that is 70 per cent Muslim with strong links to Palestine, I still take a historical disciplinary perspective and so the cultural background of the class is the same as for all other enquiries.'

'Students need to be taught tolerance and acceptance which is aided by mixing with diverse groups.'

'[Cultural diversity] increases awareness that there are potentially many victims of modern holocausts/genocides or racism and it encourages awareness of the need to try and empathise.'

(Pettigrew et al., *Teaching about the Holocaust in English Secondary Schools*, pp. 88–89)

What techniques can help a multicultural class engage with the Holocaust?

Although the facts of the Holocaust do not change according to the demography of a teacher's class, there are various techniques, methodologies and practices which can be employed when teaching this subject and that are likely to increase the attention and engagement of a culturally diverse class. This does not mean that a different or more palatable history is taught, but that methods are employed which facilitate inclusive learning and engagement with the subject, two principles which are sound pedagogy.

1. Explain why studying the Holocaust matters

One of the main reasons why teaching about the Holocaust can be challenging within a multicultural setting is because students do not appreciate its relevance to the modern world or to them as individuals. Taking the time to explain why studying the Holocaust matters can help dispel the myth in their minds that this is something which is of no significance to them. This is something which is helpful for all students, irrespective of their background, culture or ethnicity. Disaffected and apathetic students are unlikely to engage if they do not realise why studying the Holocaust matters.

This means that students need to recognise that despite the fact that the Holocaust was a Jewish tragedy, it also has a global significance which applies to all of humanity. The attempted mass murder of all of Europe's Jews challenged the very foundations of civilised society and reinforced the idea that human nature is fundamentally evil. The theological impact of the Holocaust also relates to God's impassibility and his engagement with the world. The legal legacy of the Holocaust is also profound. Of particular relevance is the UN *Convention on the Prevention and Punishment of the Crime of Genocide* which was ratified in 1948. In addition to this, the Nuremberg Trials demonstrated that individuals were culpable for crimes against humanity and that redress of such heinous acts should be sought on a legal basis with evidential documentation. This set a precedent which has been followed ever since.

Students also need to realise that the Holocaust matters because it shows the dangers of unchecked power and government without accountability. It shows how far a regime may go if left unchecked and the importance of individuals and organisations speaking out against that which is morally wrong. Similarly, it shows where racism, prejudice and discrimination can potentially lead. This is not to say that name calling in the playground if left unchecked would descend into genocide, but it is to suggest that students can see how attitudes, stereotyping and prejudice can descend into violence, persecution and eventually mass murder. These few examples, which are far from exhaustive, can demonstrate to students why the Holocaust is so significant and worthy of study. Such cases suggest that the subject is significant not because of their own ethnicity, identity or race, but because they are members of the human race. By doing this, learners recognise that the Holocaust is not simply being studied because they happen to be in Europe or North America but because it has global relevance.

Students from diverse backgrounds may be particularly interested to learn about Holocaust education programmes in their parts of the world (e.g. through the Aladdin Project). This helps them realise that members of the community and country of origin with which they associate also learn about and recognise the worth of Holocaust education.

2. Acknowledge the history of the learners

Another way of helping students to engage with the Holocaust and to not actively oppose learning about it is for teachers to acknowledge and appreciate the different histories of their own students. This helps adolescents realise that their own cultural identity and their own nation's past is not being undermined, marginalised or suppressed by learning about the Holocaust. Gryglewski comments:

> Many immigrant youths have the feeling that their personal family history stands in competition with the remembrance discourse of mainstream society. In their eyes, the majority population is not interested in the history of their families or the country their families came from.
>
> (Gryglewski 2010: S46)

This does not mean that Holocaust education takes a back seat while students narrate their own histories. Instead it is about teachers adopting an attitude which is welcoming of different cultures and identities, demonstrating the absence of cultural competition. Teachers may encourage students to ask their family about their own histories, further showing the learners that there is space within society for different backgrounds and cultures.

3. Appreciate the differences within groups

It is easy for teachers who are operating within a culturally diverse environment to group students from the same region of the world or who share the same religion, and consequently fail to appreciate the different histories, outlooks and identities within the group. This often leads practitioners into the danger of making incorrect assumptions based on their misconceptions. One common mistake that teachers make is to fail to see the differences which exist between Muslim students. Short noted that 'Muslim youth are not a monolithic entity but are divided in their attitude towards learning about the Holocaust' (Short 2013: 130). Gryglewski's research supports this, and she remarks that 'students with a Turkish background, on the whole, did not mention the Israeli–Palestinian conflict. In contrast, mixed groups with students of both Turkish and Palestinian/Arab origin manifested a sense of solidarity and did tend to mention the conflict' (Gryglewski 2010: S44). Only by appreciating the differences that exist within a cultural or religious group will a teacher be able to understand the variety and intricacy of the opportunities and challenges which multicultural education brings. This is particularly relevant, it seems, regarding learners' attitudes towards Jews and towards Israel.

4. Broaden the study beyond Europe

When teaching the Second World War many teachers focus on the European theatres and ignore the Eastern front, North Africa or the conflict in the Far East. While the Holocaust was less global than World War II and the essence of it did occur in Europe, consideration of non-European countries can also be included. Students from Turkish, Arab or North African descent are likely to be interested in the role and attitudes of Muslim countries and their leaders towards the Nazi regime and their treatment of the Jews. At present it seems that this is a useful learning strategy which has been seldom used and would help learners of non-European descent find the Holocaust more relevant. Moreover, they would feel that their own national or ethnic identity is not being ignored or marginalised.

This more inclusive approach should supplement rather than replace more traditional Holocaust curricula. Students need to know and understand that the Holocaust was first and foremost a European phenomenon; however, some consideration of where and how it touched other nations may be helpful when teaching in a multicultural setting.

If teachers choose to include in their lessons some consideration of the Holocaust in non-European countries, then it is important that what they select is not driven by an ideological agenda and that there is sufficient balance and historical integrity. While it may be beneficial for Muslim students to see how some Muslims rescued Jews during the War, especially in countries like Bosnia and Algeria, they will then also need to learn that Haj Amin al-Husseini, the grand mufti of Jerusalem, helped create a Muslim SS division in Bosnia and influenced the creation of an SS task force which planned to murder the 500,000 Jews living in British-mandated Palestine (Gilbert 2010: 185–86). In addition to providing balance, teachers should also try to provide sufficient depth and detail to Jewish–Muslim relations during the Holocaust. Without exception there are complexities and national and local circumstances to consider, which defy generalisations. In many cases there would be Muslims both supporting and opposing the persecution and murder of Jews, as Gilbert demonstrates in his account of the fate of Iraqi Jews during the Second World War:

178 Jews had been murdered in Baghdad and nine outside the city. Several Muslims who had tried to come to the defence of their Jewish neighbours were also murdered. Several hundred Jewish women and young girls were raped. More than 240 were orphaned and at least two thousand were badly wounded. In addition 911 Jewish homes and 586 Jewish-owned shops and stores were looted, as were four ancient synagogues.

(Gilbert 2010: 193)

Clearly, teachers need to approach this subject thoughtfully and intelligently if it is to be a worthwhile and historically valid exercise. Box 10.2 provides some specific examples and ideas which teachers may want to research further and include in their teaching. The website of the Aladdin Project (www.projetaladin.org), which was set up to tackle Holocaust denial and prejudice as well as advance intercultural dialogue, also provides a great deal of useful information on this subject.

Box 10.2 Broadening the sudy beyond Europe: some examples and ideas

- During the Holocaust a number of Jews sought refuge in Muslim-majority Albania, which was the only country in Europe where there were more Jews living after the war than had been before it.
- The Nazis and their allies controlled North Africa during the early 1940s and implemented a number of anti-Jewish policies. Had this territory not been liberated, then Jews living in countries such as Libya, Egypt and Palestine among others would have been murdered.
- Joel Brand's 'Blood for Goods' involved negotiations taking place between various parties in Istanbul and Aleppo among other places.

Examples of rescuers	Examples of collaborators
Khaled Abdul Wahab	Haj Amin el Husseini
Si Ali Sakkat	Muhamed Hadžiefendić
Dervis Korkut	

---

5. Study the Holocaust in the context of broader themes

Such an approach to teaching the Holocaust is becoming increasingly popular, especially in schools with culturally diverse classes. Rather than simply study the Holocaust by itself, it is taught within a broader unit which looks at themes such as racism or genocide. The idea behind doing this is that it means students can look at more historical events such as Srebrenica and the Rwandan Genocide, which may consequently attract higher levels of engagement and be nearer to some of the countries of origin of some of the students. Other curricula, especially in citizenship and religious studies classes, include looking at themes such as prejudice and racism and drawing out examples from the Holocaust. This may involve students looking at the treatment of the Jews in Germany followed by the racial prejudice of 1950s and 1960s America, succeeded by a study of contemporary racism.

This approach to teaching the Holocaust is not without numerous problems, and if it is to avoid marginalising or grossly simplifying the Holocaust, then great skill and care is needed. Many academics within the field of Holocaust education have shown concern about this method, as it can often fail to provide sufficient historical depth and can encourage students to make inappropriate and unhelpful comparisons and contrasts between the Holocaust and other events in history, without them being grounded in historical context and understanding. Moreover, it could be argued that this approach is unnecessary, because if taught well, the Holocaust can and should be made relevant to all learners, irrespective of their cultural, ethnic or religious backgrounds.

Conclusion

In the same way that politicians and policy-makers lack consensus on how to respond to cultural diversity, so those involved in Holocaust education often demonstrate differences. Ultimately, practitioners should maximise the benefits of having a multicultural class and overcome the potential challenges with thoughtful, engaging and carefully constructed teaching which shows the relevance and significance of the Holocaust to all learners.

Recommended reading

Avraham, D. (2008) 'The Challenges of Teaching the Holocaust in a Multicultural Setting', *Yad Vashem Quarterly*, 51, October: 4. Available at: www.yadvashem.org/yv/en/pressroom/magazine/pdf/yv_magazine51.pdf

Gryglewski, E. (2010) 'Teaching about the Holocaust in Multicultural Societies: Appreciating the Learner', *Intercultural Education*, 21, S1: S41–S49.

Short, G. (2013) 'Reluctant Learners?: Muslim Youth Confront the Holocaust', *Intercultural Education*, 24, 1–2: 121–32.

Chapter 11

Combating antisemitism

Antisemitism is hatred, discrimination or prejudice which is directed towards Jews on account of their religion, culture or heritage. Although the word only originated in 1879, antisemitism has existed for many millennia and continues to occur today. Prejudice against Jews has taken many forms throughout the centuries including expulsion, ghettoisation and pogroms. Many attacks against Jews were sparked by accusations of blood libel – the idea that the blood of Christian children was being used for Jewish rituals and practices. Historically, European antisemitism had strong Christian connections, with Jews being blamed for the death of Christ and thus being guilty of deicide. Throughout the nineteenth century, the emergence of nationalism led to new forms of antisemitism which were racially based and accused Jews of being disloyal to the new nation states as well as a threat to the purity of the Aryan race. This particular form of antisemitism, which was the type manifested in Nazism, played on traditional myths of Jewish global conspiracies and built on long-established stereotypes.

Antisemitism in its various guises has not been eradicated in the post-Holocaust world, although within many parts of the Western world it has been pushed to the fringes of society. Since the end of the Second World War, the already complex issue of antisemitism was given a new geo-political dimension through the creation of, and opposition to, the State of Israel. While it may be nice to think that it didn't, Schweber is absolutely correct in remarking that 'Israel's role in the Israeli-Palestinian conflict and the Middle East generally, matter in terms of Holocaust education, both globally and nationally' (Schweber 2006: 51). While opposition to Israel is not the same as antisemitism, there is a complex relationship which can often play out within the classroom, especially when teaching the subject of the Holocaust.

What types of antisemitism can be found in schools?

Although antisemitism can take many forms and often defies simplistic categorisation, the following three types of prejudice seem to exist. Only when teachers are conscious of how antisemitism manifests itself, are they in a position to tackle it and combat it within the classroom and the school setting more generally.

Ignorant antisemitism

While all forms of hatred and discrimination towards Jews are based on misinformation and a lack of knowledge, ignorant antisemitism is perhaps the most common form which exists in schools. Box 11.1 shows some of the ideas that characterise it. Ignorant antisemitism is the latent negative approach to Jews, which has been built up by playground terminology and historical stereotypes. This includes using the term 'Jew' as an insult to non-Jewish children, calling someone 'Jewish' if they are fiscally frugal or pick up money from the floor. It is important to remember that most children who engage in what they would perceive to be 'harmless banter' are reinforcing negative images of Jews and constructing harmful preconceptions with which they will approach their study of the Holocaust. For such students, their notion of Jewishness is determined by American TV sitcoms like *The Big Bang Theory* or cartoons like *The Simpsons*; and many of them have never even met someone who is Jewish.

Box 11.1 Ignorant antisemitism

I always think of Jews as having dark hair and dark eyes.

(William, aged 11)

Hitler did not like the Jews because as a race they were quite clever and had quite a lot of money.

(Loretta, aged 15)

No one in Germany liked the Jews because they had lots of money from starting banks and took up all the good jobs like lawyers and doctors.

(Shazad, aged 13)

Targeted antisemitism

Distinctly more sinister is targeted antisemitism, which actively pursues a prejudiced agenda on the basis of wilful discrimination, rather than ignorance. While ignorant antisemitism will no doubt have a negative effect on any Jewish students who witness it in their school, targeted antisemitism maliciously and purposefully seeks to ostracise, demonise and alienate Jews. Such extreme forms of prejudice are obviously very rare. Any student pursuing them will almost certainly have been indoctrinated with anti-Jewish messages from home or from elsewhere.

New antisemitism

What is generally described as 'new antisemitism' is a prejudice against Jews which manifests itself in the form of virulent and excessive abuse of Israel. As we have previously acknowledged, opposition to Israel is not antisemitism. New antisemitism, however, is when criticism is directed towards Israel *because* it is a Jewish state and thus intentional antisemitism is disguised by seemingly political debate. This type of prejudice is often seen when the actions of Israel are purposefully compared to the Nazis. This form of antisemitism occurs on the extremes of the political left and right, as well as within the radical elements of Islam.

How prevalent is antisemitism within schools?

When seeking to answer this question it is important to take into account the various forms of antisemitism. While negative stereotypes of Jews may be frequently perpetuated and while the term 'Jew' is thrown around as a term of abuse on the playground just like the word 'gay', there appear to be very limited amounts of genuine antisemitism within schools. In a recent study of over 2,000 teachers in England, it did not emerge that prejudice against Jews was a common or noteworthy problem for those engaged in Holocaust education (Pettigrew et al. 2009: 90). To some extent this was supported by a study conducted by Short on the heads of history in fifteen Muslim-majority schools in Southeast England. He noted that:

> Many Muslim students have no objection to learning about the Holocaust and seem as likely as any other group of students to benefit from their learning. They may well be antagonistic to Israel, but they are able and willing to separate that country's conflict with the Palestinians from the fate of the Jews in Nazi-occupied Europe.
>
> (Short 2013: 128–29)

Nevertheless, Short also found that 'some Muslim students are reluctant to learn about the Holocaust and are most unlikely to learn from it because of their own antisemitism' (ibid.: 129), while he also found that within a few schools, 'negative stereotyping of Jews was said to be endemic' (ibid: 125). Clearly, far more research is needed in this area.

One valuable source on the extent of antisemitism is the Community Security Trust (CST) which records all reported incidents of antisemitism within the United Kingdom. Their 2013 report stated that 529 antisemitic incidents were recorded that year, with 32 of them targeting Jewish schools, schoolchildren or teachers. They noted that '13 affected Jewish schoolchildren on their journeys to and from school; 13 took place at the premises of Jewish faith schools; and 6 involved Jewish children or teachers at non-faith schools' (CST 2014: 4). According to the CST, antisemitism increases when it is triggered by certain events such as prominent acts of antisemitism or heightened tension in the Middle East. Consequently, teachers ought to be especially observant during these occasions in order to tackle antisemitism.

Can teaching the Holocaust help combat antisemitism?

Teaching the Holocaust is not a magic formula for removing antisemitism or any other form of prejudice or discrimination. Short correctly asserts:

> The Holocaust will not necessarily fill those who learn about it with revulsion. It will have this effect only if Jews are regarded as fundamentally the same as other people and thus no more deserving of an unpleasant fate than anyone else. In the light of this caution it will be essential, before teaching the Holocaust, to expose the mythical quality of any antisemitic stereotypes with which children may be familiar.
>
> (Short 1994: 402)

Despite this warning, a number of researchers have suggested that teaching the Holocaust will make society more tolerant and liberal minded, although many of these conclusions have been drawn from studies with questionable methodologies. Maitles and Cowan provided an appropriate summary of the research to date when they remarked:

> We must recognise that education on its own cannot be a panacea for racism in general and antisemitism in particular, although there has been some evidence that learning about the Holocaust can have a positive impact on the outlook of young people.
>
> (Maitles and Cowan 2007: 431)

Rather than generalising about the relationship between teaching the Holocaust and contemporary antisemitism, it seems fair to say that teaching the Holocaust well can displace the ignorance which breeds prejudice and discrimination, while teaching the subject poorly can reinforce stereotypes and myths which enhance and increase the nature and likelihood of antisemitism. Yet in order to have a positive effect on existing antisemitism, teachers need to know and understand the existing stereotypes and be able to recognise this prejudice if it manifests itself in the classroom. Moreover, practitioners need the confidence and boldness to confront and challenge antisemitism, for if they ignore it they are implying that it is acceptable. Alongside this is *how* we teach the Holocaust. This really matters and there are various things which we should and shouldn't do if we want our lessons to have a positive effect on our learners and challenge rather than strengthen existing antisemitism.

Things to avoid when teaching the Holocaust

1. Reinforcing antisemitic stereotypes

It is important to remember that for many students, their own conceptions of Jews will have emerged solely from stereotypes and thus teachers should ensure that these are not reinforced. One commonly held view is that all Jews are religious, while many adolescents think that all Jews are orthodox and can be identified by their dress and practices. While many of Europe's Jews during the Second World War were indeed very religious, students need to learn that this was not universally the case and that Nazi policy was directed towards Jews on 'racial' rather than religious grounds. When showing photographs of Jews in Europe during the 1930s and 1940s, it seems that showing both religious and non-religious Jews will help dispel this assumption.

There are many other Jewish stereotypes which teachers should be aware of and consequently avoid re-enforcing. One of these is that Jews all share similar characteristics, such as dark curly hair and large, hooked noses. Another of these is that Jews are rich, powerful or greedy. A third is that Jews typically hold jobs as bankers, lawyers or doctors. Teachers should make efforts to dispel and challenge such ideas.

One of the most effective means of teaching about the Holocaust is to use stories of individuals or families, which make their experiences far more personal than the vast figure of 6 million. When doing this, teachers may wish to choose examples which challenge existing stereotypes rather than reinforce them.

2. Using Nazi propaganda without thinking about the effects

While it is perfectly legitimate to study Nazi propaganda, considerable care should be taken to ensure that the messages of National Socialist indoctrination do not prop up existing stereotypes or misinform learners. It is very easy for teachers to assume that all children are capable of discerning the vulgarity and crudity of Nazi propaganda while this does not seem to be the case. What may seem obvious to an enlightened and educated practitioner is not always the case for an impressionable teenager who may not understand the historical context and nature of what they are being exposed to.

Moreover, the messages of Nazi posters, children's books and the like, will only be rejected if the audience has a pre-existing understanding that this is inaccurate, offensive and morally repugnant. After all, the messages of Nazi propaganda were produced for the German public not because they were stupid or ignorant but because their messages were often believable, because they resonated with their misconceptions and played on their prejudices. Children who have never met Jewish children and who have only heard the word used as a term of abuse, are unlikely to reject wholesale the message of Nazi propaganda and may well be negatively influenced by it.

Even those students who are able to reject the extreme messages of Nazi propaganda can easily believe that antisemitism in Germany was ubiquitous and that there must have been logical reasons for it. Two major studies, one conducted by Lange in Sweden (2008) and one by Pettigrew et al. (2009) in England highlight that the vast majority of teachers thought that Jews made up a large percentage of the 1933 population in Germany. A study conducted on nearly 300 teenagers in England also found that over half of the them believed that Jews made up between 21 and 40 per cent of the German population when Hitler came to power (Gray 2014: 194). Why is it that both teachers and students alike assume that there were so many Jews living in Germany when the census of June 1933 found that Jews made up less than 1 per cent of the German population? Is it possible that even in the twenty-first century, the Nazi-peddled myth that Jews were taking all the jobs and dominating the economy in the Great Depression that followed the Wall Street Crash still exists in popular consciousness? If so, then using Nazi propaganda without carefully deconstructing it and highlighting its inaccuracies and prejudices may well reinforce traditional myths and beliefs.

In addition to this, those students who already hold antisemitic views may find the message of the propaganda resonating with their own ideologies and consequently reinforcing and strengthening their existing prejudices.

Using Nazi propaganda in the classroom – a little like using perpetrator testimonies – needs to be done thoughtfully, carefully, judiciously and selectively. When it features in lessons without sufficient consideration of its effects, then the consequences have the potential to be damaging and to strengthen rather than combat antisemitism.

3. Always presenting Jews as victims

When teaching about the Holocaust, it is obviously impossible to do so without talking about Jews and about antisemitism. Many students ask 'Why did Hitler hate Jews?' or even 'Why have people always hated Jews?' In attempting to answer these questions, practitioners will often set the origins of the Holocaust in their historic context, perhaps talking about the expulsion of Jews from England in 1290 or from Spain in 1492, perhaps including how Jews were blamed for the outbreak of the Black Death in the fourteenth century, the writings of Luther, Wagner and even American industrialist Henry Ford, the Dreyfus Affair in France or the anti-Jewish pogroms in the Russian empire during the late nineteenth and early twentieth centuries. Whether such an eclectic mix provides a context for the Holocaust or simply a potted history of anti-Jewish prejudice is a separate issue, but what seems likely is that students will come away with the sense that Jews are always the victims in history. This may in turn lead them to wonder why this is so and potentially think that there must be some inherent fault with Jews. When approaching the important subject of historic antisemitism teachers needs to look at the reasons *why* Jews were specifically targeted, such as mistrust and rumours, fear of difference, xenophobia, Christian rhetoric and a suspicion of Zionism. This more sophisticated approach not only satisfies the curiosity of the student more effectively, but it helps to demonstrate that Jews did not possess a fundamental and intrinsic flaw. At the same time, antisemitism should not be presented as something that was or is inevitable but rather something which can and should be rejected.

4. Dehumanising Jews

Closely connected to perpetually seeing Jews as victims, is the frequency with which some teachers dehumanise Jews by showing graphic images of the Holocaust. Exposing adolescents to photographs of naked skeletal figures in Auschwitz or corpses being bulldozed in Bergen-Belsen may (or may not) shock students but is unlikely to develop their understanding of the Holocaust. Instead they are likely to see the victims of the Holocaust as very far removed from their own world and fail to recognise the ordinary nature of those who perished from their experiences at the hands of the Nazis. The aim of that regime was to dehumanise Jews, to suggest that they were radically and fundamentally different from non-Jews. While it is valuable for adolescent learners to understand the brutality and extremity of what Jews endured and experienced, this should only be done in a way that does not dehumanise them and lead to patronising sentiment rather than historical understanding. Salmons expressed this sentiment when he wrote:

> Some history departments still use explicit photographs of Nazi atrocities in an attempt to communicate the full horror of the Holocaust. But should our objective be to shock and horrify? What do young people actually learn from such an approach? Too often Jews become defined by the Holocaust, dehumanised and objectified.
>
> (Salmons 2001: 35)

5. Ignoring Jewish resistance

The erroneous notion that Jews went to their deaths, in the language of the prophet Isaiah, as 'lambs to the slaughter' helps to reinforce the concept that Jews were a homogeneous victim group, who acted with religious passivity in the face of genocide. Understanding the extent and multifaceted nature of Jewish resistance helps to show students that Jews were not all the same and to defy simplistic or stereotypical generalisations. By showing their bravery and courage through acts of defiance and rebellion, Jewish identity is made more sophisticated and prevents it from being reduced to monolithic concepts of victimhood and dehumanisation.

Another advantage of highlighting Jewish resistance is that it shifts attention away from an Auschwitz-centric (or camp-centric) approach to the Holocaust. Despite the famous *Sonderkommando* uprising in Birkenau, as well as rebellions in Sobibor and Treblinka among other camps, a great deal of Jewish resistance occurred in the ghettos and through partisan activity which is often seldom known about among students or rarely taught in Holocaust curricula.

6. Defining Jewish identity solely in terms of the Holocaust

When teaching the Holocaust, students should not be left thinking that Jewish identity is dependent upon, or solely determined by it. Jews were obviously not defined by the Holocaust for the thousands of years that preceded the Nazi programme of mass murder, and in the post-war era their identity can be independent of it. This is not to say that the Holocaust was not a momentous event within the history of the Jewish people, but it is to say that Jewish identity is not dependent upon it to exist or to be defined, and students should complete their Holocaust education programmes aware of this.

7. Getting side-tracked onto Middle Eastern politics

A number of practitioners involved in Holocaust education have noted how some students are very keen to shift the focus away from the Holocaust and onto events in the Middle East (Nates 2010: 24). Other have noted how some adolescents with connections to that part of the world find it difficult to distinguish between the fate of Europe's Jews and the policies and practices of the State of Israel. In a major international report entitled *Education on the Holocaust and on Antisemitism*, educators reported 'passive defence mechanisms or active sabotage in the classroom, in part due to the suspicion that a one-sided pro-Israel stance on the Middle East conflict is driving Holocaust education' (ODIHR 2005: 38). While there is no doubt a place in contemporary Western education for discussion of the Middle East, this is a subject which is very distinct from the Holocaust. Consequently, teachers should avoid being side-tracked onto these issues, especially when the motive for doing so is antisemitism, anti-Zionism or a combination of both. Many students from the Middle East who have been taught that Israel – as a Jewish state – is an aggressor, have difficulty sympathising with Jews and this is not going to be aided by becoming side-tracked onto contemporary developments in that particular region of the world.

Things to include when teaching the Holocaust

1. Explain who Jews are

Teachers should not assume that students have a sufficient grasp of who Jews are or what makes someone Jewish. After all, there is a lack of consensus among many Jews about whether they are a religious, ethnic or cultural group. Undoubtedly Jews have a shared history and culture, and even if religion is not central to some contemporary Jews, the impact and influence that it has had on their forebears cannot be ignored. Yet being Jewish goes beyond shared religious beliefs and practices; it is connected to ethnicity, culture, history and consanguinity, which cannot be ignored if a sufficiently accurate conception of Jewishness is to be developed in the minds of learners. By exploring the complex question of 'Who are Jews?', teachers will be able to expose existing preconceptions, stereotypes and myths which can then be deconstructed and tackled. Such an approach also helps students to realise that Jews could not simply convert or deny their faith in order to save themselves.

2. Challenge stereotypes and misconceptions

When talking about Jews it is often helpful to challenge common stereotypes. For example, rather than citing Marx, Einstein or Freud as examples of famous Jews, it is perhaps better to use Natalie Portman, Scarlett Johansson or Esti Mamo, who defy popular ideas about what Jews may look like, what they may wear or even the colour of their skin. Similarly, when talking about Jews within pre-war Europe, it is important to highlight that many were poor. In his political history of Jews in Europe, Vital writes that 'the truly salient feature of eastern European Jewry (its steady increase in absolute numbers apart) was of a people plagued by endemic and ever deepening poverty' (Vital 1999: 302). By using examples of pauperised Jews labouring in domestic service or depending on the charity bestowed at Passover, the Nazi-propagated myth that Jews were the architects and operators of capitalism involved in a global conspiracy is undermined and challenged.

Other stereotypes and misconceptions that can be confronted are those which suggest that German Jews were all recently arrived immigrants who remained isolated from the rest of society. The first record of Jews living in Germany dates back to AD 321, while as Gilbert writes: 'The Jews of Germany had been among Europe's most assimilated, most cultured, most active contributors to the national life of the state in which they lived. Hundreds of thousands of them had become an integral part of German society' (Gilbert 1987: 35).

One further misconception that it is often beneficial to challenge is the size of the Jewish population both in pre-war Germany and also globally. Jews make up around only 0.2 per cent of the world's population, which is one in approximately every 500 people.

3. Demonstrate the positive aspects of Jewish history

While explaining the origins and roots of antisemitism is important, this can be harmful if it is not balanced by equal recognition and attention to the positive aspects of Jewish history. Mention might be made of the invaluable work of Jews in every academic discipline, ranging from physics to psychoanalysis, from literature to linguistics. Moreover, the Judaic Ten Commandments, as well as the teaching of both Jesus and the apostle Paul (both of whom were Jewish) lie at the very heart of Western moral thinking as well as being the foundation of many of our laws and customs.

Research suggests that at present, many teachers fail to teach about the positive aspects of Jewish history or their contribution to pre-war European life. In a study conducted by the HEDP in 2009, only 21 per cent of teachers who taught the Holocaust included 'the contribution of the Jews to European social and cultural life before 1933' while 44 per cent said that they included 'the long history of antisemitism' in their teaching (Pettigrew et al. 2009: 124). Failure to highlight the rich and varied contribution of Jews, Judaism and Jewishness in the history of humanity threatens to strengthen negative ideas that students may have about Jews – views which can be enhanced by providing a history of antisemitism without offsetting it with a history of Jewish successes and contributions.

4. Use individual examples and case studies

Comprehending the figure of 6 million is almost impossible for anyone, and in many senses a teacher of the Holocaust cannot really expect an adolescent to be able to do so. What many leading Holocaust organisations have consequently done, is to tell the story of the Holocaust through individuals' lives, using their testimonies and accounts to illustrate the experiences of Jews throughout Europe. One of the main problems with doing this is that a number of students can end up thinking that the experiences of the individual in the case study were typical of all Jews. Using a number of very different stories (e.g. a German, Polish, Latvian and Hungarian Jew) would help adolescents to see the wide range of experiences that Jews endured throughout Nazi-occupied Europe. Moreover, the availability of post-war testimonies means that many teachers focus on the experiences of survivors, which are, by their very existence, untypical. One way of resolving this problem is to focus on the story of the relative of a survivor, rather than the survivor, which still enables the power of the testimony to be used in the classroom.

The advantages of using individual accounts in combating antisemitism are manifold. The students learn about their pre-war lives; their childhood and their upbringing; they may learn about how and when they met their spouse; their first home and the children they had. In other words, this is not an emaciated and dehumanised object heading for the gas chamber, devoid of background or history, but rather a perfectly normal, unremarkably average human being who is murdered because of who their grandparents happened to be. This resonates and affects adolescents and challenges the generic stereotypes that they may have of Jews. Moreover, the individual that they have learned about is not too dissimilar to themselves. While they may have had a typical 1930s haircut or have worn what may be considered by the contemporary adolescent as 'old-fashioned clothes', they shared the same experiences of attending school, shared the same aspirations of getting a job, having a home, perhaps starting a family. In other words, students no longer see them as simply part of an incomprehensible statistic, but rather as a fellow human being, at least a little like themselves.

Conclusion

By the time that students have finished learning about the Holocaust, their understanding of Jews and Jewish identity should be much better informed and sufficiently detailed as to have eroded the ignorance and negative stereotypes which form the basis of so much existing antisemitism. As has been acknowledged, Holocaust education is not and will never be the cure for all prejudice and discrimination. Nevertheless, if practitioners are thoughtful and considerate in their teaching of the Holocaust, there should be a greater chance that existing antisemitism is reduced rather than enhanced.

Recommended reading

Gray, M. (2013) 'Exploring Pupil Perceptions of Jews, Jewish Identity and the Holocaust', *Journal of Modern Jewish Studies*, 12, no. 3: 419–35.

Maitles, H., Cowan, P. and Butler, E. (2006) *Never Again!: Does Holocaust Education Have an Effect on Pupils' Citizenship Values and Attitudes?* (Edinburgh: Scottish Executive, Department of Social Research).

Short, G. (1994) 'Teaching the Holocaust: The Relevance of Children's Perceptions of Jewish Culture and Identity', *British Educational Research Journal*, 20, no. 4: 393–405.

Chapter 12

Dealing with Holocaust denial and distortion

Holocaust denial and distortion are extreme forms of antisemitism. They are typically motivated by hatred of Jews and seek to perpetuate the historic anti-Jewish stereotypes of a global conspiracy and ambitions of worldwide domination. Nevertheless, the prevalence and rise of Holocaust denial and distortion have merited the subject a chapter in its own right, independent of – but connected to – the remarks in the previous chapter on combating antisemitism. It seems that for many teachers – especially those with less experience of teaching the subject – facing Holocaust deniers and distorters in the classroom, as well as countering their arguments convincingly and effectively, is one of the most serious concerns that they hold. This chapter aims to give a clear and up-to-date picture of the current scene and provide practitioners with the arsenal they need to challenge this antisemitic agenda robustly and vigorously.

What is Holocaust denial and distortion?

The USHMM defines Holocaust denial as 'an attempt to negate the established facts of the Nazi genocide of European Jewry' (USHMM website). The IHRA, in its working definition of Holocaust denial and distortion, notes that: 'Holocaust denial is discourse and propaganda that deny the historical reality and the extent of the extermination of the Jews by the Nazis and their accomplices during World War II, known as the Holocaust or the Shoah' (IHRA website).

It is often difficult to distinguish Holocaust denial from Holocaust distortion, the latter of which is the alteration, falsification and rejection of certain historical facts about the Holocaust, which are beyond any reasonable doubt in light of the compelling and convincing burden of historical proof. Holocaust distortion, like denial, rejects the figure of 6 million and in contradiction to the evidence, grossly minimalises the death toll. In addition to this however, those who distort the Holocaust attempt to:

- Deny that there was a systematic programme of extermination against the Jews.
- Absolve Hitler or the Nazi regime of knowledge of the deaths.
- Lay the blame for the Holocaust on the Jews.
- Purposefully reduce the significance of the Holocaust.

Typical of Holocaust denial and distortion is the propagating of the idea that the Holocaust is a myth that has been fabricated by the Jews as part of a global conspiracy. Similarly, it is proposed that the subject is dogmatically protected by the Jews, who will not permit any consideration of alternative views. In addition they argue that the notion of the Holocaust was created for political and economic gain.

When explaining what Holocaust denial and distortion is, it is also helpful to highlight what it is not. At this juncture, it is worth highlighting the distinction between Holocaust distortion and Holocaust trivialisation. The latter of the two makes inappropriate comparisons between the Holocaust and an event which clearly has no genocidal intent. Trivialisation also involves evoking the terminology of the Holocaust for political advantage. While doing so is a misuse of the Holocaust and often suggests ignorance, it is not necessarily motivated by antisemitism, although, of course, it can be.

In addition to it being distinct from trivialisation, Holocaust denial and distortion is also independent of the scholarly revision of ideas and interpretations which historians undertake. Academics refine their knowledge and understanding of the past, they do not deny its existence – certainly not when an overwhelming body of evidence is before them. Therefore, while deniers may wish to be called revisionists, this seems an inappropriate term. The vast corpus of scholarly literature on the subject since the end of the Second World War has constantly revised our understanding of the Holocaust – for example, the decision-making processes, the importance of local initiatives and the role of collaborators – yet it has not denied the key events or actions which make up the Holocaust. Consequently, 'denial' is a more accurate and appropriate term to use than 'revisionism'.

Is Holocaust denial and distortion a problem in schools?

Assessing the extent of Holocaust denial, especially within schools, is a difficult task and one which has been largely ignored by scholars within the field of Holocaust education. In a report published by the UK government in late 2012, it was stated that 'currently there is no specific data on incidents of Holocaust denial in the UK' (Foreign and Commonwealth Office 2012).

The same report also observed that 'the Internet (in particular Facebook and Twitter) is used as a forum for hate speech, Holocaust denial and antisemitic material'. The freedom with which one can express extreme ideas and the ease of maintaining anonymity has made the internet the key outlet of Holocaust denial. In his empirical study on the subject in America, Darnell found that there were thirty-one Facebook groups which have 'the denial of the Holocaust as their central or predominant purpose' (Darnell 2010: 33). These groups collectively have 4,853 members.

It seems that the easy access that students have to the internet and the frequency with which they use it, coupled with the fact there are so many Holocaust denial sites online, means that the likelihood of adolescent learners encountering the ideas of deniers and distorters has significantly increased in recent years. Teachers need to appreciate this and be sufficiently equipped to try and tackle and challenge it. In addition to rebutting the remarks of those who have been influenced by such online propaganda, dealing effectively with the problem may also need to include providing students with the hyperlinks to reliable online sources and resources for their research on the Holocaust, such as the USHMM website or the Yad Vashem website.

Although it is difficult to know whether or not Holocaust denial is a problem in schools, Google Trends highlights that during the last decade there has been an alarming shift. Darnell writes:

While the relative popularity of searches of the term 'Holocaust' has trended downwards since 2004, the relative popularity of searches of 'Holocaust denial' is on the rise. Specifically, over the past year, the use of 'denial' as a related search term to the Holocaust has increased by seventy percent. In the United States, it has increased by sixty percent.

(Darnell 2010: 33)

While it is impossible to know exactly why people are searching for Holocaust denial as well as whether this is common among young people, it nevertheless suggests that greater exposure to Holocaust denial material is occurring which is likely to be having some effect on adolescent learners.

Why do some people deny or distort the Holocaust?

There are many reasons why people choose to deny or distort the Holocaust and various organisations and individuals clearly operate with different – and at times conflicting – motives. Nevertheless, the central theme which appears to run throughout the entire Holocaust denial movement is the hatred of Jews. Shermer and Grobman astutely remarked: 'like all ideologically driven movements, Holocaust denial is complex and multifaceted, featuring diverse motives and personalities, but we maintain that the antisemitic theme returns over and over' (Shermer and Grobman 2000: 87). This antisemitism, which manifests itself in various ways, is connected to various motives and aims.

They want to reduce public sympathy for Jews

Much of the literature produced by deniers and distorters argues that the idea of the Holocaust has been constructed by Jews to serve their own ends. This is strongly linked to the idea that there is a global Jewish conspiracy; that Jews are controlling society, governments and institutions, which consequently prop up the idea of the Holocaust. Antisemitism lies at the heart of this, with deniers and distorters hoping that public sympathy for Jews will be reduced if people accept this position. Moreover, they want increased suspicion of Jews and in many cases, their removal from any offices of authority. Ultimately, such conspiracy theories echo the propaganda of the Nazi regime itself – that Jews cannot be trusted and that their loyalties lie to their own ends.

They want to destroy the State of Israel

While opposition to Israel – either in terms of its policies or very existence – may be driven by political or religious beliefs, many deniers and distorters seek to undermine the Holocaust with the intention of destroying Israel. This is most common in the Middle East, where the Holocaust is typically viewed through the prism of the Arab–Israeli conflict. Perhaps the clearest example of this were the outspoken comments of former Iranian president Mahmoud Ahmadinejad, who called the Holocaust a 'myth'. In 2006 Tehran also hosted a pseudo-academic conference called 'Review of the Holocaust – Global Vision' which drew papers from Holocaust deniers from around the world. In the working draft of a document produced by the USHMM and Salzburg Global Seminar, the following was stated:

Awareness of the Holocaust in the Middle East and North Africa is limited, but public officials in many of these states – largely in response to political concerns *vis-à-vis* Israel – have made seriously distorted and patently false claims about documented evidence of the systematic murders perpetrated by the Nazis during World War II.

(USHMM and Salzburg Global Seminar 2013: 24)

Deniers and distorters claim that the establishment of the State of Israel was the product of Western sympathy and guilt for the Holocaust. They thus argue that if the Holocaust is 'disproved' then the justification for Israel won't exist and it can then be destroyed. It seems that in this instance, the wish to destroy Israel is first and foremost because it is a Jewish state and thus is underpinned by virulent antisemitism.

Teachers need to be aware that while anti-Israel sentiment is obviously not *de facto* antisemitism, some anti-Israel rhetoric is fuelled by antisemitism, which can at times manifest itself as Holocaust denial or distortion.

They want to defend extreme political ideologies

A significant element of Holocaust deniers and distorters supports radical political groups such as neo-Nazi organisations or fascist parties. By suggesting that the Holocaust did not occur – or at least that it was not a systematic programme of mass murder organised and conducted by the Nazi regime – they believe that the reputation of their own organisations and the legitimacy of their own racial ideology will be enhanced. In such instances, they are denying or distorting history to serve contemporary political ends. Many young people who come across the websites of such organisations are unlikely to recognise this agenda and efforts should be made to expose the reasoning behind their propaganda.

They want to rehabilitate racial theory and Aryan ideology

The foundations of the Holocaust were the Nazis' core ideological beliefs about race and put simply, that some races were superior to others. They believed categorically that one's character and nature was also racially determined and that the Aryan ideal lay at the very pinnacle of racial and biological hierarchy. Contemporary racists – those who believe that one race is superior to another – may find the denial or distortion of the Holocaust is beneficial to the advancement of their ideology. Along similar lines, some deniers and distorters wish to 'rehabilitate' the Aryan identity from the crime of the Holocaust. Consequently, Holocaust denial and distortion is very common among white supremacist groups both within the United Kingdom and the United States of America.

Should teachers address or ignore Holocaust denial or distortion?

The extent to which teachers should address Holocaust denial and distortion in the classroom, if at all, is a controversial issue. On the one hand, there are those who believe that Holocaust curricula should specifically target the claims of deniers and provide students with a robust defence of the past. Conversely, others suggest it is acceptable to completely ignore the claims and arguments of deniers and distorters in the classroom. A happy medium somewhere in between seems to me to be the most beneficial and practical response. Deniers should not be setting the agenda of our curricula and it must be remembered that their views represent a minority position. Moreover, there are so many topics competing for time and space on a Holocaust programme that addressing deniers' and distorters' arguments should only make up a very small amount of it. Despite this, burying one's head under the sand and refusing to address the arguments themselves does not appear to be doing anyone any favours, least of all the students who have come to learn about the subject in its entirety or who may have questions on the issue. Clearly, one would not want a student with an obvious agenda driving the lesson, but neither should they be ignored. Shermer and Grobman put forward a convincing case for tackling the issue and confronting the arguments:

> Why, some people ask, do we need to respond at all to the Holocaust deniers? Can't we just dismiss them all as a bunch of antisemitic neo-Nazi thugs? No, we can't ... To resort to labels is to misunderstand what is really going on and therefore to swat down straw men. We think it is time to move beyond name calling and present the evidence. Failure to do so might create serious consequences ... We must be forthright and honest about what we know and do not know about the Holocaust.
>
> (Shermer and Grobman 2000: 16–17)

Despite this, it is important to recognise that there are both advantages and disadvantages of addressing Holocaust denial in school. While these are discussed below, there is a responsibility on practitioners to do their best to avoid, or at least minimise, the potential negative effects of addressing the subject in the classroom.

The advantages of addressing Holocaust denial and distortion

The truth will prevail

One of the best arguments for confronting Holocaust denial is that truth will always prevail and therefore has nothing to fear from those who seek to refute the Nazis' crime against Europe's Jews. If classrooms are to be a forum for debate, discussion and learning, then there needs to be public space for all views, however unpalatable they may be to the majority. While Holocaust denial is a crime in countries such as France and Austria, future generations are surely better equipped if they reach their opinions through evidence-based knowledge rather than official sanction. Moreover, the banning of ideas by the state sets a dangerous precedent and seems to undermine the liberal democratic values which should characterise modern society. In his preamble to the Declaration of Independence, Thomas Jefferson wrote:

> Truth is great and will prevail if left to herself; that she is the proper and sufficient antagonist to error, and has nothing to fear from the conflict unless by human interposition disarmed of her natural weapons, free argument and debate; errors ceasing to be dangerous when it is permitted freely to contradict them.
>
> (Quoted in Jayne 1998: 155)

Most students will come across the subject anyway

The large number of Holocaust denial websites which exist on the internet and the ease with which they can be stumbled upon, even when asking legitimate historical questions in search engines, strongly suggests that most students will come across the arguments and ideas of those who deny or distort the Holocaust. If this is the case, then it seems far better that students can have a dialogue about the subject in their classrooms, which is more beneficial than an online propaganda monologue. A student who comes across Holocaust denial material is far more likely to reject its arguments and dismiss its ideas if he or she has already been educated about the aims and agendas of the movement and presented with the appropriate counter-arguments.

It shows there are answers to the deniers' arguments

By refusing to engage with the arguments of those who deny and distort the Holocaust, some students may come to the conclusion that there is no evidence for the Nazis' mass murder of the Jews. Surely teachers do a disservice to their students when they simply provide an *ad hominem* attack on deniers without refuting the actual claims that they make. Most students can see through this and will recognise that the issues have not been addressed satisfactorily. Furthermore, by providing evidence which counters the original claims, students not only learn that the arguments for the Holocaust are robust and secure, but will also acquire the ability to make their own defence of them if ever called upon to do so.

It reduces the appeal of the Holocaust denial movement

When I was a teenager and my history teacher told me that Peter Wright's book *Spycatcher* had originally been banned in the United Kingdom, I could not get hold of a copy quickly enough. Its appeal lay exclusively in the fact that this was something that 'authority' didn't want me to read. In a similar way, it seems probable that students will be more likely to engage with the work of Holocaust deniers – something which is so easy to do online – simply because to do so is an act of rebellion or defiance against their teacher, school or society at large. If engaging with Holocaust denial literature and repeating its arguments in the classroom is seen as ignorant rather than risqué or 'edgy', then it seems that its appeal will diminish considerably.

Moreover, by raising the issue of Holocaust denial and distortion *before* a student does so, the teacher demonstrates a willingness to discuss the issue and reduces the likelihood of an adolescent doing so to try and push the boundaries. In addition, this helps to prevent a situation where members of a class rally around the initial student who generated the discussion and a seemingly ideologically combative situation emerges between a teacher and his or her learners. By raising the issue first it also suggests that a teacher is intellectually comfortable talking about the subject and this may give his or her answers greater weight in the eyes of their learners.

It may help to diminish the ability of Holocaust deniers to find new supporters

All movements of any longevity depend upon the recruiting of new supporters to continue or increase their success. Dismissing the denial movement out of hand has not led to the collapse of the movement and in so many ways has been an unsuccessful and counter-productive policy within Holocaust education in schools. Surely Holocaust deniers will find it much harder to persuade young people to support their cause if students have been grounded in the evidence and have learnt about the flawed nature of their case.

The disadvantages of addressing Holocaust denial and distortion

It can legitimise the work of Holocaust denial and distortion

One of the most persuasive counter-arguments to explicitly addressing Holocaust denial in schools is that it can legitimise the cause, characters and case of the movement. While students of the Third Reich and the Holocaust have often studied the debate between intentionalist historians and structuralist historians, there is a risk that they may see a new deliberation between deniers and 'actualists' (or whatever term is the antonym of the denial movement). Deniers and distorters have spent decades working towards a facade of scholarly legitimacy and by discussing their ideas in schools their cause could be greatly helped.

A very challenging balancing act surely exists for teachers who choose to address Holocaust denial and distortion in their classroom. If practitioners take their arguments seriously and scrutinise their validity, they do risk the danger of giving them unmerited kudos. Yet on the other hand, if they preach against (rather than teach about) Holocaust denial, they run the very serious risk of alienating or disengaging their students. While care and wisdom are obviously needed, it is surely the case that when the arguments put forward by deniers and distorters are scrutinised and put under the microscope of historical investigation, their case will not stand the test of the evidence and any potential legitimacy acquired by the process of investigation will be more than countered by the conclusions that the students have drawn.

It can raise awareness of the movement

Although the argument was put forward that most students will come across Holocaust denial irrespective of whether or not it is discussed in schools, it will no doubt be the case that some learners – perhaps a minority – would never have even been aware of it had it not been raised by their teacher. The argument that raising awareness of Holocaust denial and distortion is always a negative thing makes two assumptions. First, that raised awareness of Holocaust denial is likely to lead to raised support for it. While one cannot support something one is not aware of, it does not follow that raised awareness will lead to raised support, for the reasons given above. Second, it assumes that in this instance, ignorance is preferable to knowledge. Yet surely one of the purposes of education is to dispel ignorance – even ignorance of the morally objectionable. After all, the Holocaust itself was extremely morally objectionable and teachers strive to dispel ignorance concerning what happened. It seems therefore,that raising awareness of it should not be a cause for concern.

It may generate curiosity to visit Holocaust denial websites

While it may be the case that those who come across the issue of Holocaust denial in their lessons may choose to visit denial websites out of curiosity and thus read their arguments, this should not be a serious concern. First, it is surely better that adolescents have knowledge of the debates and counter-arguments *before* going on their websites. Second, they are more likely to read the ideas of deniers with a critical approach if they are familiar with the various agendas of the movement and the evidence which contradicts their viewpoints.

What arguments do deniers and distorters make and how can they be combated?

While there are many claims and ideas put forward by deniers and distorters, a number of them rest upon the idea that one cannot be certain about anything in history. The theory of knowledge, also known as epistemology, is a branch of philosophy that has existed for millennia before the Holocaust even took place. While it would be impossible to discuss the ideas of Locke, Berkely and Hume in distinction to Plato, Descartes and Spinoza in any meaningful sense here, it suffices to say that the discipline of history has developed methodological procedures to test the validity of a proposition about the past on the basis of evidence. This includes the sources' internal and external authenticity, its coherence with other accepted propositions and the weight that can be afforded to it. Importantly, those who seek to deny and distort the Holocaust seem to place great weight on a single testimony or emphasise an obscure detail upon which their argument hangs, while remaining unconvinced by the coherence of tens of thousands of other sources of evidence which contradict their central argument. Nevertheless, there are three key arguments which are put forward by those who seek to deny or distort the Holocaust.

1. There were no gas chambers that were used for genocide

The views of the deniers and distorters regarding the gas chambers is twofold. Some argue that gas chambers were built after the war, for example the Americans built those at Dachau and the Polish at Auschwitz. Others such as Kollerstrom have written that 'well-designed cyanide gas chambers were indeed present at Auschwitz, and did work efficiently, but that they were operated for purposes of hygiene and disinfection, in order to save lives and not take them' (Kollerstrom 2008). Deniers and distorters are keen to point out that neither photographic nor video evidence of Jews being gassed exists. While this seems remarkably unsurprising, the digital examination of aerial photographs taken by the Allies on 31 May 1944 and 25 August 1944, does show a group of people being marched into Crematorium V. Allied aerial photographs were taken on five different dates and the three occasions when people are not being marched into the gas chambers correspond with Danuta Czech's *Auschwitz Chronicle: 1939–1945* which explicitly records all the activities of the camp on a day-to-day basis, drawn from all the key records, post-war trials and testimonies.

Deniers and distorters also have no answer to the testimonies of the *Sonderkommando*, those who were forced to operate in and around the gas chambers. Shlomo Venezia, for example, who worked as a *Sonderkommando* in Auschwitz, is very clear in expressing what happened:

> Finally, the German bringing the gas would arrive. It took two prisoners from the *Sonderkommando* to help him lift up the external trapdoor, above the gas chamber, then he introduced the Zyklon B through the opening … Once the gas had been thrown in, it lasted about ten to twelve minutes, then finally you couldn't hear anything anymore, not a living soul.
>
> (Venezia 2009: 68–69)

If this was not enough, the post-war testimonies of perpetrators such as SS sergeant Perry Broad as well as Auschwitz commandant Rudolf Hoess are further evidence, as well as the way that the accounts of survivors and perpetrators corroborate so compellingly.

2. There were not 6 million Jews killed in the Holocaust

The suggestion that 6 million Jews did not perish in the Holocaust is a common claim of deniers and distorters. Robert Faurisson remarked, 'I have good enough reason to think that the figure of the dead at Auschwitz (Jews and non-Jews) amounts to around 50,000 and not to 4 million, as has been pretended for a long time'. He also stated that 'as to the number of dead in all the concentration camps from 1933 to 1945, I think that it ought to be 200,000 or, at the most, 360,000' (IHR website). Deniers and distorters suggest that there were never 6 million Jews under Nazi occupation and that there is a much smaller difference in the pre-war and post-war Jewish population figures than 6 million. They also claim that millions of Jews fled into the Soviet Union and did not come under Nazi rule.

There are many compelling counter-arguments as to why 6 million is not a fabricated number. One of these is that Nazi perpetrators themselves have concurred with the figure. The Nazi physician Dr Wilhelm Hoettel, for example, stated at the Nuremburg Trials that 'in the various concentration camps approximately four million Jews had been killed, while about two million were killed in other ways, the majority of these having been killed by the action squads of the security police' (quoted in Shermer and Grobman 2000: 175). 'The security police' is a reference to the *Einsatzgruppen*, mobile killing squads consisting of SS and police units which murdered Jews by firing squad throughout the East. The records of *Einstazgruppe A* alone highlight the huge numbers of Jews murdered in countries such as Latvia and Lithuania, which total over 200,000. Other ways of proving the figure to be around 6 million is by detailed comparisons of population demographics before and after the war; birth and death records, the number of those recorded as being transported to camps and the number of those who survived. For specific details on how figures have been calculated, see the appendix in the revised edition of Raul Hilberg's *The Destruction of the European Jews*. While historians have revised their figures from around 5 million up to about 6 million, perhaps the most authoritative figure has been produced by German historian Wolfgang Benz, who estimated that between 5.29 and 6.2 million Jews were murdered by the Nazis (Benz 1999). Ultimately, deniers and distorters need to answer the question of where all the Jews went if they were not murdered, something which to date they have been unable to do.

3. The Nazis did not conduct a systematic policy of extermination

This particular argument does not deny that Jews – perhaps even considerable numbers of Jews – died during the Second World War but contends that this was not a systematic policy of murder. Rather it was the product of disease and infection, which spread through the camps. Deniers and distorters also claim that because no document signed by Hitler ordering the murder of Europe's Jews exists, it therefore either did not happen or Hitler did not know it was going on. According to his own website, David Irving has offered $1,000 for proof that Hitler knew of the Holocaust. Of course, proof exists; it's just that for deniers and distorters, their definition of proof is quite different from the ordinary or legal understanding.

On 30 November 1941 Hitler put a stop to a particular liquidation, as seen from the telephone notes of Heinrich Himmler. The order came: 'Jewish transport from Berlin: No liquidation'. If Hitler was not aware of the policy of systematic extermination then why would he have chosen to have stopped this transportation or felt the need to do so? Moreover, this also indicates that liquidation had become normalised.

In addition to this, the post-war testimony of Rudolf Hoess is very insightful. He explicitly stated that when Himmler gave the order to conduct the 'Final Solution' this command had ultimately been given by Hitler.

> In the summer of 1941, I cannot remember the exact date, I was suddenly summoned to the Reichsführer SS, directly by his adjutant's office. Contrary to his usual custom, Himmler received me without his adjutant being present and said in effect: 'The Führer has ordered that the Jewish question be solved once and for all and that we, the SS, are to implement that order ... The Jews are the sworn enemies of the German people and must be eradicated. Every Jew that we can lay our hands on is to be destroyed now during the war, without exception.'
>
> (Hoess 1947: 183)

Other evidence that Hitler had ordered the mass murder of Europe's Jews is found in speeches made by senior Nazi figures, such as that delivered by Himmler at Posen on the 4th and 6th of October 1943. While deniers and distorters have sought to interpret the word he used, 'Ausrotten', as 'root out' rather than 'exterminate', this is inconsistent with the common usage of the word and suggests that they are clutching at straws.

Conclusion

It appears that if Holocaust denial and distortion is to be successfully overcome, then it needs to be confronted. When shown the evidence, students can see the flaws in the arguments and recognise the compelling weight of evidence that exists. Rather than fear a student raising the matter, teachers should take the lead in introducing the subject, tackling the issues and enhancing the success and effectiveness of Holocaust education.

Recommended reading

Evans, R. J. (2000) *In Defence of History?* (New York: W. W. Norton).
Lipstadt, D. (1994) *Denying the Holocaust: The Growing Assault on Truth and Memory* (New York: Penguin).
Lipstadt, D. (2005) *History on Trial: My Day in Court with David Irving* (New York: HarperCollins).
Shermer, M. and Grobman, A. (2000) *Denying History: Who Says the Holocaust Never Happened and Why Do They Say It?* (Berkeley: University of California Press).

Chapter 13

Schemes of work

This chapter contains detailed schemes of work for teaching the Holocaust in the subjects of history, religious studies and citizenship. Each lesson in the schemes of work has a corresponding lesson plan which is found in the next chapter.

SCHEME OF WORK FOR HISTORY: THE HISTORY OF THE HOLOCAUST

This scheme of work is a general guide for practitioners who wish to teach about the Holocaust in history lessons. It is divided into ten lessons which work through the subject in chronological order, including thematic lessons on subjects such as resistance. It also includes an optional eleventh lesson on the post-Holocaust world. This scheme of work does not need to be followed precisely but provides a suitable and appropriate way of teaching about the Holocaust. Teachers who are preparing their classes for public examinations should ensure that they have covered the syllabus provided by the exam board. Those using this scheme of work with younger or less able classes may wish to use fewer examples and reduce the amount of content.

Lesson 1: Jews, Jewish identity, history, religion and culture

Learning objectives	Content
• To highlight students' preconceptions and initial ideas and understandings about Jews, Jewish identity and the Holocaust. • To enable learners to appreciate who Jews are, their history, religion and culture. • To provide context to the study of the Holocaust; to show the lives and experiences of Jews in Europe prior to the rise of Hitler and the Second World War. • To restore individuality and agency to those who lived in the past.	• Jewish identity, history, religion and culture. • Jews in Western Europe; their high levels of assimilation, small percentage of population. • Jews in Eastern Europe; greater focus on separate identity; *shtetls*; large Jewish populations in the Soviet Union, Poland, Hungary and Romania. • Contribution of Jews to European life and society. Examples might include Gabriel Lippmann who invented colour photography and won the Nobel Prize for Physics; Gustav Mahler, the romantic composer; or Franz Kafka, the author of novels and short stories.

Points to note

- It is helpful to explore students' prior conceptions about Jews, Jewish life and identity. It is worth remembering that many learners will have had minimal interaction if any with Jews or Jewish communities and many of their existing ideas will have come from popular media forms.
- When teaching about Jewish life before the war it is important to recognise the diversity that existed. Practitioners should make efforts to reflect that in their teaching and try to challenge stereotypes.

Suggested resources

'Jewish Calendar' and 'Celebrating Passover' – Activities available from the website of the Jewish Museum, London (www.jewishmuseum.org.uk).

'Pre-War Jewish Life' – Lesson plan and resources available from the Holocaust Educational Trust website (www.het.org.uk).

'Pre-World War II European Jewish Life Photo Project' – Lesson plan available from the USHMM website (www.ushmm.org).

Lesson 2: Nazi attitudes and actions towards Jews (1933–39)

Learning objectives	Content
• To demonstrate the historical roots and origins of antisemitism. • To examine the nature of Nazi propaganda directed at Jews and the use of stereotyping to try and shape popular opinion. • To enable students to think about why Nazi propaganda was sometimes successful; when people would be most vulnerable to its messages, and the types of methods that were employed. • To show the evolution of Nazi antisemitic policies and practices and to highlight the gradual worsening of the lives of Jews in Germany from 1933 and in Austria from 1938.	• Nazi racial theory and antisemitism as well as its roots and origins throughout European history. • Antisemitic propaganda used within Germany; the range of methods used (e.g. children's books such as *The Poisonous Mushroom*, films such as *Die Rothschilds* or *Der Ewige Jude* as well as posters, speeches and radio broadcasts), the messages contained within it and its effectiveness within Germany. • Nazi policies, practices and legislation directed against Jews between 1933 and 1939. This should include the boycott of Jewish shops (1 April 1933), the burning of Jewish books (10 May 1933), the Nuremberg Laws (15 September 1935) and *Kristallnacht* (9–10 November 1938).

Points to note

- Although students need to appreciate the long history of antisemitism, persecution of Jews should in no way be seen as inevitable.
- Care should also be taken to ensure that Jews are not simply seen as victims throughout history.
- Remember that some students lack the contextual knowledge and ability to critically approach propaganda. Teachers should thus make sure that Nazi stereotyping of Jews does not reinforce any existing prejudices or misconceptions that students may already hold.

Suggested resources

'"Germany's Sculptor": Propaganda and the Visual Arts in the Third Reich' – Lesson plan and resources available from the Yad Vashem website (www.yadvashem.org).

'Stages of Persecution' – Lesson plan and resources available from the Holocaust Survivors' Friendship Association website (www.holocaustlearning.org).

Lesson 3: Jewish emigration

Learning objectives	Content
• To show how things within Germany had become so bad for Jews that most sought to escape Nazi persecution. • To demonstrate that the Nazi regime encouraged Jews to leave and at this point did not have a plan for systematic mass murder. • To enable students to appreciate the difficult situation facing Jews who had to leave their homes, business and livelihoods behind. • To highlight the different responses of countries towards Jewish emigration.	• The plight of Jews in Germany and Austria during 1938 and 1939. • The response of the international community to the Jewish refugee situation and the Evian Conference of July 1938. This should include the tightening of quotas in countries across the world and the need for visas (although no visa was required for Jews to enter Shanghai). • The policy of Britain to severely restrict Jews from emigrating to British-mandated Palestine and to block any 'illegal' immigration there. • The sinking of the ship *Struma* after it was prevented from sailing to Palestine and the return to Europe of the liner *St Louis*. • The *Kindertransport* and the experiences and difficulties faced by Jewish children entering the UK.

Points to note

- Many students make the mistake of thinking that Jews could freely emigrate to Israel. Teachers should take the time to explain that the modern State of Israel was not established until 1948 and that before this date it was known as Palestine and controlled by the British on behalf of the League of Nations.
- It is worth pointing out that only 800,000 Jews in total (less than one in seven of those murdered) had the opportunity to escape from Nazi-occupied Europe.
- Emphasise that many of the children who entered Britain on the *Kindertransport* could not speak English, would have missed their parents and in many cases were the only ones in their families to survive the Holocaust.

Suggested resources

'*Kindertransport*: Saving Refugee Children' – Sources and explanatory teacher notes available from the UK National Archives website (www.nationalarchives.gov.uk).

'Britain, Refugees and the Kindertransport' – Lesson plan and resources available from the website of the Holocaust Educational Trust (www.het.org.uk).

'Map 13' on pp. 27–28 of Martin Gilbert's book: *Holocaust: Maps and Photographs*. It provides a map of the world with the number of Jews who were allowed into each country along with accompanying notes.

Lesson 4: The Polish ghettos

Learning objectives	Content
• To set Nazi policies towards Jews within the context of the early stages of the war • To highlight the notion of the 'Judenfrage' (Jewish question) and how mass emigration was not viable for Poland's Jews • To explain the range of antisemitic measures put in place within Poland and other occupied territories • To enable students to understand what a ghetto was, its nature, function and purpose for the Nazi regime • To show students the horrific conditions of the ghettos, but also the range of activities and experiences which existed within them	• The Nazi invasion of Poland in September 1939, which meant that there were then about 3,000,000 Jews under Nazi rule • The passing of antisemitic legislation in occupied Poland including the wearing of the Star of David and the forced eviction of Jews from their homes into the ghettos • Life within the ghettos, e.g. Warsaw, Krakow and Łódź. Case studies might include looking at the life of Janusz Korczak and his orphanage, the controversial role of the Judenrate or the cultural life that existed in the Warsaw ghetto.

Points to note

- It is important to present the evolution of Nazi antisemitic actions within the context of the war. Moreover, the invasion of Poland brought a new problem to the regime, namely 'What to do with Poland's Jews?'
- It is necessary for learners to appreciate that a programme of systematic mass murder was not inevitable nor, at this point, yet planned.
- Students are unlikely to have a grasp of what a ghetto was like and so individual studies may be helpful.
- Learners should realise the awfully crowded conditions as well as the starvation and diseases that were rife, in addition to the threat of deportation.

Suggested resources

'Children in the Ghetto' – Interactive animated street tour of the ghetto with accompanying resources available at http://ghetto.galim.org.il/eng/street.html.

'Defiant Requiem' – 2012 documentary on Rafael Schächter, who organised the performance of Verdi's *Requiem* in Theresienstadt.

'Inside the Warsaw Ghetto' – Lesson plan and resources available from University of Southern Florida, http://fcit.usf.edu/holocaust.

Lesson 5: War in the East and the evolution of the 'Final Solution'

Learning objectives	Content
• To show how the invasion of the Soviet Union led to a new phase of the Holocaust. • To demonstrate the popular antisemitism in many parts of Eastern Europe and the Soviet Union and how this led to pogroms and collaboration. • To highlight the role of the *Einsatzgruppen* and the start of systematic mass murder. • To explain the development and evolution of Nazi policy and how this emerged from a combination of local initiatives as well as central planning from Berlin. • To recognise that there is scholarly debate about the importance of certain events such as the Wannsee Conference in the development of the 'Final Solution'.	• The invasion of the Soviet Union by Germany and the brutality of the war on the Eastern front. • The history of antisemitism in the Russian Empire during the nineteenth and early twentieth centuries, e.g. the Kishinev pogrom in 1903, and the Pale of Settlement. • The pogroms against Jews in newly occupied Nazi territory in the East (Bialystok, Riga and Lvov). • The structure and role of the *Einsatzgruppen*, the Babi Yar massacre and the early experiments with gas vans. • The Wannsee Conference (20 January 1942).

Points to note

- Teachers need to show how the evolution of the Holocaust was connected to this new stage of the war.
- Students should know something of the history of antisemitism in the East, but recognise that this was actively encouraged by the Nazi regime.
- Some students may think that the first use of gassing was directed against Jews in the camps. Teachers should point out that gassing had first been used against the mentally incapacitated and was then used by *Einsatzgruppe* members after complaints of mental anguish at having to shoot women and children en masse. Gassing in concentration camps was seen to be the most efficient method of killing.
- The importance of Wannsee in the decision-making process should be debated. Neither Hitler nor Himmler were present and in many senses the meeting coordinated policy decisions which could not have been made on that occasion. The minutes of the meeting are very significant, however, in revealing the Nazis' plan to murder all of Europe's Jews.

Suggested resources

'Lesson 5: 1942–45, Genocide' – Lesson plan and resources available from Holocaust and Human Rights Education Center website (www.holocausteducationctr.org).

'Survivor Stories: Val Ginsburg – The Fate of my Community' – Account and testimonial video available from the Holocaust Survivors' Friendship Association website (www.holocaustlearning.org).

'The Road to Treblinka' – Part of the BBC documentary series *The Nazis: A Warning from History*.

Lesson 6: The camp system

Learning objectives	Content
• To demonstrate the wide range of different camps which existed in the German empire and where they were located. • To recognise that the Nazi regime created camps which were exclusively designed for the murder of Jews and other 'undesirables'. • To enable students to understand the experiences of different individuals within the camp system. • To understand how the various camps operated, including the process of selection and gassing. • To highlight the routines within the camp and how the conditions were created to reduce the likelihood of survival. • To understand how the camps benefited the Nazi regime and fitted into the context of the war.	• The evolution of the camp system and its history in the early days of the Third Reich (e.g. Dachau). • The 'Final Solution', Operation Reinhard and the liquidation of the ghettos. • The construction of the death camps (e.g. Treblinka, Sobibor and Belzec); the reason for their creation, the nature of the operations and the extent of the killing that went on there as well as their subsequent destruction. • The variety of camps which existed (e.g. Drancy, Westerbork and Mauthausen) and their locations throughout Europe. • Life in the camps, the routines, work programmes, desperate food shortages, selection processes, disease, etc. • The relationship between the war effort and the camps.

Points to note

- Many students make the mistake of thinking that all the camps operated in the same way; that inmates would either work or be gassed. Practitioners should explain the different functions of the camps.
- It is common for students to think that the practices at Auschwitz (such as the tattooing of numbers) occurred in every camp, which was not the case.
- Students often fail to realise how many camps there were and how these were spread throughout Europe including in Germany, France, Austria and even the Channel Islands.
- Extracts from survivors can provide a personal and engaging insight into life in the camps, although it is worth acknowledging to learners that their experiences were untypical by virtue of the fact that they survived.

Suggested resources

If This Is a Man – The autobiography of Holocaust survivor Primo Levi.
'Learning and Remembering about Auschwitz-Birkenau' – Lesson plan available from Yad Vashem website (www.yadvashem.org).
'Personal Histories: Camps' – Video testimonies of experiences in the camps. Available from USHMM website (www.ushmm.org).
'The Forgotten Camps' – Website containing testimonies, accounts, daily routines and details of the various camps (www.jewishgen.org).

Lesson 7: Case study

Learning objectives	Content
• To focus in on the experiences of one individual and his or her family. • To generate agency to the victims of the Holocaust and to enable students to see the victims as individual people rather than a collective group. • To provide dignity, character, colour and personality to the individuals who perished in the Holocaust through the use of testimonies, letters, diaries and case studies. • To highlight the varying experiences of those who suffered in the Holocaust and to explain how no two stories are identical.	• The background of the individual before the war; where they lived, their job, their family, interests and aspirations (the amount of information will vary according to the example chosen). • How the individual's life was affected by the policies, legislation and actions of the Nazis. • The experiences of the individual and how this impacted on their family. • If the individual chosen survived the Holocaust then the case study should include what happened to them in the immediate aftermath of the war and how they lived in the post-1945 years, whether they remarried, had children, etc.

Points to note

- Teachers can select from a wide range of individuals, and it is worth spending time considering what one wants to achieve from the case study before choosing the example.
- It can be helpful to use examples which challenge stereotypes and preconceptions or which introduce students to aspects of the Holocaust with which they are less familiar.
- It is worth remembering that although survivors can provide excellent insight into what life was like in the camps, their experiences were not always typical and it is more representative to use an individual who did not survive. Conversely, the impact of the Holocaust is particularly evident when studying a survivor who lost his or her family.
- If the individuality and dignity of the victims are to be appreciated by learners then it is particularly important that teachers build up a picture of the individual before the Holocaust.

Suggested case studies

Leon Greenman – An English Jew who settled in the Netherlands and was sent to Auschwitz. He survived the war, although his wife and son did not. There are many case studies already designed about his life and experiences, for example by the Jewish Museum in London (www.jewishmuseum.org.uk), and 'Ordinary Things' by the Institute of Education's Centre for Holocaust Education (www.holocausteducation.org.uk).

Janusz Korczak – A Polish Jew who ran a Jewish orphanage in the Warsaw ghetto. Refusing to allow the orphans to be deported without him, he accompanied them to Treblinka where he, along with them, was murdered.

Rabbi Menachem Ziemba – An eminent rabbi who was murdered by the Nazis during the Warsaw ghetto uprising in 1943.

Alternatively, case studies could be conducted of specific incidents or groups of people murdered by the Nazis such as the 'The Children of Izieu'.

Lesson 8: Resistance

Learning objectives	Content
• To enable students to understand that resistance can take many forms and go beyond force and violence. • To explore the circumstances that existed and why resisting the Nazi regime was extremely difficult and involved such considerable risks. • To demonstrate the places where resistance occurred such as the ghettos and the camps. • To consider the successes and failures of the resistance movement and to evaluate what constitutes success and failure in the context of the Holocaust. • To provide examples of specific individuals and organisations who conducted resistance against the Nazi regime and their collaborators.	• The nature and types of resistance; this might include violent resistance, acts of spiritual and cultural identity, suicide, attempts to remain humane amidst the killing, etc. Examples might include the keeping of Passover in the ghettos or camps, the circulation of ghetto newspapers, the recording of events by organisations such as *Oneg Shabbat* or the suicide of Adam Czerniaków, leader of the Warsaw ghetto *Judenrat*. • The brutal punishments for those who resisted and the suffering that it might cause for others. • Key examples of uprisings including the Warsaw ghetto uprising of 1943, the revolts in Sobibor and Treblinka in 1943 and the *Sonderkommando* uprising in Auschwitz-Birkenau in October 1944; partisan resistance throughout Europe. • Key individuals and organisations including Emmanuel Ringelblum, *Tekumah* (a secret Hebrew language society in the Warsaw ghetto), and the Bielski partisans. • Success and failure in resistance, which might include analysing the number of lives saved, the moral value of resistance and the value of recording the Nazis' crimes; concepts of *Kiddush ha-hayyim* and *Kiddush ha-Shem*.

Points to note

- Many students may struggle to appreciate the value of non-violent resistance and thus it is worth spending time examining exactly why other forms of Jewish opposition were important.
- Mini case studies of individuals help learners appreciate the range of considerations which one had to take into account before deciding whether or not to participate in a form of resistance, such as the welfare of their family.
- In order to understand the complexity of the situation, students should appreciate that resistance typically led to horrific retaliatory acts by the Nazi regime.
- In order to provide a balance, resistance should be considered within the context of the ghettos, the camps and within Europe generally, including partisan resistance in the forests.

Suggested resources

'Defiance' – A 2008 film produced and directed by Edward Zwick which tells the story of the Bielski partisans during the Nazi occupation of Belarus.

'Individual Responsibility and Resistance during the Holocaust' – Lesson plan available from the USHMM website (www.ushmm.org).

'Unit Four: Jewish Resistance' – Lesson plan and resources available from the Holocaust Memorial Resource and Education Center of Florida website (www.holocaustedu.org).

Lesson 9: Perpetrators, victims, bystanders, rescuers and collaborators

Learning objectives	Content
• To enable students to realise that in some instances those who were involved in the Holocaust cannot be simply classified as 'bystander' or 'collaborator'. • To understand the context and complexity of the decision-making processes of those involved in the Holocaust. • To explain how (with a few exceptions) those who implemented the Holocaust were not psychopaths but ordinary, rational and often highly intelligent and cultured individuals. • To examine the complex reasons why non-Jewish people helped Jews, stood by, actively collaborated or chose different responses on different occasions. • To engage students in the process of historical enquiry and empathy through looking at examples of individuals in the past.	• Jewish cooperation with the Nazi regime with specific focus on the functions of the *Judenrate*, the Jewish ghetto police, *Kapos* and *Sonderkommando*. • The collaboration of local people in areas such as the Baltic States in rounding up and murdering Jews. • The extent to which 'ordinary people' in Germany and other countries knew what was going on in the Holocaust and the extent to which they wanted to know; Roosevelt and Churchill's knowledge of the Holocaust and Auschwitz-Birkenau. • Police Battalion 101 and the obedience of 'ordinary men' in participating in the killing and not opting out when given the opportunity to do so. • The normality of key perpetrators like Adolf Eichmann and Rudolf Hoess and Hannah Arendt's concept of the 'banality of evil'. • The motives and actions of individuals such as Oskar Schindler, Raoul Wallenberg and Carl Lutz.

Points to note

• Learners should understand the difficult position that members of the *Judenrate* were put in, their typically limited knowledge of the death camps and the variety of moral judgements that were made.

• Students should appreciate that there is no evidence of a Nazi ever being punished for refusing to murder Jews and that there was an obedient acquiescence from those involved in the killing.

• It is important that students understand that most Jews were not rescued and that by contrast, most Jews were murdered.

• Some attention should be drawn to the wide range of motives demonstrated by those involved with the Holocaust, which often included financial incentives or career advancement.

• Students should appreciate that it is often not possible to simply place individuals into the neat categories of perpetrator, victim, bystander, rescuer or collaborator.

Suggested resources

'Reflections' – Educational pack published by the Imperial War Museum and available for purchase from the website (www.iwmshop.org.uk).

'Rethinking Perpetrators, Bystanders and Rescuers' – Lesson plan and resources available from the USHMM website (www.ushmm.org).

'Unit Five: Rescuers' – Lesson plan and resources available from Holocaust Memorial Resource and Education Center of Florida website (www.holocaustedu.org).

Lesson 10: The ending of the Holocaust

Learning objectives	Content
• To understand the ending of the Holocaust in the context of the Second World War. • To appreciate that the destruction of Jews continued right up until the final days of the war. • To explain how the Nazis sought to remove the evidence of their crimes by destroying the gas chambers. • To highlight how tens of thousands of Jews died of illness and over-eating in the immediate aftermath of the liberations. • To demonstrate the difficulty of the circumstances which faced survivors, the creation of Israel and the experiences of survivors after 1945.	• The advances of the Allied forces and the retreat of the Nazis; the subsequent dismantling of the camps and destruction of the gas chambers at Auschwitz-Birkenau. • The death marches and the experiences of those who endured them. • The reports of the Allied soldiers upon discovering the camps and the world's subsequent reaction. • The experiences of survivors; the high death rates of survivors and the difficulties that they faced (this should include the loss of their families and their homes, as well as their physical and mental health, and also the continuation of popular antisemitism). • The creation of the State of Israel and the closure of the displaced person camps.

Points to note

• Some students think that Hitler's death triggered the ending of the Holocaust. Dispelling misconceptions on this point is important for learners to develop an understanding of the ending of the Holocaust in the context of the war.

• Students should understand that survivors could not simply go home. They need to appreciate that survivors were often thousands of miles from their country of birth; that their homes had been annexed by others and that violent antisemitism still existed in many parts of Central and Eastern Europe.

• When addressing the creation of the State of Israel, care must be taken to ensure that students do not simply think that it was a sympathetic reaction to the Holocaust, but rather appreciate that it was a culmination of myriad, often long-term factors.

Suggested resources

'Liberation and Survival' – Lesson plan available from the Yad Vashem website (www.yadvashem.org).

'Survivor Testimonies' – Available from the USC Shoah Foundation YouTube Channel and website (http://sfi.usc.edu).

'What Did Zigi Do After the Holocaust?' – Lesson plan and resources available from the Holocaust Education Trust website (www.het.org.uk).

Lesson 11: The post-Holocaust world (optional lesson)

Learning objectives	Content
• To highlight the fate of the perpetrators of the Holocaust and the importance of post-war justice. • To show that the Holocaust has had a major impact on various aspects of post-war society. • To demonstrate to students why the Holocaust is such an important part of history and its relevance to the modern world. • To consider the way that the Holocaust has been remembered and the relationship between the past and the present.	• The details and outcome of the Nuremberg Trials and their judicial precedence; other post-war trials, e.g. the Eichmann trial and its significance in the development of Holocaust consciousness. • The impact of the Holocaust on the creation of the United Nations Convention on the Prevention and Punishment of the Crime of Genocide (1948) and the International Criminal Court (2002). • The remembrance and representation of the Holocaust, e.g. *Schindler's List*, Holocaust Memorial Day, IHRA.

Points to note

- Many students do not understand how the legacy of the past has influenced the world in which they live. This lesson helps students to appreciate the legacy, importance and relevance of the Holocaust and enables them to understand how it has shaped the modern world.
- This lesson is a useful bridge for teachers who want to move on to a study of post-war conflicts or genocides.

Suggested resources

'Nuremberg Trials Project: A Digital Document Collection'. Harvard Law School Library (http://nuremberg.law.harvard.edu).

SCHEME OF WORK FOR RELIGIOUS STUDIES:
THE HOLOCAUST – PREJUDICE, ETHICS AND RELIGION

The Holocaust appears in the syllabi of various religious studies courses, including those on Judaism, ethics and the problem of evil. This particular scheme of work seeks to draw together these strands and create a programme where the central themes are the issues, questions, moral dilemmas and personal choices which emerged and continue to emerge from the Holocaust. This programme does not need to be followed consecutively or systematically. Many of the ideas contained within it could be integrated into existing schemes of work where appropriate. Teachers who are preparing their classes for public examinations should ensure that they have covered the syllabus provided by the exam board.

Lesson 1: Prejudice, discrimination and antisemitism

Learning objectives	Content
• To understand the meaning of the terms prejudice, discrimination and antisemitism. • To consider why prejudice and discrimination sometimes exist. • To reflect on antisemitism within Germany and Nazi-occupied Europe and its place in contemporary society.	• Key terms: 'prejudice', 'discrimination' and 'antisemitism'. • The reasons for prejudice and discrimination, such as racism, sexism, etc.; ignorance; fear; suspicion; religious and political beliefs; propaganda and education; cultural or social values. • The treatment of Jews in Germany and the escalation of antisemitism from 1933 to 1939.

Points to note

- Explain that discrimination is not intrinsically wrong, but that often the reason why discrimination occurs is wrong. We can legitimately discriminate between the quality of essays but not the colour of one's skin.
- Try to develop a complex understanding in learner's minds about the reasons for discrimination. It is too simplistic to label everyone as 'racist' or 'sexist'. Think about how someone may have legitimate fears or grievances and how these can easily turn into something more damaging and corrosive.

Suggested resources

'Confronting Antisemitism Project' – Sample lesson plan available from the Anti-Defamation League website (http://archive.adl.org/).

'Fighting the Fires of Hate: America and the Nazi Book Burnings' – Educational activities available from the USHMM website (www.ushmm.org).

'Remembering the Holocaust and Confronting Xenophobia on January 27th' – Lesson plan available from the Yad Vashem website (www.yadvashem.org).

'Strategies in Facing Antisemitism: An Educational Resources Guide' – Available from the Simon Wiesenthal Center website (www.wiesenthal.com).

Lesson 2: Combating prejudice

Learning objectives	Content
• To evaluate whether or not prejudice and discrimination continue to exist and why that may be the case. • To reflect upon why prejudice, discrimination and antisemitism are wrong. • To consider a number of ways in which prejudice, discrimination and antisemitism can be prevented and combated.	• Post-war examples of prejudice: these might include racial segregation and discrimination in the USA, apartheid in South Africa or genocide in Rwanda. • The reasons why prejudice and discrimination are wrong; these might include: it is unfair; it makes people feel disrespected and unwanted; it breeds resentment, hatred and violence; it can lead to physical oppression; it divides a society. • The advantages and disadvantages of various measures to combat prejudice and discrimination such as affirmative action, legislation, education, etc.

Points to note

• When selecting examples of post-war prejudice, choose ones which will interest and resonate with the majority of the class. Remember that one is not comparing these examples to the Holocaust but looking at the common themes of prejudice and discrimination as well as how they occur in different contexts.

• Avoid generalisations. Choose a few examples and study them in detail. Remember that the reasons for prejudice and discrimination in one context may be very different in another, although there are often common themes and ideas which run through the different situations.

Suggested resources

'Hatred, Propaganda and War' – Lesson plans and resources available from the Survivors' Fund website (www.survivors-fund.org.uk).

'The Road to Civil Rights' – Lesson plans and materials available from the iCivics website (www.icivics.org).

Lesson 3: Moral dilemmas and the Holocaust

Learning objectives	Content
• To recognise the meaning of the term 'moral dilemma' and to be able to recognise examples. • To understand that extreme situations such as the Holocaust are likely to generate some very severe examples of moral dilemmas. • To reflect upon the decision-making processes and the factors which need to be taken into consideration when attempting to deal with a moral dilemma.	• The meaning of the term 'moral dilemma' along with various examples from contemporary life and the Holocaust. • The options that are available for individuals who are caught in moral dilemmas. • The options available for those who see other people caught in a moral dilemma.

Points to note

• In order to help learners grasp the meaning of the term 'moral dilemma', contemporary examples which are relevant to their own lives could be used before moving on to examples from the Holocaust.

• In relating this to the Holocaust, the teacher can introduce the idea of the bystander who sees what is happening but does not act. Some discussion could be had about the concept of moral duty.

Suggested resources

'Teaching or Preaching: The Holocaust and Intercultural Education in the UK' – Article by P. Salmons on a case study of students who look at moral dilemmas in the Holocaust (*Intercultural Education*, 14, no. 2 (2003): 139–49). Available from the Imperial War Museum website at http://archive.iwm.org.uk/upload/pdf/TeachingorPreaching.pdf.

'What Were Some of the Dilemmas Faced During the Holocaust?' – Lesson plan and resources available from the Holocaust Educational Trust website (www.het.org.uk).

Lesson 4: Dealing with moral dilemmas

Learning objectives	Content
• To strengthen understanding about the meaning of moral dilemmas by introducing students to more examples. • To enable students to recognise that various thinkers have sought to introduce ethical systems which help people in moral dilemmas to find an answer. • To encourage students to apply these ethical systems to specific moral dilemmas from the Holocaust and to pass judgement on their relative effectiveness.	• Various ethical beliefs and systems which can be used to try and deal with moral dilemmas: – Utilitarianism – Kantian ethics – Theistic ethics – (Aristotelian) virtue theory. • The advantages and disadvantages of each of these systems as well as something about their origins and use in the modern world.

Points to note

• The number of moral theories which are discussed, as well as the level of depth and detail which are applied, will be dependent on the ability of the class.

• Things can be simplified to looking at the intentions behind an action and the consequences of an action, as well as the discussion regarding whether or not there are absolutes in morality.

Suggested resources

'Holocaust and Human Behaviour' – *Facing History and Ourselves* resource book (www.facinghistory.org).

Lesson 5: Applying moral theories to the Holocaust

Learning objectives	Content
• To strengthen existing knowledge and understanding of ethical theories. • To recognise how these theories can be applied to moral dilemmas from the Holocaust and to see the benefits and problems of doing so. • To reflect on the reasons behind the decisions that were made by those in moral dilemmas during the Holocaust.	• The way in which moral theories are applied in real life situations. • The other factors which affect the decision-making process. • The concept of historical empathy (understanding why people made the decisions they did, even if one does not agree with the morality of that decision).

Points to note

• It is important to recognise that in the real world, moral theories are not applied in a vacuum. Individuals making decisions during the Holocaust had a range of competing concerns of varying significance which also impacted upon the decisions that they made.

Suggested resources

'Compassion within the Ghetto Walls' – Lesson plan and resources available from the Yad Vashem website (www.yadvashem.org).

'Janusz Korczak Case Study' – Resources available from the Holocaust Memorial Day Trust website (www.hmd.org.uk).

Lesson 6: Justice and the Holocaust

Learning objectives	Content
• To consider the meaning of the term justice and the requirements that are necessary to achieve justice. • To consider how justice can be achieved in the post-Holocaust world. • To evaluate whether or not it is ever possible to achieve justice after the horrors of the Holocaust. • To see the response of survivors, Israel and the international community to surviving Holocaust perpetrators.	• Justice – its definition and application in relation to the Holocaust. • The different views regarding what should happen to surviving perpetrators of the Holocaust. • The work that has been done to try and achieve justice after the Holocaust. This should include a look at the Nuremberg Trials and the work of the Conference on Jewish Material Claims Against Germany. • Case studies of individual cases. These should include Adolf Eichmann but might also look at individuals such as Oswald Pohl, Hermann Höfle, Erwin Lambert and Josef Mengele.

Points to note

• When choosing individual case studies, it is helpful to select a variety of different examples. These might include people like Josef Mengele who managed to escape justice.

• Search for any recent news stories of elderly individuals who have been arrested and discuss whether or not they should be put on trial. This will help students to understand the relevance and importance of the discussion. It is also possible to use examples of those accused of being perpetrators of the Rwandan Genocide who live in the UK.

Suggested resources

'Justice after the Holocaust' – Lesson 16 available from the Facing History and Ourselves website (www.facinghistory.org).

'Justice and Fairness' – Lesson plan and resources available from the USC Shoah Foundation website (http://sfi.usc.edu).

'The Trial of Adolf Eichmann' – Lesson activities and resources from http://remember.org/ eichmann.

Lesson 7: An introduction to forgiveness and the Holocaust

Learning objectives	Content

• To understand the meaning of the term 'forgiveness'.
• To consider the criteria which are required to enable forgiveness and the difficulty of doing so (especially for large and personal crimes).
• To appreciate the complexity and sensitivity of relating forgiveness to the Holocaust and whether or not it is ethical or possible to offer forgiveness on behalf of the dead.
	• Forgiveness – its meaning and relationship to the Holocaust.
	• The factors that affect an individual's decision of whether or not to forgive
	  – The relationship with the person who committed the wrong deed
	  – The seriousness of the deed
	  – The intention of the person
	  – The consequences of the deed
	  – The reaction of the person who has committed the wrong deed.

Points to note

- To some students, the idea of relating forgiveness to the Holocaust may be offensive and thus sensitivity and care is needed.
- It is important to ask students about their own views on this subject and to recognise the complexity of the situation. While they may not be able to conceive of forgiving leading Nazi perpetrators, does this apply to all those involved in some way with the Holocaust? What about those who repent of their crimes?
- Consider with students the fact that the dead are not able to forgive, and thus whether or not to forgive on their behalf is not for us to decide (or potentially a betrayal of their memory).

Suggested resources

'Candles Holocaust Museum, Indiana' – A range of podcasts and information on the power of forgiveness and the Holocaust, set up by Holocaust survivor Eva Kor, available from the Candles Holocaust Museum website (www.candlesholocaustmuseum.org).

Lesson 8: Forgiveness and the Holocaust

Learning objectives	Content
• To reflect upon the advantages and disadvantages of forgiveness for the victim and the perpetrator. • To recognise the different religious and philosophical approaches to the concept of forgiveness. • To understand that different approaches have been adopted towards the idea of forgiving those who carried out the Holocaust.	• The reasons why people may forgive someone who has wronged them or their family, e.g. religious beliefs; sense of liberation; response to repentance, etc. • The reasons why people may not forgive someone who has wronged them or their family, e.g. lack of repentance; demand for justice; natural enmity against the perpetrator, etc. • The advantages and disadvantages of forgiveness to both the person who has been wronged and the person who committed the wrong. • The Judaic view of forgiveness and how this relates and applies to the Holocaust.

Points to note

- Help students to consider what enables one individual to forgive and another not to be able to do so. Also consider what prevents one person from being able to forgive and not another.
- Encourage students to think about whether or not the Judaic view of forgiveness expects individuals to forgive irrespective of all other factors.
- Discuss the relationship between forgiveness and justice. Does forgiveness come at the expense of justice? If so, is this a problem?

Suggested resources

'Moral Dilemma – Excerpts from *The Sunflower*' – Lesson plan available from the Tennessee Holocaust Commission website (www.tennesseeholocaustcommision.org).

'The Forgiveness Project' – A travelling exhibition, set of resources and stories available from the Forgiveness Project website (http://theforgivenessproject.com).

Lesson 9: The Holocaust and the problem of evil

Learning objectives	Content
• To enable students to recognise the meaning of the phrase 'the problem of evil'. • To help students appreciate why and how the Holocaust caused a problem for Jewish (and Christian) theologians and philosophers. • To examine the responses that have been made by theologians and philosophers and to assess their credibility.	• The theological and philosophical issues that the Holocaust (and evil generally) creates regarding the existence and nature of God. • Whether or not the Holocaust demands new responses to the problem of evil and if so, why. • The answers and responses that theologians and philosophers have put forward to the Holocaust and the problem of evil.

Points to note

- Teachers should remember that the Holocaust has the potential to undermine or challenge an individual's faith. Care should be taken to be sensitive and to be balanced.
- Ensure that students are not simply given the major theological and philosophical questions about the Holocaust and the problem of evil, but also the answers that have been offered to these questions. If the answers are not provided too, then learners with a faith may feel isolated or bewildered.

Suggested resources

'Faith in *Night*' – Lesson plan on the subject of faith in Elie Wiesel's *Night*, available from http://teachingnight.com.

'Religious Education Resources' – Video of survivor Eugene Black describing the impact of the Holocaust on his life and faith. Available from the Holocaust Learning website (www.holocaustlearning.org).

Lesson 10: The churches and the Holocaust

Learning objectives	Content
• To recognise the existence of both Protestant and Roman Catholic churches in Germany during the Third Reich. • To help students appreciate the risks and consequences that were involved in resisting the Nazi regime. • To consider what students would expect the churches should do and would do. • To explore the lives of individuals within the church who opposed the policies and actions of the regime and the subsequent consequences.	• The distinction between Protestant and Catholic churches and their role within German society. • The reasons why many Christians in Germany supported the Nazis. • The role of the German Evangelical Church and the creation of the Confessing Church; Dietrich Bonhoeffer and Martin Niemöller. • The 1933 Concordat between the Vatican and the Nazi government; the policies and silence of Pope Pius XII; Bishop Galen; Maximilian Kolbe. • The Nazis' increased opposition to the churches in Germany.

Points to note

• Most Germans within Germany were at least nominally Christian, with around 20 million people belonging to the Roman Catholic Church and approximately 40 million to Protestant churches.

• It is easy to make generalisations about the church when there were obviously those who supported and opposed the regime to varying extents within both the Protestant and Catholic churches.

• It is also difficult to assess popular support for a dictatorship, although the official position of the church hierarchy is often a useful gauge.

Suggested resources

'Response to the Holocaust: Resistance and Rescue' – Lesson plan and resources available from the Holocaust and Human Rights Center website (www.holocausteducationctr.org).

'When They Came for Me' – Lesson plan and resources on Martin Niemöller available from the National WWII Museum website (www.nationalww2museum.org).

SCHEME OF WORK FOR CITIZENSHIP:
THE HOLOCAUST AND OTHER GENOCIDES

This scheme of work is aimed at practitioners who wish to teach about the Holocaust in the context of other genocides, and is especially focused for teachers of citizenship. Alternatively, parts of this scheme of work could form part of a history curriculum. This programme of work does not need to be followed prescriptively but can be used as a helpful guide for the successful delivery of Holocaust education within the context of citizenship. Teachers who are preparing their classes for public examinations should ensure that they have covered the syllabus provided by the exam board. In this scheme of work, comparative lessons have been constructed on the Holocaust and the Rwandan Genocide. When comparing the Holocaust to other events and phenomena, great care is needed and practitioners should read Chapter 9 for further help in this area. This scheme of work would particularly work for students in key stages 4 or 5, although it can be modified to accommodate younger students.

Lesson 1: Defining the Holocaust

Learning objectives	Content
• To recognise that there are a number of different definitions of the Holocaust. • To consider the key differences in these definitions and to think about which definition is the most appropriate. • To understand why the definition of the Holocaust matters and why its definition can have important political implications.	• What was the Holocaust? • Should the definition include all those who were persecuted by the Nazi regime or only those who were killed? Thus when did the Holocaust start? • Should the definition include those who died of disease or over-eating after the liberation of the camps? Thus when did the Holocaust end? • Should the definition include only Jewish victims or all those who suffered at the hands of the Nazi regime and its collaborators? Where does one draw the line? • Why have definitions of the Holocaust often been considered so important and why do they continue to matter today?

Points to note

- This can be a particularly sensitive issue if students feel that their ethnic or religious group is being excluded from the Holocaust. Care should be taken to ensure that students are thoughtful and considerate.
- Students often arrive with preconceived or simplistic ideas about what the Holocaust was. It is important to challenge these and to help students appreciate that defining the Holocaust can be a very problematic and difficult thing to do.
- Help students to appreciate that there continues to be significant disagreement over seventy years later.

Suggested resources

'Introduction to the Holocaust' in the USHMM's *Holocaust Encyclopedia*. Available from the USHMM website (www.ushmm.org).
'The Holocaust: Definition and Preliminary Discussion'. Available from the Yad Vashem website (www.yadvashem.org).

Lesson 2: Was the Holocaust unique?

Learning objectives	Content
• To recognise that there are contrasting views on whether or not the Holocaust was unique. • To develop a sophisticated understanding of what 'uniqueness' means with reference to the Holocaust. • To consider why the Holocaust has become such a powerful term of reference and how this can be open to abuse or exploitation. • To reflect on what (if anything) can be acceptably compared with the Holocaust.	• The definition of uniqueness with specific reference to the Holocaust. • The arguments put forward on both sides of the debate regarding whether or not the Holocaust is unique. • The reasons why the Holocaust has become such a powerful and sensitive point of reference. • The exploitation of the Holocaust, the motives behind such exploitation and the reasons why this is problematic.

Points to note

- Learners need to recognise that there are different uses of the term 'unique' and that it is necessary to understand what is meant when one says that the Holocaust is unique.
- It is important that students try to appreciate why different schools of thought exist and understand the arguments on both sides. Again, this can be a sensitive issue and care should be taken when teaching this lesson.

Suggested resources

Kinloch, N. (2001) 'Parallel Catastrophes? Uniqueness, Redemption and the Shoah', *Teaching History*, 104: 8–14.

Lesson 3: What is genocide?

Learning objectives	Content
• To understand the origin and meaning of the term 'genocide'. • To recognise the lack of consensus around the UN definition and to consider whether subsequent definitions are more appropriate. • To consider that genocide has continued in the post-Holocaust world. • To analyse various historical events and assess whether or not they should be defined as genocide.	• Raphael Lemkin and his role in the creation of the UN Convention on the Prevention and Punishment of the Crime of Genocide. • Other scholarly definitions of the term which have emerged since 1948. • Examples of post-war genocide and the uncertainty which has surrounded the application of the term 'genocide' to various historical and contemporary events .

Points to note

- It is important to show that the concept of genocide emerged as a consequence of the Holocaust but that genocide has continued in the post-war world.
- Remember that many students may not have a clear understanding of what the UN is or its role in the world.
- This lesson provides teachers with an opportunity to explore a number of different events in various continents and go beyond European or Western history.

Suggested resources

Various online teaching resources are available at the One Million Bones website (www.onemillionbones.org).

'Who Is Responsible When Genocide Occurs?' – Lesson plan available at the USHMM website (www.ushmm.org).

Lesson 4: Assessing genocide

Learning objectives	Content
• To understand that definitions of genocide have to be applied to both historical and contemporary events. • To recognise that there is often disagreement as to whether or not something should be defined as genocide. • To appreciate that there are sometimes conflicting political, social, religious or national interests in defining certain events as genocide.	• Various events which under some definitions and interpretations might be considered genocide: – The Stalinist purges (1934–41) – The famines in China (1958–63) – The Cultural Revolution (1966) – The Khmer Rouge (1975–79) – The anti-Sikh riots (India 1984) – Srebrenica (1995). • The political and national sensitivities involved in defining events as genocide (e.g. the Armenian Genocide and Franco–Turkish relations); explanations of post-war genocide and measures that might be employed to try to prevent it.

Points to note

• Students may not have heard of some of these events prior to the lesson. Consequently, it may well be necessary to provide some sort of context to these events if the presentations fail to do so adequately.
• Encourage students to think broadly and imaginatively when considering ways in which genocide might be prevented, e.g. education, gun control, greater levels of democracy, etc.

Suggested resources

'Genocide Watch' – An organisation that aims to predict, prevent, stop and punish genocide (www.genocidewatch.net).
'The Crisis in Darfur: Is Genocide Occurring?' – Lesson plan available from 'The Genocide Teaching Project' webpage from the American University Washington College of Law's Center for Human Rights and Humanitarian Law (www.wcl.american.edu/humright/center).

Lesson 5: Comparative genocide – the background to the Holocaust and the Rwandan Genocide

Learning objectives	Content
• To understand that despite the UN Convention on the Prevention and Punishment of the Crime of Genocide, genocide has continued to take place. • To recognise that there are similarities and differences between the Holocaust and the Rwandan Genocide. • To appreciate the specific contexts of both the Holocaust and the Rwandan Genocide.	• The history of Jews in Europe; their culture, identity and religion. • The historical relationship between Hutu and Tutsi. • The significance of racial theory in marginalising and persecuting different groups within Nazi Germany and Belgian-controlled Rwanda. • The introduction of identity cards in Rwanda and the post-colonial legacy up to 1994.

Points to note

• Comparing genocides can be a very worthwhile activity, although, if done badly, it can do more harm than good. It is important to read Chapter 9 on 'Comparing the Holocaust to other genocides' before teaching this module.
• In order to prevent unhelpful or meaningless comparisons, context is very important.
• There should be an emphasis on the differences as much as on the similarities.

Suggested resources

'Rwanda' – Lesson plan and resources available from the Holocaust Memorial Day Trust website (www.hmd.org.uk).
'The Origins of the Rwandan Genocide' – Lesson plans and resources available from the Survivors' Fund website (www.survivors-fund.org.uk).

Lesson 6: Comparative genocide – the Holocaust and the Rwandan Genocide

Learning objectives	Content
• To enable students to understand the role that propaganda played in both the Holocaust and the Rwandan Genocide. • To reflect upon the motives and actions of the perpetrators and the experiences of the victims. • To evaluate the difficulties faced by survivors and the importance of justice.	• Antisemitism, racial theory and the hatred and propaganda employed by the Nazi regime and Hutu extremists to marginalise and persecute their targets. • The ghettos, *Einsatzgruppen* and death camps in the Holocaust; the roadblocks, *Interhamwe* militias and the slaughter of the Rwandan Genocide. • The Nuremberg Trials and the role of the international community in confronting the horrors of Nazism; the criticisms of the International Criminal Tribunal for Rwanda and the *Gacaca* courts.

Points to note

- If students have already studied the Holocaust in history, more time can be spent on the Rwandan Genocide, with which most students will be wholly unfamiliar.
- Encourage students to think about how such actions were possible. Try to avoid simplifying the explanations.
- Consider why justice is necessary for the dead and the survivors, as well as the challenges of trying to achieve it.

Suggested resources

'Hatred, Propaganda and War' – Lesson plans and resources available from the Survivors' Fund website (www.survivors-fund.org.uk).

'Rwandan Genocide' – Lesson plan available from the Holocaust Museum Houston website (www.hmh.org).

Chapter 14

Lesson plans

The following lesson plans correspond with the lessons contained in the schemes of work found in the previous chapter. The resources to which they refer are catalogued in the next chapter.

LESSON PLANS FOR: THE HISTORY OF THE HOLOCAUST

Lesson 1: Jews, Jewish identity, history, religion and culture

Learning objectives

- To explore students' preconceptions and misconceptions about Jews and Jewish identity.
- To understand the long and complex history of the Jewish people and the different experiences of Jews at various points in history.
- To contextualise the Holocaust and demonstrate the experiences of Jews living in pre-war Europe.
- To ensure students see Jews as individuals with agency who lived ordinary lives and to not view them simply as a collective victim group of Nazis.

	Lesson details	Materials needed
Starter	• Show students photographs of famous Jews from the past and present. This might include Nobel Prize winners, but should also include actors, musicians and models. • Discuss with students the following questions: – What makes a person Jewish? – Are Jews a religious group or an ethnic group? (10 minutes)	• Photographs of famous Jews. This might include: Amy Winehouse, Scarlett Johannson, Albert Einstein, Sacha Baron Cohen.
Main	• Split the class into groups of three or four and give each group a photograph depicting an aspect of pre-war Jewish life in Europe. • Ask each group to write down what is happening in the photograph and anything they can infer from pre-war Jewish life. • Give each group 2–4 minutes with each photograph and encourage discussion within the group. (25 minutes)	• Photographs of pre-war Jewish life. Available from 'Jewish life in Europe before the Holocaust' in the USHMM's *Holocaust Encyclopedia* (www.ushmm.org) to add to the 'Jews, Jewish identity, history, religion and culture' worksheet (pp. 168–169)
Plenary	• Students to write a summary of what life was like for Jews living in pre-war Europe. (10 minutes)	
Homework	• Research one of the following people and explain their contribution to European society: – Gabriel Lippmann – Gustav Mahler – Franz Kafka.	

Lesson 2: Nazi attitudes and actions towards Jews (1933–39)

Learning objectives

*   To understand the nature of discrimination and persecution implemented by the Nazis.
*   To show the deterioration of living standards imposed on the Jews.
*   To consider the different propaganda methods that were employed.
*   To demonstrate the historical roots of antisemitism.

	Lesson details	Materials needed
Starter	• Ask students to try and explain the following words: 'Persecution', 'Discrimination' and 'Prejudice'. • Students given quotations from Martin Luther and Heinrich von Treitschke. Discuss the history of antisemitism using the quotations as a stimulus. (15 minutes)	• 'Nazi attitudes and actions towards Jews' worksheet (pp. 169–170)
Main	• Show the students a photograph of the boycott of Jewish shops and allow them to discuss the questions in pairs. • Share ideas as a class. • Show the students a photograph of a Jewish passport in 1939. Explain that the Nazis made all Jews with non-Jewish names adopt 'Israel' (for males) and 'Sara' (for females). • Discuss why names are important and how they shape identity. Mention can be made of how the Nazis gave Jews numbers in Auschwitz. • Show students Star of David photographs and allow them to work through the questions. Explain how font on Star was supposed to represent the Hebrew characters. (25 minutes)	• Photograph of Jewish shop during the 1 April 1933 boycott • Photographs of Jewish passport showing 'J' stamped on it and insertion of middle name 'Israel' or 'Sara' • Photographs of Star of David badge • German star = 'Jude' • Frence star = 'Juif' • Dutch star = 'Jood'
Plenary	• Show students excerpts from the Nazi children's book *Der Giftpilz* and discuss the impact that this might have on children's thinking about Jews. (5 minutes)	• Images from *Der Giftpilz*

Lesson 3: Jewish emigration

Learning objectives

- To show the rapid deterioration of the lives of Jews within Germany and Austria.
- To demonstrate the difficulty of the decision-making process involved in leaving one's home country.
- To highlight the response of other countries towards Jewish emigration and the restrictions that were established.

	Lesson details	Materials needed
Starter	• Discuss with the class why people may leave their home country and the challenges and difficulties of doing so. (5 minutes)	
Main	• Give students a copy of the 'Jewish Emigration' worksheet. • Project onto the board each new development and ask students to complete the respective row on the table. (It is likely to be necessary to explain each of the developments to ensure every student understands.) After each event, discuss with the class what decision they made and encourage debate about what option is best. (35 minutes)	• 'Jewish emigration' worksheet and accompanying teacher sheet (pp. 171–172)
Plenary	• Explain to students the restrictions that different countries placed on Jewish emigration. (5 minutes)	• 'Map 13' in Gilbert's *Holocaust: Maps and Photographs*

Homework	• Ask students to research the following two events and describe what happened:
	  – The voyage of the *St Louis*
	  – The *Struma* disaster.	

Lesson 4: The Polish ghettos

Learning objectives

- To understand Nazi policies towards the Jews within the context of the Second World War.
- To explain the establishment of ghettos and its relation to the 'Jewish question'.
- To demonstrate the antisemitic measures that the Nazis introduced against Poland's Jews.
- To enable students to begin to understand what life was like in a ghetto and the nature of the conditions that existed.

	Lesson details	Materials needed

Starter	• Play students an excerpt from the film *The Pianist* (2002) and then discuss the following questions:
	  – How would you describe the conditions of those in the film?
	  – What examples are there to show these conditions?
	  – Why are they living in such a way?
	  – Where is this and when?
	  – Why did the Nazis create ghettos?
	(20 minutes)
		• *The Pianist* (2002), extracts 15:12–19:38 and 32:32–33:49

Main	• Using 'Children in the Ghetto' animation, work through the different experiences of children living in the ghetto and ask students to complete the worksheet 'The Polish ghettos'. (20 minutes)	• http://ghetto.galim.org.il/eng/street.html • 'The Polish ghettos' worksheet (p. 173)
Plenary	• Narrate the story of Janusz Korczak and his orphanage in the Warsaw ghetto. Students can then fill in the final box of the worksheet. (5 minutes)	
Homework	• Ask students to produce a piece of extended writing on what life was like in the Warsaw ghetto. They can use their class notes and further research.	

Lesson 5: War in the East and the evolution of the 'Final Solution'

Learning objectives

- To explore the role and motives of collaborators and the *Einsatzgruppen* in murdering Jews in the East.
- To show the evolution of policy towards the Jews in the context of the war in the East.
- To learn about the Wannsee Conference and consider its importance within the Holocaust.

	Lesson details	Materials needed
Starter	• Show students the first two minutes of *Conspiracy* (2001) and discuss the situation in the war and the background to the Wannsee Conference. (10 minutes)	• *Conspiracy* (2001)
Main	• Give students a copy of 'War in the East and the "Final Solution"' worksheet. Read through the extracts of the minutes and discuss the questions. (10 minutes) • Explain the role of the *Einsatzgruppen*. • Project onto the board the Jäger Report (extracts of which can be downloaded from www.yadvashem.org) and sensitively discuss the motives and methods of killing. • Alternatively, appropriately selected testimonies of survivors regarding *Einsatzgruppen* activities could be read or listened to. (See for example the YouTube channel of the USC Shoah Foundation.) (20 minutes)	• 'War in the East and the evolution of the "Final Solution"' worksheet (pp. 174–175) • Various websites
Plenary	• Explain how Nazi soldiers were emotionally and psychologically struggling with shooting women and children at close range and the testing of gassing as an alternative method of murder. • (See 'The Road to Treblinka' on the BBC DVD *The Nazis: A Warning from History*.) (5 minutes)	
Homework	• Ask students to produce a timeline of key events in the evolution of the Holocaust between September 1939 and January 1942.	

Lesson 6: The camp system

Learning objectives

- To demonstrate the reasons for the camps and the different types of camps which existed throughout Nazi-occupied Europe.
- To help students understand the conditions and experiences of those who lived, worked and died in the camps.
- To appreciate the centrality of the camps to the Holocaust and the speed and efficiency of the murder programme.

	Lesson details	Materials needed
Starter	• Ask students to write down what they know about life in the camps. Discuss their ideas and challenge generalisations and misconceptions. Explain that there were different types of camp. (5 minutes)	
Main	• Divide the class into six groups and provide each group with details of a particular camp. • Choose different types of camp in different parts of Nazi-occupied Europe. This could include: – Treblinka – Theresienstadt – Westerbork – Mauthausen – Ravensbrück – Chełmno. • Ask each group to work through the material and to prepare a 3-minute presentation on the camp. Students can use 'The camp system' worksheet to structure their preparation and take notes from the presentations of the other groups. (15 minutes)	• 'The camp system' worksheet (p. 176) • Various resources about the camps (See the websites of the Jewish Virtual Library, USHMM and Yad Vashem)
Plenary	• Group presentations. (25 minutes)	
Homework	• Ask students to answer the following question: • Explain some of the different types of camp that existed and how they fitted into the Nazi programme of mass murder.	

Lesson 7: Case study

Learning objectives

- To help students understand that the victims of the Holocaust were individuals rather than a collective group.
- To provide agency and dignity to the victims.
- To demonstrate that the experiences of different people varied and to show the individuality of each story.

	Lesson details	Materials needed
Starter	• Choose three everyday objects, such as a photograph, an item of clothing or a book. Think what people in the future might want to know about these items. • Ask students to think about why a particular item may be of sentimental value. (10 minutes)	

Main	• Look at the background of the individual
	• Think about the following questions:
	  – Where did they live?
	  – What was their occupation?
	  – How old were they when the war started?
	(10 minutes)
	  – Watch a video about the individual or a testimony from a surviving member of their family.
	(10 minutes)
		• Sources about the individual's life

Plenary	• Ask students to write a biography of the individual's life (10 minutes)	

Lesson 8: Resistance

Learning objectives

- To enable students to understand that resistance can take many different forms and go beyond the use of force.
- To appreciate the dilemmas and difficulties involved with resisting the Nazis.
- To explore the extent of resistance during the Holocaust and to analyse whether or not it was successful.

	Lesson details	Materials needed
Starter	• Ask students to try and produce a definition of resistance. • Discuss what it meant to resist in the context of the Holocaust. Ask students to think of all the different ways that one might have been able to resist. (10 minutes)	
Main	• Give students a copy of the 'Resistance' worksheet. Ask them to read through the sheet and to answer the questions. (20 minutes) • Explain how the opportunities and means of resistance varied depending on location and context, e.g. ghetto, camp, etc. (5 minutes)	• 'Resistance' worksheet (p. 177)
Plenary	• Show extract from the film *Defiance* (2008). Explain the different types of resistance that are being juxtaposed in the scene. (10 minutes)	• *Defiance* (2008), extract 1.05:05–1.09:30
Homework	• Ask students to read about the Warsaw Ghetto Uprising (1943) and the Birkenau *Sonderkommando* Uprising (1944) and to evaluate the ways in which these were both successful and unsuccessful.	

Lesson 9: Perpetrators, victims, bystanders, rescuers and collaborators

Learning objectives

* To enable students to recognise the complexities associated with terms such as 'victim' and 'perpetrator' and to understand that simplistic labelling can be problematic.
* To appreciate the complexities associated with decision-making and to explain why certain choices were made.

	Lesson details	Materials needed

Starter	• Discuss with students definitions for the following terms:
	  – Victim
	  – Perpetrator
	  – Rescuer
	  – Bystander
	  – Collaborator.
	(10 minutes)	

Main	• Provide students with a copy of the 'Perpetrators, victims, bystanders, rescuers and collaborators' worksheet. Ask students to read the four examples and fill in the table. • Ask students to compare their answers with each other and to explain why they chose those terms. • Discuss and answer why it is difficult to categorise individuals with simple labels. (20 minutes)	• 'Perpetrators, victims, bystanders, rescuers and collaborators' (pp. 178–179) worksheet
Plenary	• Explain the role and function of the Judenräte, Kapos and the Sonderkommando. • Alternatively, briefly explain the story of Oskar Schindler. Discuss why the awarding of Schindler with the title of 'righteous among the nations' was seen as controversial. (15 minutes)	
Homework	• Ask students to read the extract about Churchill on the worksheet and to answer the questions.	

Lesson 10: The ending of the Holocaust

Learning objectives

- To understand the ending of the Holocaust in the context of the war.
- To explain the death marches and the attempts by the Nazis to destroy the evidence of their crimes.
- To ensure that students understand the difficulties and problems faced by survivors after the Holocaust.

	Lesson details	Materials needed

Starter	• Ask students to read the extracts written by Elie Wiesel and Primo Levi on 'The ending of the Holocaust' worksheet.
	• Discuss the following questions:
	  – What are the authors describing?
	  – Why did Germans evacuate the camps?
	  – What happened to those in the camps?
	  – What challenges did survivors face?
	(15 minutes)
		• 'The ending of the Holocaust' worksheet (p. 180)

Main	• Ask students to complete the rest of the worksheet and discuss their answers. (10 minutes) • Read the report of the 42nd Infantry Division's liberation of Dachau (available from the USHMM website). • Discuss the impact of the findings on the soldiers and on the general public of the Allied countries. (15 minutes)	• USHMM website
Plenary	• Explain how many of the survivors remained in displaced persons camps until the creation of the State of Israel in 1948. (5 minutes)	
Homework	• Ask students to listen to the testimony of a survivor on what life was like for them after the Holocaust. (See the USC Shoah Foundation YouTube Channel.)	

Lesson 11: The post-Holocaust world (optional lesson)

Learning objectives

- To learn about the fate of the leading Holocaust perpetrators.
- To consider the legacy and impact of the Holocaust on post-war society.
- To reflect upon the way that the Holocaust should be remembered and commemorated in contemporary society.

	Lesson details	Materials needed

Starter	• Discuss with students the following question:
	  – Why was it considered important to put the leading Nazis on trial?
	  (5 minutes)	

Main	• Show students 'Letter to Heinrich Himmler concerning X-ray and surgical sterilization' (item no. 119) from the Nuremberg Trials Project (http://nuremberg.law.harvard.edu/).
	• Discuss with students the following questions:
	  – What does this document prove?
	  – Why was it important to compile evidence against the Nazi perpetrators?
	  (15 minutes)
	• Give students a copy of the UN definition of genocide and explain how this emerged as a consequence of the Holocaust. Ask students whether this is a suitable definition and whether or not it has been suitably enforced.
	  (10 minutes)
		• Item 119 from the Nuremberg Trials Project
		• Article 2 of the UN Convention on the Prevention and Punishment of the Crime of Genocide

Plenary	• Ask students to work in groups to consider three ways in which society can ensure that the Holocaust is appropriately remembered. (15 minutes)	
Homework	• Give students a copy of 'The post-Holocaust world' worksheet. Ask them to complete the sheet.	• 'The post-Holocaust world' worksheet (p. 181)

LESSON PLANS FOR: THE HOLOCAUST – PREJUDICE, ETHICS AND RELIGION

Lesson 1: Prejudice and discrimination

Learning objectives

- To acquire a knowledge and understanding of key terms, such as 'prejudice', 'discrimination' and 'antisemitism'.
- To develop an understanding of some of key reasons why discrimination and prejudice exist and to see how these have manifested themselves in specific historical contexts.
- To acquire a knowledge and understanding of how the Nazis persecuted and discriminated against Jews in Germany during the 1930s.

	Lesson details	Materials needed
Starter	• Give students a copy of the worksheet 'Prejudice and discrimination'. Ask them to complete the first two definitions. Discuss their answers and provide a model answer if necessary. (10 minutes)	• 'Prejudice and discrimination' worksheet (p. 182)
Main	• Ask students to produce a spider diagram on why prejudice and discrimination might exist. Encourage specific examples to support their answers. (10 minutes) • Ask students to produce the timeline using the worksheet. (15 minutes)	
Plenary	• Explain the meaning and origin of the term 'antisemitism' and how the Nazis gave it a racial rather than a linguistic meaning. (5 minutes) • Discuss whether or not antisemitism still exists today. (5 minutes)	
Homework	• Complete the homework on the sheet by visiting the Community Security Trust website and answering the questions.	• www.thecst.org.uk

Lesson 2: Combating prejudice

Learning objectives

- To consider examples of post-war prejudice and to see the common themes and trends which exist.
- To evaluate the effectiveness of various measures that could be used to try and combat prejudice in the modern world.
- To recognise the negative effects of prejudice on an individual, group and society as a whole.

	Lesson details	Materials needed
Starter	• Ask students to come up with examples of post-war prejudice. Encourage students to go beyond racial and ethnic prejudice. • Explain two or three examples and assess the common themes. (15 minutes)	
Main	• Working in pairs, ask students to imagine that they were making the constitution for a new country. What five laws would they introduce to combat prejudice? (10 minutes) • Think about the restrictions on freedom that exist within these constitutions and discuss the advantages and disadvantages of non-legislative measures such as education and affirmative action. (10 minutes)	• 'Combating prejudice' worksheet (p. 183)
Plenary	• Ask students to complete the table on the negative effects of prejudice on individuals, groups and society as a whole. (10 minutes)	

Lesson 3: Moral dilemmas and the Holocaust

Learning objectives

- To understand the concept of a moral dilemma through the use of examples.
- To recognise that extreme situations like the Holocaust generate a number of moral dilemmas.
- To appreciate the difficulties associated with weighing up various options in a moral dilemma.

	Lesson details	Materials needed
Starter	• Give the students a contemporary moral dilemma and ask them what they would do in such a situation and why. (10 minutes)	
Main	• Ask them to define a moral dilemma and discuss the definitions. • Distribute 'Moral dilemmas and the Holocaust' worksheet and ask students to complete the paragraph. • Students should read the moral dilemma and copy and complete the table by stating the positive and negative consequences. • In pairs, students then read the four Holocaust-related dilemmas and answer the questions. (N.B.: Teachers should explain the terms 'ghetto', 'Judenrat', 'Sonderkommando', 'concentration camp' and 'death camp' before the activity to provide sufficient historical context and understanding.) (30 minutes)	• 'Moral dilemmas and the Holocaust' worksheet (pp. 184–185)
Plenary	• Pairs compare answers with other pairs: – Did both pairs decide on the same choice? – Did they justify their decisions using the same arguments? (10 minutes)	

Lesson 4: Dealing with moral dilemmas

Learning objectives

- To develop their understanding of moral dilemmas by looking at new examples.
- To recognise that philosophers and theologians have developed different and conflicting ethical theories and systems which can be used to answer moral dilemmas.
- To learn to apply some of these ethical theories to moral dilemmas.

	Lesson details	Materials needed
Starter	• Show the following two excerpts, which highlight moral dilemmas: • *The Pianist*, 43:37–44:50 • *Sophie's Choice*, 2:07:00–2:13:13. • Discuss why the decisions were made. (15 minutes)	• *The Pianist* (2002) • *Sophie's Choice* (1982)

Main	• Provide students with a contemporary moral dilemma. It may be as simple as what to do when given a present that you don't like but asked whether or not you like it. Alternatively, it could be a Holocaust-related dilemma.
	• Explain the meaning of the following terms and apply them to the above dilemma:
	  – Utilitarianism
	  – Kantian ethics
	  – Theistic ethics
	  – Virtue Theory.
	• After explaining each theory, ask students to work in groups to discuss the advantages and disadvantages of it.
	(25 minutes)	

Plenary	• Ask each group which ethical system they think is the most effective in dealing with moral dilemmas. (5 minutes)	
Homework	• Ask students to answer the question: 'Which ethical theory is the most effective and why?' Ask them to include discussion of all the theories covered during the lesson in their answer.	

Lesson 5: Applying moral theories to the Holocaust

Learning objectives

- To develop existing understandings of ethical theories and to consider how these can be applied to real life situations.
- To recognise the advantages and disadvantages of moral theories to a particular moral dilemma.
- To reflect on why different people make different choices to similar dilemmas.

	Lesson details	Materials needed
Starter	• Ask students to think about the types of factors that may affect how individuals apply moral theories to their own moral dilemmas (e.g. family considerations, conscience, religious beliefs, social pressure, etc.). (10 minutes)	

Main	• Show students once again the moral dilemmas from *The Pianist* and *Sophie's Choice*
	  – *The Pianist* 43:37–44:50
	  – *Sophie's Choice* 2:07:00–2:13:13.
	• Discuss whether the application of each moral theory would have led to the same choices as were made in *The Pianist* and *Sophie's Choice*.
	(20 minutes)
		• *The Pianist* (2002)
		• *Sophie's Choice* (1982)

Plenary	• Ask students to copy and complete the table at the end of the 'Moral dilemmas and the Holocaust' worksheet. (15 minutes)	• 'Moral dilemmas and the Holocaust' worksheet (pp. 184–185)

Lesson 6: Justice and the Holocaust

Learning objectives

- To understand the meaning of the term 'justice' and to think about how it differs from revenge.
- To consider the different responses that have existed regarding what should happen to those who perpetrated the Holocaust.
- To learn about the outcomes of those who have been captured.

	Lesson details	Materials needed
Starter	• Distribute a copy of the worksheet 'Justice and the Holocaust'. Ask students to define the terms 'justice' and 'revenge' and work in pairs to discuss and complete the table. (15 minutes)	• 'Justice and the Holocaust' worksheet (p. 186)
Main	• Discuss with students the different ways that justice could be acquired for Holocaust survivors (examples could include the arrest and execution of Nazi perpetrators; the restoration of money and possessions lost in the Holocaust; financial compensation from Germany, etc.). (10 minutes) • Explain the crimes of Adolf Eichmann, his escape to Argentina and the Mossad operation to capture him. • Show students an excerpt (32:19–37:25) from the film *The Man Who Captured Eichmann* (1996). (10 minutes)	• *The Man Who Captured Eichmann* (1996)
Plenary	• Ask students to complete the activity on the worksheet and to reflect on their own view about justice and the Holocaust. (10 minutes)	
Homework	• Research the work of the Conference on Jewish Material Claims Against Germany. How effective has it been in achieving justice for Holocaust survivors?	

Lesson 7: An introduction to forgiveness and the Holocaust

Learning objectives

* To understand the meaning of the term 'forgiveness'.
* To recognise the complexities and difficulties in deciding how forgiveness is applied and to whom, and when is the correct time to apply forgiveness.
* To consider what factors help an individual to decide whether or not to forgive and their relative importance.

	Lesson details	Materials needed
Starter	• Distribute a copy of the 'An introduction to forgiveness and the Holocaust' worksheet. • Discuss with students the meaning of the word forgiveness and provide them with a dictionary definition. (5 minutes)	• 'An introduction to forgiveness and the Holocaust' worksheet (pp. 187–188)
Main	• Ask students to work in pairs and to read through each scenario and to discuss with their partner their answers to the questions. Encourage students to challenge their partner's views if they disagree. (Students can be given a straight 25 minutes for this activity, or alternatively, given 5 minutes for each scenario with 3 minutes for a whole class discussion after each scenario). (25 minutes)	
Plenary	• Explain to students how different factors can affect our approach to forgiveness. Ask students to complete the box at the bottom of the second page of the worksheet. (15 minutes)	

Lesson 8: Forgiveness and the Holocaust

Learning objectives

- To understand the reasons why an individual might choose to forgive another and the reasons why an individual might not choose to forgive another.
- To realise that there are potential advantages and disadvantages for both the victim and the perpetrator in relation to forgiveness.
- To apply what students have learnt about forgiveness to real life scenarios and contexts from the Holocaust.
- To understand the moral dilemmas that the Holocaust generated within the context of Judaic teaching.

	Lesson details	*Materials needed*
Starter	• Distribute a copy of the 'Forgiveness and the Holocaust' worksheet. • Discuss with students some of the reasons why people might choose to forgive and why they might choose not to. Ask students to write their reasons on the worksheet. (10 minutes)	• 'Forgiveness and the Holocaust' worksheet (pp. 189–190)
Main	• Ask students to discuss with their partners the advantages and disadvantages of forgiving and to complete the box. (Encourage students to think about the immediate and long-term impact.) • Ask as many pairs as possible to share one advantage or disadvantage with the class. (15 minutes)	
Plenary	• Ask students to read the second page of the worksheet and to answer the questions. (If time permits, encourage a few students to share their responses to question 3.) (20 minutes)	
Homework	• Ask students to visit the website of 'The Forgiveness Project' and to read the four stories relating to the Rwandan Genocide.	• http://theforgivenessproject.com/stories/

Lesson 9: The Holocaust and the problem of evil

Learning objectives

- To recognise the moral, philosophical and theological problems generated by evil in the world.
- To consider how the extent and extremity of the Holocaust challenges theological assumptions about the existence and nature of God.
- To consider whether or not new responses to these challenges are needed and to assess the credibility of the answers that have been put forward to the questions regarding the problem of evil.

	Lesson details	Materials needed

Starter	• Distribute a copy of 'The Holocaust and the problem of evil' worksheet. Ask students to read the quotation by Elie Wiesel and to discuss with a partner why the Holocaust might impact on an individual's faith in the existence and nature of God.
	• Share the ideas as a class and ensure that discussion includes the questions:
	  – Why did God not stop the Holocaust?
	  – Was God unable to stop the Holocaust?
	  – Did God not want to stop the Holocaust?
	(10 minutes)
		• 'The Holocaust and the problem of evil' worksheet (pp. 191–192)

Main	• Explain to students that suffering is typically caused by human action or the natural world. Ask students to provide examples of each and to consider whether God is responsible for preventing both or either of these. Ask students what the impact of this would be (i.e. on our free will). (15 minutes)	
Plenary	• Using the second page of the worksheet, ask students to read through the theological and philosophical responses to the questions discussed earlier and to explain which of these is the most convincing and why. (20 minutes)	

Lesson 10: The churches and the Holocaust

Learning objectives

- To understand the nature and character of German Christianity and the reasons why some Nazi ideas were attractive to the churches while others were repugnant.
- To recognise that there were individuals within both the Protestant and Roman Catholic churches who supported the Nazis and that there were others who opposed them by speaking out and helping to rescue Jews during the Holocaust.
- To explore the roles of individual characters from within the churches who resisted the Nazis' antisemitic measures.

	Lesson details	Materials needed
Starter	• Explain to students that most Germans belonged to either a Protestant church (around 40 million) or the Roman Catholic Church (around 20 million). • Ask the class to describe the attitudes that they would expect the church to have towards the Nazis and why. (10 minutes)	
Main	• Distribute a copy of 'The Churches and the Holocaust' worksheet and ask students to complete the activity box. (10 minutes) • Using the web link, explain the importance of the 1933 Concordat and look at the agreements that were made. (15 minutes)	• 'The Churches and the Holocaust' worksheet (p. 193) • www.concordatwatch.eu/kb-1211.834
Plenary	• Distribute 'The Churches and the Holocaust (2)' worksheet. Ask students to read about the actions of the Nazi regime and the churches and to complete the activity. (5 minutes)	• 'The Churches and the Holocaust (2)' worksheet (p. 194)
Homework	• Ask students to complete the research activity (question 2) on 'The Churches and the Holocaust (2)' worksheet	• 'The Churches and the Holocaust (2)' worksheet (p. 194)

LESSON PLANS FOR: THE HOLOCAUST AND OTHER GENOCIDES

Lesson 1: Defining the Holocaust

Learning objectives

*   To enable students to understand why definitions matter and to appreciate that 'Holocaust' has been a difficult and contentious word to define.
*   To consider when the Holocaust began and when it ended.
*   To reflect on whether 'the Holocaust' should be used to define only Jewish victims of Nazism or also include a range of other groups.

	Lesson details	Materials needed
Starter	• Give students a copy of the 'Defining the Holocaust' worksheet and ask them to write a definition of the Holocaust. (5 minutes)	• 'Defining the Holocaust' worksheet (pp. 195–196)
Main	• Ask students to discuss with their partner why they think the definition of the Holocaust matters. • Ask each pair to feedback ideas and discuss together. (10 minutes) • Ask students to read out their definitions and ask students if they can see any differences. (10 minutes) • Discuss the events listed in the box on the worksheet and ask students to put a tick in the right hand column if their definition of the Holocaust includes that event. (15 minutes)	
Plenary	• Ask students whether or not they would now like to change their definition and why or why not. (5 minutes)	
Homework	• Complete the sentences and justify their definitions on the second page of the worksheet.	

Lesson 2: Was the Holocaust unique?

Learning objectives

- To examine the meaning of the term 'unique' in specific reference to historical events and the Holocaust in particular.
- To recognise the range of arguments that have been put forward by both sides regarding the Holocaust's uniqueness.
- To consider which events (if any) can legitimately be compared (and contrasted) with the Holocaust.

	Lesson details	Materials needed
Starter	• Ask students to define what is meant by the term unique and then introduce them to dictionary definitions. • Discuss what uniqueness means with regards to the Holocaust (i.e. can it legitimately and meaningfully be compared with other historical or contemporary events?). (10 minutes)	• Dictionary definitions of 'unique'
Main	• Distribute copies of the 'Was the Holocaust unique?' worksheet and ask students to answer the questions. (15 minutes) • Show students news reports on PETA's 'Holocaust on the Plate' campaign and Pope John Paul II's comparison of abortion to the Holocaust. • Discuss with students why the Holocaust was chosen as a point of comparison and whether such comparisons are problematic. (15 minutes)	• 'Was the Holocaust unique?' worksheet (p. 197) • News reports of PETA's 'Holocaust on the Plate' campaign and the Pope's comparison of abortion to the Holocaust
Plenary	• Discuss what (if any) can be legitimately and meaningfully compared with the Holocaust. Consider the difference between appropriate and inappropriate comparisons. (5 minutes)	

Lesson 3: What is genocide?

Learning objectives

*   To understand the meaning of the word 'genocide' and consider its origins within the context of the Holocaust.
*   To reflect upon alternative definitions and whether or not they are more effective than the UN definition.
*   To enable students to think about the continuation of genocide in the post-Holocaust world.

	Lesson details	*Materials needed*
Starter	• Ask students if they know the meaning of any of the following words and then explain their etymology: – Regicide – Homicide – Genocide. (5 minutes)	
Main	• Watch 'The Genocide Word by Raphael Lemkin' on YouTube. • Give students a copy of the 'What is genocide?' worksheet and discuss with them the strengths and weaknesses of the UN definition. (10 minutes) • Ask students to read the alternative definitions and answer the two questions. (10 minutes) • Split the class into groups and assign each group one of the following events: – The Stalinist purges (USSR, 1934–41) – The famines in China (1958–63) – The Cultural Revolution (China, 1966) – The Khmer Rouge (Cambodia, 1975–79) – The anti-Sikh riots (India 1984) – Srebrenica (Bosnia-Herzegovina, 1995). Ask students to research the event and present a brief overview of it and state whether or not it would be classified as genocide under each of the various definitions. (20 minutes plus homework)	• 'What is genocide?' worksheet (pp. 198–199)

Lesson 4: Assessing genocide

Learning objectives

- To understand the meaning of the word 'genocide' and consider its origins within the context of the Holocaust.
- To reflect upon alternative definitions and whether or not they are more effective than the UN definition.
- To enable students to think about the continuation of genocide in the post-Holocaust world.

	Lesson details	Materials needed
Starter	• Distribute the 'Assessing genocide' worksheet and ask students to also have out in front of them the various definitions of genocide from the previous lesson. Explain that every group will give a presentation on an event and that they are to consider whether or not the event qualifies as genocide under each of the definitions. (5 minutes)	• 'What is genocide?' and 'Assessing genocide' worksheets (pp. 198–200)
Main	• Ask each group to make their presentation. After each presentation, discuss with the students whether or not the event that they have just learned about should be classified as genocide under each of the definitions. (30 minutes)	• 'What is genocide?' worksheet (pp. 198–199)
Plenary	• Ask students why certain groups may want their suffering to be classified as 'genocide'. • Discuss with students why genocide continues to exist today and what measures might be taken to prevent it. (10 minutes)	

Lesson 5: Comparative genocide – background to the Holocaust and the Rwandan Genocide

Learning objectives

- To demonstrate that despite the post-war rhetoric of 'never again', genocide has taken place since the Holocaust.
- To consider the history and context of the Holocaust and the genocide in Rwanda.
- To examine the similarities and differences that exist between these two historical events.

	Lesson details	Materials needed
Starter	• Explore students' preconceptions and existing ideas by asking them to summarise the Holocaust and to write anything they know about the Rwandan Genocide or history of Rwanda. • Encourage students to share their ideas and ask students to point out Rwanda on a map. (10 minutes) • Provide a brief synopsis of the Rwandan Genocide. (10 minutes)	• World map
Main	• Distribute the boxes from the worksheets (these should already have been cut up and placed in a random order). • Working in pairs or threes, ask students to match up corresponding boxes regarding the background to and context of the Holocaust. • Ensure students have matched the boxes correctly and discuss any issues raised by students. (10 minutes)	• 'Comparative genocide: the background to the Holocaust and the Rwandan Genocide' (A) and (B) worksheets (pp. 201–202)
Plenary	• Discuss the key similarities and differences and compile a table. (10 minutes)	

Lesson 6: Comparative genocide – the Holocaust and the Rwandan Genocide

Learning objectives

- To show the importance of propaganda in shaping attitudes and prejudice towards Jews and Tutsis in Germany and Rwanda respectively.
- To explain the nature of the killings and the methods and motives of those who perpetrated them.
- To help students understand the experiences of the victims and the extent of the suffering.
- To reflect upon the importance of post-genocide justice and the challenge that this posed in the aftermath of the Holocaust and the Rwandan Genocide.

	Lesson details	Materials needed
Starter	• Provide students with a copy of the worksheet and ask students to answer the first two questions. (10 minutes)	• 'Comparative genocide: the Holocaust and the Rwandan Genocide' worksheet (p. 203)
Main	• Watch excerpt 2, 'In the face of evil', and excerpt 3, 'Heroes and bystanders' from the PBS documentary *Ghosts of Rwanda* (www.pbs.org/wgbh/pages/frontline/shows/ghosts/video). (30 minutes)	• *Ghosts of Rwanda* documentary
Plenary	• Discuss the meaning of justice and the difficulties associated with achieving it. (5 minutes)	
Homework	• Ask students to write down the problems that are faced by survivors of the Rwandan Genocide. • Ask students to research the following: – The International Criminal Tribunal for Rwanda – The *Gacaca* courts – Survivors' Fund.	

Chapter 15

Worksheets

The following worksheets correspond with the schemes of work and the lesson plans from the previous two chapters. They are arranged for teaching the Holocaust in history, religious education and citizenship, although some of the worksheets might be used interchangeably between the subject areas.

JEWS, JEWISH IDENTITY, HISTORY, RELIGION AND CULTURE

What makes a person Jewish?

What is happening in the photograph? What can you learn about pre-war Jewish life?

Photograph 1	
Photograph 2	
Photograph 3	
Photograph 4	
Photograph 5	
Photograph 6	
Photograph 7	
Photograph 8	

What was life like for most Jews living in Europe before the war?

NAZI ATTITUDES AND ACTIONS TOWARDS JEWS (1933–39)

Try to define the following terms:

Discrimination

Persecution

Prejudice

Let the magistrates burn their synagogues and let whatever escapes be covered with sand and mud. Let them be forced to work, and if this avails nothing, we will be compelled to expel them like dogs.

Martin Luther (1543), Concerning the Jews and Their Lies

The Jews are our misfortune.

Heinrich von Treitschke (1881), A Word about Our Jews

Look at the photograph of the Jewish shop in Germany in April 1933 and discuss the following questions:

1   What is the word *Jude* written on the building? What does it mean?
2   Why has a Star of David (Jewish symbol) been painted on the building?
3   Why are Nazi men in brown shirts standing outside?
4   How is this going to make Jewish shop owners feel?
5   How will this affect business?

Look at the photograph of the passports in Germany in 1939 and discuss the following questions:

1   How can you tell that these passports belong to Jews?
2   Why do you think that the Nazis wanted Jews to stand out?
3   What do you notice about the middle name on the passport?
4   Who normally gives an individual their name?
5   Why are names important?

Look at the photograph of the Star of David and discuss the following questions:

1   What is the Star of David?
2   Why do you think the Nazis made Jews wear the Star of David on their clothes?
3   What do you notice about this style of font?
4   Why do you think they used this style?
5   Why did the Nazis want the Jews to stand out?

JEWISH EMIGRATION

Background: David and Eva are Jewish. Their families have lived in Germany for as far as they can trace back. They enjoy living in Berlin with its theatres, shops and cinemas. David and Eva have two children who are both at school a few blocks away from their house. David enjoys working as a dentist in Berlin. David and Eva have never left Germany before and all their friends and family live in Germany.

Year	Event	Should David and Eva leave Germany?	Why? / Why not?
1933			
1934			
1935			
1936			
1937			
1938			
1939			

JEWISH EMIGRATION
(TEACHER SHEET)

Year	Event
1933	Hitler becomes chancellor of Germany. One-day boycott of Jewish shops and business. Jews barred from holding jobs in the civil service or universities. Public burning of Jewish books.
1934	Jews barred from national health insurance. Jews are banned from the German Labour Front. Jews are prohibited from getting legal qualifications.
1935	Jews no longer allowed to serve in the German armed forces. Nuremberg Laws: Jews no longer considered German citizens; Jews could not marry 'Aryans'; Jews could not fly a German flag. Jewish performers and artists forced to join Jewish cultural unions.
1936	Berlin Olympics: Brief period of respite for the Jews in Germany. Doctors banned from practising medicine in German institutions.
1937	Jews banned from various professional occupations including dentistry, accountancy and the teaching of German children. Jews are no longer allowed child allowances or tax reductions.
1938	Jews forced to register all property held within Germany. International conference held in Evian, France to discuss the plight of Jewish refugees. All Jewish passports are marked with the letter 'J'. *Kristallnacht*: hundreds of synagogues burnt and Jewish businesses looted. Jewish pupils expelled from German schools.
1939	Jews are forced to hand over all gold and silver items. Jews lose their rights as tenants. Jews are forbidden to be outdoors after 8 p.m. in winter and 9 p.m. in summer.

THE POLISH GHETTOS

What did the Nazis do to mark Jews? Why did they do this?	Were Jews allowed to leave the ghettos? What stopped them from leaving?
How did Jews spend their time throughout the days?	How did Jews keep up their religious practices in the ghetto?
Why were children used in smuggling?	Who was Janusz Korczak and what did he do?

WAR IN THE EAST AND THE EVOLUTION OF THE 'FINAL SOLUTION'

> The Wannsee Conference was a meeting of senior Nazi officials (although neither Hitler nor Himmler was present) where the details of the 'Final Solution' were discussed. Extracts from the minutes of the meeting are below.

TOP SECRET

30 copies

Discussion about the final solution of the Jewish question which took place in Berlin, 20th January 1942:

… The Chief of the Security Police and the SD then gave a short report of the struggle which has been carried on thus far against this enemy, the essential points being the following:

(a) the expulsion of the Jews from every sphere of life of the German people,
(b) the expulsion of the Jews from the living space of the German people.

In carrying out these efforts, an increased and planned acceleration of the emigration of the Jews from Reich territory was started, as the only possible present solution.

Approximately 11 million Jews will be involved in the final solution of the European Jewish question, distributed as follows among the individual countries:

A.	B.
Germany proper 131,800	Bulgaria 48,000
Austria 43,700	England 330,000
Eastern territories 420,000	Finland 2,300
General Government 2,284,000	Ireland 4,000
Bialystok 400,000	Italy including Sardinia 58,000
Protectorate Bohemia and Moravia 74,200	Albania 200
Estonia – free of Jews	Croatia 40,000
Latvia 3,500	Portugal 3,000
Lithuania 34,000	Rumania including Bessarabia 342,000
Belgium 43,000	Sweden 8,000
Denmark 5,600	Switzerland 18,000
France / occupied territory 165,000	Serbia 10,000
unoccupied territory 700,000	Slovakia 88,000
Greece 69,600	Spain 6,000
Netherlands 160,800	Turkey (European portion) 55,500
Norway 1,300	Hungary 742,800
	USSR 5,000,000
	Ukraine 2,994,684
	White Russia
	excluding Bialystok 446,484

Under proper guidance, in the course of the final solution the Jews are to be allocated for appropriate labour in the East. Able-bodied Jews, separated according to sex, will be taken in large work columns to these areas for work on roads, in the course of which action doubtless a large portion will be eliminated by natural causes.

The possible final remnant will, since it will undoubtedly consist of the most resistant portion, have to be treated accordingly, because it is the product of natural selection and would, if released, act as the seed of a new Jewish revival.

QUESTIONS

1   Why did the Nazis use the term 'Final Solution' and what did it mean?

2   What do you think the Nazis intended to do with the Jews that were listed in the table?

3   Why does it say that Estonia was 'free of Jews'?

THE CAMP SYSTEM

Camp	Location	Date of operation	Type of camp	Additional details
Treblinka				
Theresienstadt				
Westerbork				
Mauthausen				
Ravensbrück				
Chełmno				

RESISTANCE

In no place did Jews resist the slaughter. They went passively to death and they did it, so that the remnants of the people would be left to live, because every Jew knew that lifting a hand against a German would endanger his brothers from a different town or maybe from a different country.

Not to act, not to lift a hand against Germans, has since then become the quiet, passive heroism of the common Jew.

Ringelblum notes, 17 June 1942: Joseph Kermish, 'Emmanuel Ringelblum's Notes, Hitherto Unpublished', Yad Vashem Studies, VII, Jerusalem 1968, pp. 178–80.

At Kedainiai, on August 28, an *Einsatzkommando* unit drove more than two thousand Jews, among them 710 men, 767 women and 599 children, into a ditch. Suddenly, a Jewish butcher jumped up, seized one of the German soldiers, dragged him into the ditch, and sank his teeth into the German's throat with a fatal bite. All two thousand Jews, including the butcher were then shot.

Martin Gilbert (1986) The Holocaust: A Jewish Tragedy, p. 184.

Problems associated with resisting the Nazis:

* Joining a partisan group would mean abandoning one's family.
* It could lead to the Nazis conducting reprisal killings to act as a deterrent.
* It would mean defying the authority of the *Judenrat* and Jewish police in the ghetto.
* The chances of success were minimal.
* It was difficult to acquire weapons and Jews were untrained and inexperienced in using them.

Questions

Making reference to the sources above, explain why Jewish resistance was often unsuccessful.

Why was the decision of whether or not to resist a very complex one?

PERPETRATORS, VICTIMS, BYSTANDERS, RESCUERS AND COLLABORATORS

Produce a definition for the following terms:

Victim

Perpetrator

Rescuer

Bystander

Collaborator

Heinrich is a member of the Nazi Party and a successful businessman. In 1936 he informed the authorities that his business rival was trading with Jewish suppliers and opposed the removal of Jews from German public life. During the war, Heinrich moves to Nazi-occupied Poland and employs lots of Jews in his factories because they are cheap labour. By doing so, his workers avoid the gas chambers. As Heinrich begins to understand what the Nazis are doing to Jews he begins to become disillusioned with the Nazis and decides to employ more Jews than he needs.

Martin was a Nazi official who became a member of the Nazi Party in order to help his career. Martin provided falsified documents to two Jewish families who were his wife's friends. During the war, Martin helped to organise the ordering of supplies to Auschwitz-Birkenau.

Joseph worked as a train driver and had not voted for the Nazis. Joseph did not like the antisemitic measures that were taking place. During 1942, Joseph drove the trains from the Warsaw ghetto to Treblinka, transporting thousands of Jews to their deaths. Joseph did not ask what was happening to the Jews upon their arrival although he strongly suspected that they were being killed. After the war he regretted his involvement in the Holocaust and committed suicide.

Leib was a Jewish man who lived in Poland when the Nazis invaded in 1939. He was forced into the ghettos where he volunteered to work as a policeman, enforcing order and discipline. In 1941 he heard about a planned revolt in the ghetto and offered to give the Nazis the names of the ringleaders in exchange for the safety of his family. The ringleaders were shot and Leib and his family were soon deported to Belzec death camp.

Read the four extracts and tick the boxes which you think describe each character. (You may tick more than one box for each individual.)

	Victim	Perpetrator	Rescuer	Bystander	Collaborator
Heinrich					
Martin					
Joseph					
Leib					

Explain why it is often difficult to describe individuals using only one term.

The British could have done nothing, even if they had wanted to, to save the European Jews from annihilation, but clearly they didn't want to. They could have done important things on the margin: they could have permitted more Jews to escape from the Balkans to Palestine – which they refused to do ... The conclusion, at any rate, is that the Allies did not really care; and even if they cared, it is doubtful whether large numbers of Jews could have been saved.

Y. Bauer (2001) Re-Thinking the Holocaust (New Haven: Yale University Press), pp. 217–22.

Questions

1   What sort of things might the Allies have done to have stopped the Holocaust or to have at least slowed down the rate of killing?

2   What arguments might they have put forward for their inaction?

3   What was 'Operation Anthropoid'? Was it successful?

THE ENDING OF THE HOLOCAUST

18 January. During the night of the evacuation the camp-kitchens continued to function, and on the following morning the last distribution of soup took place in the hospital ... Outside it must have been at least 5 degrees Fahrenheit below zero; most of the patients had only a shirt and some of them not even that.

... The Germans were no longer there. The towers were empty.

19 January ... We got up at dawn ... I felt ill and helpless, I was cold and afraid.

Primo Levi, Survival in Auschwitz (New York: Touchstone), pp. 157–58.

The battle did not last long. Toward noon everything was quiet again. The SS had fled and the resistance had taken charge of the running of the camp. At about six o'clock in the evening, the first American tank stood at the gates of Buchenwald.

Our first act as free men was to throw ourselves on to the provisions. We thought only of that. Not of revenge, not of our families. Nothing but bread. And even when we were no longer hungry, there was still no one who thought of revenge.

Elie Wiesel, Night (London: Penguin), pp. 125–26.

When the camps were liberated, many survivors were stuck in a foreign country, hundreds or thousands of miles from their country of origin. In many instances, their entire family had been murdered by the Nazis. They themselves were close to death; weak, often ill and vulnerable to various diseases.

Write down some of the questions that a survivor in this situation might be thinking.

1 ....

2 ....

3 ....

4 ....

5 ....

THE POST-HOLOCAUST WORLD

Match the person with their role within the Third Reich and their post-war fate. Copy and complete the following table:

Person	Role	Post-war fate

ADOLF HITLER

COMMITTED SUICIDE IN A BUNKER IN BERLIN ON APRIL 30, 1945

HERMANN GOERING

FLED TO ARGENTINA WHERE HE WAS SECRETLY ARRESTED BY ISRAELI AGENTS. HE WAS THEN PUT ON TRIAL IN JERUSALEM, FOUND GUILTY AND EXECUTED IN 1962.

JOSEPH GOEBBELS

SENTENCED TO DEATH AT THE NUREMBERG TRIALS AND HANGED IN OCTOBER 1946.

REICHSMARSCHALL AND LEADER OF THE GERMAN AIR FORCE

ADOLF EICHMANN

LEADER OF NAZI GERMANY

SENTENCED TO DEATH AT THE NUREMBERG TRIALS. COMMITTED SUICIDE THE NIGHT BEFORE HE WAS DUE TO BE HANGED.

MINISTER FOR PROPAGANDA

GOVERNOR-GENERAL OF OCCUPIED POLAND'S 'GENERAL GOVERNMENT'

HANS FRANK

CAPTURED BY THE ALLIES IN MAY 1945 AND COMMITTED SUICIDE

SENTENCED TO DEATH IN ABSENTIA AT NUREMBERG. CLAIMS ABOUT HIS DEATH AND BODY CONTINUE TO BE DISPUTED.

REICHSFUEHRER-SS

COMMITTED SUICIDE ON MAY 1, 1945

MAJOR ORGANISER OF THE HOLOCAUST

MARTIN BORMANN

HEINRICH HIMMLER

HITLER'S SECRETARY

PREJUDICE AND DISCRIMINATION

Prejudice is ....

....

Discrimination is ....

....

Draw a timeline from 1933 to 1939, including the events below.

September 15, 1935 Nuremberg Laws: Jews barred from German citizenship	**April 1, 1933** Boycott of Jewish shops and businesses	**September 1, 1939** Curfew for Jews in Germany; they must not be out after 8.00 p.m.
January 30, 1933 Adolf Hitler appointed chancellor of Germany	**October 5, 1938** All Jewish passports declared invalid unless stamped with the letter 'J'	**November 9, 1938** *Kristallnacht*: Jewish synagogues and homes smashed; ninety-one Jews killed
November 8, 1937 Antisemitic museum exhibition opens in Munich	**October 4, 1933** The Editors Law: prevents Jews from working in journalism	**May 10, 1934** Public burning of books by Jewish and communist authors

Homework

Go to the website of the Community Security Trust (www.thecst.org.uk). Download the latest Antisemitic Incidents Report and Antisemitic Discourse Report.

Does antisemitism still exist in the UK today? What evidence do you have to support your answer?

COMBATING PREJUDICE

Imagine you could set up a new country from scratch. What five laws would you pass to minimise prejudice?

1   ....

2   ....

3   ....

4   ....

5   ....

Instead of restricting personal freedoms and liberties, what other ways could be introduced to combat prejudice?

1   ....

2   ....

3   ....

4   ....

5   ....

Describe some of the effects of prejudice on the following:

The victim of prejudice	
The perpetrator of prejudice	
The group being prejudiced	
Society as a whole	

MORAL DILEMMAS AND THE HOLOCAUST

Complete the paragraph using the words below.

There are sometimes situations when we are _____ to make a choice between _____ options. A moral dilemma is when whatever choice we make, the results will have negative _____ that are likely to cause someone to _____ or result in something happening that we do not _____.

SUFFER	CONSEQUENCES	DESIRE	FORCED	CONFLICTING

Read the dilemma below and then copy and complete the table below:

A woman has no money to buy food and her young child is extremely hungry. As they walk past the market stall she steals some fruit. The owner of the stall catches the woman and threatens to take her to the police station. The woman explains her desperate situation and asks the owner of the stall to forgive her and let her go.

	Positive consequences	Negative consequences
Take the woman to the police station		
Let the woman go		

Look at the four moral dilemmas which occurred in the Holocaust and answer the following questions:

- What are the two possible choices in this dilemma?

- What are the positives consequences of each choice?

- What are the negative consequences of each choice?

- What choice would you make? (Give two reasons).

- Someone else may make the other choice. Explain what else you might need to know about the individual concerned before understanding the reason for their choice.

Dilemma 1:	Dilemma 2:
A rabbi living in the Krakow ghetto is encouraged by the Jewish community to join the *Judenrat* (Jewish Council) which was responsible for carrying out Nazi orders in the ghettos. This often included lists for deportation to the death camps.	A Jewish prisoner in Birkenau is told to join the *Sonderkommando* (a small group of inmates who cremated the bodies of those who had died in the gas chambers). By agreeing, he is likely to stay alive for a few more months.

Dilemma 3:	Dilemma 4:
An inmate at Mauthausen concentration camp sees a fellow prisoner who is ill and soon to die. If he steals his fellow-inmate's bread rations he is more likely to survive.	A Jewish prisoner in Auschwitz has the opportunity to join a group of other inmates in carrying out an attempt to escape. The prisoner knows that if he stays he will die but that if he escapes, ten inmates will be killed as a punishment and deterrent.

Copy and complete the table below, explaining which outcome each moral philosophy supports and why.

	Intentions	Consequences	God	Virtue
Dilemma 1				
Dilemma 2				
Dilemma 3				
Dilemma 4				

JUSTICE AND THE HOLOCAUST

Justice is ....

....

Revenge is ....

....

What are the similarities and differences between justice and revenge?

Similarities	Differences

Underneath each quotation explain whether or not you agree with it and why/why not?

'An eye for an eye makes the whole world blind.'
Mahatma Gandhi

'True peace is not merely the absence of tension: it is the presence of justice.'
Martin Luther King Jr

AN INTRODUCTION TO FORGIVENESS AND THE HOLOCAUST

Forgiveness is ....

....

Look at the following scenarios and discuss with your partner the questions underneath them.

Scenario 1

> You are playing a game of tennis with a friend. In the middle of the match they lose a crucial
> point and in anger they hit the tennis ball as hard as they can, which accidentally hits you on the
> head. They immediately apologise.

Do you forgive your friend? Why/why not?

If yes, would you forgive them if they had hit the tennis ball at you on purpose but then apologised?

If yes, would you forgive them if they had hit the tennis ball at you on purpose and not apologised?

Scenario 2

> You are cycling along a road when a car knocks you off, leading to a broken wrist and mild
> concussion. The driver stops and is arrested by the police for driving under the influence of
> alcohol. He is taken to court and found guilty. The driver admits his guilt and asks for your
> forgiveness.

Do you forgive the driver? Why?/Why not?

If yes, would you still forgive him if he had driven off after the event?

If yes, would you still forgive him if he had driven off, denied the event and refused to apologise?

Would you be able to forgive the driver if he had stopped, admitted his guilt and apologised if you were the parent of the cyclist and if the cyclist had been killed by the accident?

Scenario 3

> You are sitting in a German court room in the 1960s listening to a court case. The defendant is
> found guilty of being a guard at Auschwitz who helped to carry out the Holocaust. The
> defendant shows no emotion and is not sorry. Your parents and grandparents were all
> murdered in Auschwitz.

Do you forgive the guard? Why?/Why not?

Would your response be different if the guard confessed his crimes and asked for forgiveness?

Would your response be different if you were not Jewish and if you and your family had no connection to the Holocaust?

Is it your place to forgive on behalf of the dead?

What are the problems with doing so?

Look at your answers to the questions that you gave for the three scenarios. How did the following factors affect your approach to forgiveness?

Your relationship with the person who wronged you:

The seriousness of the action committed:

The intention of the person who committed the action:

The consequences of the action committed:

The reaction of the person who has committed the wrong:

FORGIVENESS AND THE HOLOCAUST

Someone may decide to forgive another person because:

1   ....

2   ....

3   ....

4   ....

Someone may decide not to forgive another person because:

1   ....

2   ....

3   ....

4   ....

Complete the table below.

	Advantages	Disadvantages
Victim		
Perpetrator		

O Lord, remember not only the men and women of good will, but also those of ill will. But do not remember all of the suffering they have inflicted upon us.

Instead, remember the fruits we have borne because of this suffering – our fellowship, our loyalty to one another, our humility, our courage, our generosity, the greatness of heart that has grown from this trouble.

When our persecutors come to be judged by you, let all of these fruits that we have borne be their forgiveness.

Found in the clothing of a dead child at Ravensbrück concentration camp

---

In the book *The Sunflower*, Simon Wiesenthal tells the story of when he was at Lemberg concentration camp in 1943. He was summoned to the bedside of a dying solider who wanted forgiveness from a Jew for the crimes he had committed. The soldier tells Wiesenthal how he had murdered 300 Jews in a house by setting it on fire and shooting them as they jumped out of the burning building. The soldier asked Wiesenthal for forgiveness. Wiesenthal left the room without saying a word to the soldier.

Questions

1   Which of the two responses do you find the most surprising? Explain your answer.

2   Why do you think that Simon Wiesenthal responded in the way that he did?

3   Do you think that Simon Wiesenthal made the correct response? Explain your answer.

4   Read the quotation below from the *Mishneh Torah*.

   (a) Did Simon Wiesenthal disobey this instruction or not?

   (b) Can one forgive on behalf of the dead?

It is forbidden to be obdurate and not allow yourself to be appeased. On the contrary, one should be easily pacified and find it difficult to become angry. When asked by an offender for forgiveness, one should forgive with a sincere mind and a willing spirit ... forgiveness is natural to the seed of Israel.

Mishneh Torah, Teshuvah 2:10

THE HOLOCAUST AND THE PROBLEM OF EVIL

> Never shall I forget that night, the first night in camp, that turned my life into one long night seven times sealed.
>
> Never shall I forget that smoke.
>
> Never shall I forget the small faces of the children whose bodies I saw transformed into smoke under a silent sky.
>
> Never shall I forget those flames that consumed my faith forever.
>
> Never shall I forget the nocturnal silence that deprived me for all eternity of the desire to live.
>
> Never shall I forget those moments that murdered my God and my soul and turned my dreams to ashes.
>
> Never shall I forget those things, even were I condemned to live as long as God Himself.
>
> Never.
>
> *Elie Wiesel (1958) 'Night'*

Why might the Holocaust impact on an individual's beliefs in the existence and nature of God?

Most suffering is caused by either human action or the natural world. Give examples of each in the boxes below.

Examples of suffering caused by human action	Examples of suffering caused by the natural world

Read the responses that theologians and philosophers have put forward to the problem of evil and explain whether or not you agree.

Response	Do you agree?
The Holocaust was not a unique event and does not need a unique answer. The problem of evil has always existed and continues to exist. The extent of the Holocaust was different but not the ideas and motives behind it.	
The Holocaust, like the problem of evil, is a consequence of sin and wickedness in the world, for which God cannot be blamed.	
The Holocaust and other genocides are the results of God giving us free will. If God were to intervene in the Holocaust then he would deprive humanity of free will and we would act like robots.	
The blame for the Holocaust should not rest on God who is holy. Instead, it was humans who invented and carried out the Holocaust and thus it is humanity who should receive the blame.	
God's ways are perfect and sovereign. God understands the workings of the whole universe throughout the entirety of history. We are limited and finite in our understanding and must thus trust in God through the good times and the hard times.	
The Holocaust was part of God's divine and sovereign plan to achieve a bigger purpose, e.g. to punish the Jews for their sins; to punish secular Zionists for trying to establish the land of Israel before the Messianic age; in order to bring about the establishment of the land of Israel, etc.	

THE CHURCHES AND THE HOLOCAUST

The Nazis opposed the liberal attitudes that existed in Germany in the 1920s

Antisemitism had often emerged from the Christian tradition as Jews were accused of killing Christ

The Nazis wanted to Nazify Christianity by putting swastikas in the churches

The Nazis wanted a strong Germany and were nationalistic

The Nazis opposed communism. Communism was an atheistic ideology and the communist government in the USSR had attacked the churches

The Nazis were antisemitic and rejected the Jewishness of the Christian Bible

Christians believed in the sanctity of life and the equality of all people before God

Article 4 of the 1920 Nazi Party Platform stated that it upheld 'the point of view of a positive Christianity'

Some leaders within the Nazi regime were hostile to Christianity, for example Alfred Rosenberg

Activity

Read the boxes above.

Put an 'S' in the box if it explains why a German Christian might support the Nazis and an 'O' if it explains why a German Christian might oppose the Nazis.

Discuss with your partner which reason might be the most important one in influencing a German Christian's attitude towards the Nazis and why.

THE CHURCHES AND THE HOLOCAUST (2)

The actions of the Nazi regime

The actions of the church

1933: The Nazi regime agrees to maintain the freedom of the Roman Catholic Church and the protection of its organisations and societies.

1933: The Catholic Centre Party signs a concordat (agreement) with Nazi Germany agreeing not to oppose Nazi policies.

1936: Establishing of German Reich Church. The swastika replaces the cross as its symbol.

1934: Creation of the 'Confessing Church' – a Protestant church which opposed Nazi influence.

1936–9: Parents pressured to remove their children from Catholic schools and attend Nazi-approved schools.

1937: Pope Pius XI writes 'With burning anxiety' a public statement criticising Nazi policies, which is to be read from all Catholic pulpits.

1937: Christmas carols and nativity plays are banned from schools.

1938: Priests banned from teaching religious classes in schools.

1941: Cardinal Count von Galen publicly opposes the Nazi policy of 'euthanasia'.

Activity

1   Briefly explain the relationship between the Nazis' actions and the response of the church.

2   Research the following individuals and explain who they were and how they opposed the Nazi regime:

- Martin Niemöller

- Dietrich Bonhoeffer

- Cardinal Count von Galen

- Maximilian Kolbe

DEFINING THE HOLOCAUST

Try to define the Holocaust, giving a date when it started and finished, as well as stating which victim groups it includes.

Place a tick or a cross in the right hand column if your definition includes the following events.

The boycott of Jewish shops and business	1 April 1933	
First concentration camp opened	22 March 1933	
Introduction of compulsory sterilisation	14 July 1933	
Nuremberg Laws remove Jews from being citizens of Germany	15 September 1935	
Arrest and forcible relocation of Roma from Greater Berlin	16 July 1936	
Kristallnacht – synagogues and Jewish properties destroyed. Over ninety Jewish deaths with tens of thousands arrested and sent to concentration camps	9–10 November 1938	
Jewish children expelled from schools	15 November 1938	
Start of 'Euthanasia' programme which murders those judged 'incurably sick'	1 September 1939	
Warsaw ghetto sealed off	15 November 1940	
First death camp opened at Chelmno	8 December 1941	
British prisoners of war die in the death march from Auschwitz	January 1945	
Jewish inmates die of typhus and other diseases in the camps after liberation	January–April 1945	

Complete the following sentences:

a. I think the Holocaust began in _____ because ...

b. I think the Holocaust ended in _____ because ...

c. I think the Holocaust should include all Nazi discrimination and persecution because ...

Or

I think the Holocaust should only include deaths caused by the Nazis because ...

d. I think the Holocaust should only refer to the experiences of Jews because ...

Or

I think the Holocaust should refer to all victims' experiences because ...

WAS THE HOLOCAUST UNIQUE?

Comparing the Holocaust to other events lets Germany off the hook by saying that their actions were no different to those of other countries throughout history.

The Holocaust was driven by ideological goals, which were often at the expense of practical alternatives. This has not occurred in any other event.

As a proportion of their population, the Roma probably suffered as much as the Jews during the war.

The destruction of the Tutsis in Rwanda was the state policy of the new 'government'.

The Nazis wanted to destroy all Jews – not just those within a confined geographical location.

The speed of killing in the Rwandan Genocide was faster and more intense than the Holocaust.

The Holocaust was mass murder on an industrial scale. It was systematic and without exception.

The Holocaust was the only time in history when a state sought to murder every man, woman and child of a specific group.

Even though the term did not exist before the Holocaust, genocides have occurred both before and since the Second World War.

Questions

Which of the arguments support the idea that the Holocaust was unique and which oppose it?

Which set of arguments do you find the most convincing? Explain your answer.

WHAT IS GENOCIDE?

Definition of genocide

Any of the following acts committed with intent to destroy, in whole or in part, a national, ethnical, racial or religious group, as such:

(a) Killing members of the group;
(b) Causing serious bodily or mental harm to members of the group;
(c) Deliberately inflicting on the group conditions of life calculated to bring about its physical destruction in whole or in part;
(d) Imposing measures intent to prevent births within the group;
(e) Forcibly transferring children of the group to another group.

Convention on the Prevention and Punishment of the Crime of Genocide (1948)

What are the strengths of this definition?	What are the weaknesses of this definition?
(Think about the groups that it protects and the breadth of the definition.)	(Think about what groups are excluded and whether you feel all these things should be classified as genocide.)

The crime of genocide should be recognized therein as a conspiracy to exterminate national, religious or racial groups. The overt acts of such a conspiracy may consist of attacks against life, liberty or property of members of such groups merely because of their affiliation with such groups.

Raphael Lemkin (1946)

Genocide, American Scholar, Vol. 15, No. 2, (April 1946) pp. 227–230.

Genocide is a form of one-sided mass killing in which a state or other authority intends to destroy a group, as that group and membership in it are defined by the perpetrator.

Frank Chalk and Kurt Jonassohn(1990)

The History and Sociology of Genocide: Analyses and Case Studies, New Haven: Yale University Press, 1990, p.35.

Genocide in the generic sense means the mass killing of substantial numbers of human beings, when not in the course of military action against the military forces of an avowed enemy, under conditions of the essential defencelessness of the victim.

Israel Charny (1997)

'A Proposed Definitional Matrix for Crimes of Genocide' in Andreopoulos, G. *Genocide: Conceptual and Historical Dimensions,* Philadelphia: University of Pennsylvania Press, 1997) pp. 76–77, p. 76.

Genocide is a form of violent social conflict or war, between armed power organizations that aim to destroy civilian social groups and those groups and other actors who resist this destruction. Genocidal action is action in which armed power organizations treat civilian social groups as enemies and aim to destroy their real or putative social power, by means of killing, violence and coercion against individuals whom they regard as members of the groups

Martin Shaw (2007)

What is Genocide? Cambridge: Polity Press, 2007, p.154.

Questions

1. In what ways do these definitions differ from the United Nations definition of 1948?
2. Why have scholars felt it necessary to try and re-define the term 'genocide'?

Find out about the following events in history and whether they would be classified as genocide in each of the definitions. Give reasons for your answers in the grid.

- The Stalinist purges (USSR – 1934–41)
- The famines in China (1958–63)
- The Cultural Revolution (China – 1966)
- The Khmer Rouge regime (Cambodia – 1975–79)
- The anti-Sikh riots (India – 1984)
- Srebrenica (Bosnia-Herzegovina – 1995)

ASSESSING GENOCIDE

	UN Definition (1948)	Lemkin (1946)	Chalk and Jonassohn (1990)	Charny (1997)	Shaw (2007)
The Stalinist purges					
The famines in China					
The Cultural Revolution					
The Khmer Rouge regime					
The anti-Sikh riots					
Srebrenica					

COMPARATIVE GENOCIDE: BACKGROUND TO THE HOLOCAUST AND THE RWANDAN GENOCIDE (A)

There were 67 million people living in Germany, of whom approximately 505,000 were Jewish. Jews made up less than 1 per cent of the German population. Around 80 per cent of Jews in Germany were citizens.

Jews had lived in Germany for many centuries; the earliest record dating back to an imperial decree in Cologne in AD 321.

The Nuremberg Laws defined Jews as those having three or four Jewish grandparents. If an individual had one or two Jewish grandparents they were labelled *Mischling*, which meant 'crossbreed'.

In January 1933 Hitler became chancellor of Germany. Antisemitic measures were put in place, including a boycott of Jewish shops on 1st April 1933.

Between 1933 and 1939 things became increasingly harder for Jews living in Germany. In 1935 they were deprived of German citizenship and prevented from holding certain jobs.

Many Jews emigrated from Germany during the 1930s and sought to start new lives abroad. By 1939 many countries had placed strict quotas on the number of Jews allowed to enter.

Living standards for ordinary Germans improved throughout the 1930s as the economy recovered from the Great Depression. Nevertheless, persecution and propaganda against the Jews increased.

The Jews were defenceless against the oppression of the Nazi regime. The Jews who stayed in Germany hoped that things would not get any worse.

COMPARATIVE GENOCIDE: THE BACKGROUND TO THE HOLOCAUST AND THE RWANDAN GENOCIDE (B)

The Rwandan people consisted of three different groups: the Hutus, the Tutsis and the Twa. The Hutus made up around 80–85 per cent of the population, the Tutsis around 15–18 per cent and the Twa 1 per cent.

Before Rwanda was colonised in the late nineteenth century it had a monarchy. Rwanda was colonised by the Germans and then the Belgians.

During the Belgian colonisation, a national census fixed the Rwandan people's ethnicity as Hutu, Tutsi or Twa. This was based on physical features, and everyone had to carry an identity card.

The Belgian colonists used the Tutsi ruling elites to govern the country which generated resentment amongst the Hutu majority.

By 1959 Belgium knew that it would soon leave Rwanda and decided to give power to the Hutu majority. This immediately led to mass murders of Tutsis throughout Rwanda. Many Tutsis fled to neighbouring Uganda.

In 1973 Juvenal Habyarimana took power in Rwanda and the persecution of the Tutsi minority increased. Hutu power developed, and sought the extermination of the Tutsi people.

Under Habyarimana the Rwandan economy suffered and anti-Tutsi propaganda and persecution increased. Civilian militias called the *Interhamwe* were equipped and trained with the support of the French.

The Tutsi refugees in Uganda formed a movement called the Rwandan Patriotic Front, which aimed to end Tutsi persecution by removing the Habyarimana regime.

COMPARATIVE GENOCIDE: THE HOLOCAUST AND THE RWANDAN GENOCIDE

Every Hutu should know that a Tutsi woman, whoever she is, works for the interest of her Tutsi ethnic group. As a result, we shall consider a traitor any Hutu who:

- marries a Tutsi woman
- befriends a Tutsi woman
- employs a Tutsi woman as a secretary or a concubine.

From the Hutu 'Ten Commandments', which was published in Kangura *(an anti-Tutsi, Hutu-power newspaper) in December 1990.*

A cartoon appearing in Der Stürmer (August 1935). The caption reads: 'Ignorant, lured by gold, they stand shamed in Judah's fold. Souls poisoned, blood infected. Disaster lives in their wombs.'

Questions

What are the main messages of these sources?

How are Tutsi women and the Jewish man portrayed?

Copy and complete the table below:

Similarities	Differences

Research Study:

It is estimated that approximately between 250,000 and 500,000 women were raped during the Rwandan Genocide.

1. Why do you think that sexual violence was so prolific during the Rwandan Genocide?

2. How was it connected to the propaganda messages that the Hutu extremists presented?

Bibliography

Avraham, D. (2008) 'The Challenge of Teaching the Holocaust in a Multicultural Classroom', *Yad Vashem Jerusalem Quarterly*, 51, October: 4. Available at: www.yadvashem.org/yv/en/pressroom/magazine/pdf/yv_magazine51.pdf.

Bauer, Y. (2001) *Re-Thinking the Holocaust* (New Haven CT: Yale University Press).

Benz, W. (1999) *The Holocaust: A German Historian Examines the Genocide* (New York: Columbia University Press).

Bernstein, M. (1994) 'The *Schindler's List* Effect', *The American Scholar*, 63, no. 3: 429–32.

Bloxham, D. (2009) *The Final Solution: A Genocide* (Oxford: Oxford University Press).

Boyne, J. (2006) *The Boy in the Striped Pyjamas* (Oxford: David Fickling Books).

Community Support Trust (2014) *Antisemitic Incidents Report 2013* (www.thecst.org.uk).

Darnell, S. (2010) *Measuring Holocaust Denial in the United States*. Policy Analysis Exercise (Cambridge MA: Harvard Kennedy School of Government).

Doneson, J. (2001) 'For Better or Worse: Using Film in a Study of the Holocaust', in Totten, S. and Feinberg, S. (eds), *Teaching and Studying the Holocaust* (Boston: Allyn and Bacon), pp. 194–202.

Eckmann, M. (2010) 'Exploring the Relevance of Holocaust Education for Human Rights Education', *Prospects*, 40: 7–16.

Foreign and Commonwealth Office (2012) *International Task Force Country Report of the United Kingdom of Great Britain and Northern Ireland*. Available at: https://www.gov.uk/government/uploads/system/uploads/attachment_data/file/206418/20121101_ITF_Country_Report_of_the_United_Kingdom_of_GB.pdf. Accessed 28 March 2014.

FRA (2010) *Excursion to the Past – Teaching for the Future: Handbook for Teachers* (Vienna: European Union Agency for Fundamental Human Rights).

Gilbert, M. (1986) *The Holocaust: The Jewish Tragedy* (London: Collins).

Gilbert, M. (2010) *In Ishmael's House: A History of Jews in Muslim Lands* (Toronto: McClelland and Stewart).

Gourevitch, P. (1998) *We Wish to Inform You that Tomorrow We Will Be Killed with Our Families* (New York: Farrar, Straus and Giroux).

Gray, M. (2014) 'Preconceptions of the Holocaust among Thirteen and Fourteen Year Olds in English Schools'. Unpublished Ph.D. thesis, Institute of Education, University of London.

Gryglewski, E. (2010) 'Teaching about the Holocaust in Multicultural Societies: Appreciating the Learner', *Intercultural Education*, 21, S1: S41–S49.

Hansen, J. (2013) 'Auschwitz Is Made of Lego and Hitler Hates Beckham: YouTube and the Future of Holocaust Remembrance'. Paper presented at *The Future of Holocaust Studies Conference*, Universities of Southampton and Winchester, 29–31 July 2013.

Herbert, U. (2000) 'Extermination Policy: New Answers and Questions about the History of the "Holocaust" in German Historiography'. In Herbert, U. (ed.), *National Socialist Extermination Policies: Contemporary German Perspectives and Controversies*. New York: Berghahn Books.

Hilberg, R. (1961) *The Destruction of the European Jews* (New York: Holmes and Meier).

Hoess, R. (1947) *Commandant of Auschwitz* (London: Phoenix Press).

Holocaust Memorial Day Trust (2014a) www.hmd.org.uk/genocides/holocaust. Accessed 14 January 2014.

Holocaust Memorial Day Trust (2014b) www.hmd.org.uk/news/hmdt-survey-half-uk-population-unable-name-post-holocaust-genocide. Accessed 14 August 2014.

Hondius, D. (2010) 'Finding Common Ground in Education about the Holocaust and Slavery', *Intercultural Education*, 21, supplement 1: S61–S69.

Huffington Post (2014) 'Most Young People "Can't Name a Single Genocide since the Holocaust"'. Available at: www.huffingtonpost.co.uk/2014/01/23/holocaust-genocide_n_4652428.html. Accessed 24 January 2014.

Institute for Historical Review (n.d.) 'Interview with Robert Faurisson'. Available at: www.ihr.org/jhr/v02/v02p319_Faurisson.html. Accessed 1 April 2014.

International Holocaust Remembrance Alliance (2014a) *How to Teach About the Holocaust in Schools*. Available at: www.holocaustremembrance.com/node/319. Accessed 16 January 2014.

International Holocaust Remembrance Alliance (2014b) *Working Definition on Holocaust Denial and Distortion*. Available at: www.holocaustremembrance.com. Accessed 16 January 2014.

Jayne, A. (1998) *Jefferson's Declaration of Independence: Origins, Philosophy and Theology* (Lexington: University Press of Kentucky).

Kinloch, N. (2001) 'Parallel Catastrophes? Uniqueness, Redemption and the Shoah', *Teaching History*, 104, 8–14.

Kollerstrom, N. (2008) 'The Auschwitz "Gas Chamber" Illusion'. CODOH website. Available at: http://codoh.com/library/document/684. Accessed 1 April 2014.

Lazar, A. and Litvak Hirsch, T. (2013) 'An Online Partner for Holocaust Remembrance Education: Students Approaching the Yahoo! Answers Community', *Educational Review*, DOI: 10.1080/00131911.2013.839545. Available at: www.tandfonline.com/doi/full/10.1080/00131911.2013.839545#.VGzyODSM1n0.

Le Petit, N. (2011) 'David Cameron on Multiculturalism', *Politics Review*, 21, no. 2 (November): Extension, p. 1.

Levene, M. (2008) *The Meaning of Genocide* (London: I. B. Tauris).

Lipstadt, D. (1993) *Denying the Holocaust: The Growing Assault on Truth and Memory* (London: Penguin).

Maio, H., Traum, D. and Debevec, P. (2012) 'New Dimensions in Testimony', *Past Forward*, Summer, 22–26.

Maitles, H. and Cowan, P. (2007) 'Making the Links: The Relationship Between Learning About the Holocaust and Contemporary Anti-Semitism', in Ross, A. (ed.), *Citizenship Education in Society* (London: CiCe), pp. 431–44.

McGuinn, N. (2000) 'Teaching the Holocaust through English', in Davies, I. (ed.), *Teaching the Holocaust: Educational Dimensions, Principles and Practice* (London: Continuum), ch. 9, 119–34.

Michalczyk, J. and Cohen, S. (2001) 'Expressing the Inexpressible Through Film', in Totten, S. and Feinberg, S. (eds), *Teaching and Studying the Holocaust* (Boston: Allyn and Bacon), pp. 203–22.

Nates, T. (2010) '"But Apartheid Was Also Genocide … What About Our Suffering?" Teaching the Holocaust in South Africa – Opportunities and Challenges', *Intercultural Education*, 21: S1, S17–S26.

Novick, P. (1999) *The Holocaust and Collective Memory* (London: Bloomsbury).

Office for National Statistics (2012a) *Ethnicity and National Identity in England and Wales in 2011* (London: ONS). Available at: www.ons.gov.uk/ons.

Office for National Statistics (2012b) *Key Statistics for Local Authorities in England and Wales Release* (London: ONS). Available at: www.ons.gov.uk/ons.

OSCE Office for Democratic Institutions and Human Rights (2005) *Education on the Holocaust and on Anti-Semitism* (Warsaw, Poland: OSCE). Available at: www.osce.org.

People for the Ethical Treatment of Animals (2009) 'PETA Germany's Holocaust Display Banned'. Available at: www.peta.org/blog/peta-germanys-holocaust-display-banned. Accessed 6 January 2014.

Pettigrew, A., Foster, S., Howson, J., Salmons, P., Lenga, R-A.and Andrews, K. (2009) *Teaching about the Holocaust in English Secondary Schools: An Empirical Study of National Trends, Perspectives and Practice* (London: Holocaust Education Development Programme, Institute of Education, University of London).

Salmons, P. (2001) 'Moral Dilemmas: History Teaching and the Holocaust', *Teaching History*, 104: 34–40.

Salmons, P. (2013) 'Remembering Without Knowing? The Challenge of Holocaust Memorial Day for Schools'. Institute of Education London Blog. Available at: http://ioelondonblog. wordpress.com. Accessed 21 February 2014.

Schweber, S. (2006) 'Holocaust Fatigue', *Social Education*, 7, no.1: 48–55.

Shermer, M. and Grobman, A. (2000) *Denying History: Who Says the Holocaust Never Happened and Why Do They Say It?* (Berkeley: University of California Press).

Short, G. (1994) 'Teaching the Holocaust: The Relevance of Children's Perceptions of Jewish Culture and Identity', *British Educational Research Journal*, 20, no. 4: 393–405.

Short, G. (2003) 'Lessons of the Holocaust: A Response to the Critics', *Educational Review*, 55, no. 3: 277–87, at 285–86.

Short, G. (2005) 'Learning from Genocide? A Study in the Failure of Holocaust Education', *Intercultural Education*, 16, no. 4: 367–80.

Short, G. (2013) 'Reluctant Learners? Muslim Youth Confront the Holocaust', *Intercultural Education*, 24, nos 1–2: 121–32.

Short, G., Supple, C. and Klinger, K. (1998) *The Holocaust in the School Curriculum: A European Perspective* (Strasbourg: Council of Europe).

Skloot, R. (2008) *The Theatre of Genocide* (Madison: University of Wisconsin Press).

Symer, D. (2001) 'The Internet and the Study of the Holocaust', in Totten, S. and Feinberg, S. (eds), *Teaching and Studying the Holocaust* (Boston Allyn and Bacon), pp. 223–38.

United States Holocaust Memorial Museum (2014a) 'Introduction to the Holocaust'. *Holocaust Encyclopedia*. Available at: www.ushmm.org/wlc/en/article.php?ModuleId=10005143. Accessed 14 January 2014.

United States Holocaust Memorial Museum (2014b) 'Why Teach About the Holocaust?' Available at: www.ushmm.org/educators/teaching-about-the-holocaust/why-teach-about-the-holocaust. Accessed 21 February 2014.

United States Holocaust Memorial Museum and Salzburg Global Seminar (2013) *Global Perspectives on Holocaust Education: Trends, Patterns and Practices* (working draft). Available at: https://edulibs. org/salzburg-global-seminar.

Venezia, S. (2009) *Inside the Gas Chambers* (Cambridge: Polity Press).

Vital, D. (1999) *A People Apart: A Political History of the Jews in Europe 1789–1939* (Oxford: Oxford University Press).

Index

9 781138 791008